CHADVENTURE FOR THE N-WORD PASS

Written by

MACKENTOSH DER

ISBN 9798986375786 (paperback)

First edition published 2020. Reissued edition 2024.

Published by Der Enterprise

Contents

To my family

FIRST WARNING: This book is almost entirely satire. The views and opinions expressed in this book almost always represent only those of the characters, not the author.

Prologue

SECOND WARNING: The beginning of each chapter (and the entirety of this prologue) contains a scattered but life-changing "we live in a 'sus 'iety" redsigmapill. However, I expect that a good chunk of you holding this book only picked the book up for bookshelf decoration or got it as a gag keepsake because "lol (laugh out loud) book name," and you are likely a retardingly illiterate dork who is unable to handle the "big brain" stuff here, as you probably haven't read a remotely "based" thing before. If that's the case, or you're expecting a coherent story plot at best, feel free to skip those and move on to the story sections if you want, but you'd remain an "unbased" normie—though be warned, I made the storyline to be kinda basic (Trust me bro, don't expect plot twists. Or is there?) to maybe encourage you to educate yourself instead. I may even write highly inf*rmally for the grammar commies to seethe. But don't blame me—some men just want to watch the world learn (we should live in a "big chungus brain" society). I am about to show, in brief, the oppression gamers face every day in a "modern technological society"—the truly enlightened gamer actually hates gaming (We'll finally have representation after all these years—this book is like "the black panther" but for true gamers!).

Anyway, I shall begin.
   Very rare is a thinker who articulated "social justice warrior" behavior and perhaps the origins of "no-no" words as well-put as a man whom I heard some people in "ill*gal" corners of the internet call "the man who managed to both be a good mathematician and an 'IRL (in real life) pro gamer' who did a 'bomb stealth placement' speedrun world record" (of course, I'm not justifying the acts, I am only mentioning the reputation of "anti-techer" in the "gamers rise up" community). Modern leftists, particularly the ones who burn things down to do their so-called "protests," are said to be idiologues who don't truly give a damn about the "marginalized" whom they lie about "giving a g*sh darn about." Their inane mentality is largely driven by certain dismal feelings: low self-esteem, depression, self-hatred, defeatist thoughts, and guilt.[1] These feelings are largely fueled by the sense of meaninglessness in modern society. What makes this so socially problematic is these feelings induce the leftists to insincerely and second-handedly self-insert themselves into the "marginalized" groups of people, while if anything, it is those leftists who are the hostile ones—by the way, there are studies revealing they tend to use condescending language while speaking to the minorities they claim to protect.[2]
   One could simply "criteria" genuine "rebels with a cause" by describing them as willing to defend their cause even if it may lead to disapproval,[3] and that their actions

---

[1] T. Kaczynski, *Industrial Society and its Future* (Independently published, 2018), para. 10.
[2] C.H. Dupree and S.T. Fiske, "Self-presentation in interracial settings: The competence downshift by White liberals," *Journal of Personality and Social Psychology*, 117(2019): 579–604. https://doi.org/10.1037/pspi0000166
[3] B. Monin, P.J. Sawyer, and M.J. Marquez, "The rejection of moral rebels: Resenting those who do the right thing," *Journal of Personality and Social Psychology*, 95 (2008): 76–93. https://doi.org/10.1037/0022-3514.95.1.76

would affect the world.[4] Modern leftists clearly don't fit this. In our "clown world," they are pseudo-superheroes who "fight injustices" only because it supplies them with the delusion that they are quirkily saving the world from evil. But they don't at all have THEIR own lives sorted out.[5] As such, the minorities that they "rebel" are at the back of their actual minds; they do their activism only because they are so desperate to feel differentiated and special in modern society. But it is important to acknowledge that the system in the 21st century shifted to rooting for "equal rights"—leftists, due to their lack of non-falsified historical context, are still "stunted" onto the system's older values that were popular half a century ago or more (like the caricatural stories of "black and white" times). They synchronize their activisms with the increasing new "updated" values (In gamer terms, modernity from time to time having "patch note updates" of more w*ke values), to make it look like THEIR activisms made the change. Grandly, all they do is invent their own grievances, commonly by provoking those on the other side to attack them. Then, when that party reasonably reacts to it, the leftist would "collect" that "counter-provoke" as a non-contextual piece of "data" that will be added to the next w*ke ubiquitous pieces for the state.

Are leftists ultimately just biotic expressions of the system's surveillance and totalitarian apparatuses, serving to censor stuff mindlessly? Typically, when modern leftists hear the "official formal words" originally designed to specifically refer to marginalized groups, it triggers an unthoughtful reaction in them because they tend to subconsciously think it implies there is something about their cultural values that are different from modern society.[6] Their "activism" would then morph those words into slurs (LITERALLY 1984 (but it would at least be funnier if it's "19_69_" instead lol)), because society's "modernity" is internalized as the "default" and "right side of progress" for leftists, whether they are self-aware of it or not; they think that anything anthropologically suggesting a social group didn't initiate something along this type of progress in the past suggests "this implies something negative about them, therefore we must stop calling them that." Obviously, this is self-defeating—as the modern world "tries" to become more egalitarian to increase its own efficiency, in which identical normies become the "ideal," it becomes hostile towards group, cultural, and even individual differences, as they become rendered as hindrances.

It is mainstream bugthought to say that leftists are diametrically opposed to industrialized modernity as bugman capitalism. But the fact of the matter is, facets of modern life that people perceive as "making life simple," such as automation making things so "EZ" (The off*sive gamer word for "easy," that used to "hurted" my feelings when people say it to me after a game match) has led to various mental and behavioral issues that invoke people to pretend to rebel just to feel like they are doing something "impactful." However, it shall be mentioned that these psychological problems aren't exclusive to the leftist types—they easily extend to "the rightists" as well and even most of mankind in the modern world (though it's more prevalent amongst leftists—leftism is

---

[4] E. Midlarsky, "Aiding under stress: The effects of competence, dependency, visibility, and fatalism," *Journal of Personality*, 39 (1971): 132-149. https://doi.org/10.1111/j.1467-6494.1971.tb00993.x

[5] V. McLeod, *Clown World Chronicles* (VJM Publishing, 2020), 119.

[6] T. Kaczynski, *Industrial Society and its Future* (Independently published, 2018), para. 11.

the most widely disseminated ideology in modern times due to the "democratization of function/ability" and herd morality bias inherent to modernity's technologization).

So then, is there ultimately some inherent working under modern conditions that, in turn, leads to the insidious censorship of words? Let me now attempt to fit a brief introductory explanatory reason to you "gamers," in this prologue, for why you fundamentally can't use "epic gamer words" freely.

First, be reminded that there is some inner working in modernity that leads people in society to exhibit "unnatural" and "unfree" behaviors. An easy-to-"relatable" example that parallels modern mankind is the poor orcas (animals known for their advanced minds) being in one of those shitty asshole-like tiny aquariums that entertain the public. There are stories of these captive orcas exhibiting strange behaviors such as self-harm and even self-death as a result.[7] Likewise, in a "land context," think of a donkey enclosed within an overly tight industrial-grade farming fence that must be "single-digit centimeters" away from its fellow donkeys for the sake of financial cost reduction for the farm—a very stressful surrounding! Now, whether donkeys are particularly of high nobility such that it has a need for living space as much as an orca, how come there are some rare cases where the first thing a donkey may do is sand off its own hide with rough sandpaper tongue? (A signage that it wouldn't longer use its in-built functions for intended purposes). People like to gawk at those stories as if they're alien behavior while failing to realize that they themselves likely experience similar depressive feelings in modern urban life—mankind is not so different.

We can see this reflected especially in the strange sexual behaviors in modern man (You heard me right snowflakes, I just said "seggs" but with a "xual" at the end rather than "ggs")). You tell me—most of you readers, at least if you are reading this in the 21st century, would already have a good idea of what I am talking about. I have consistently observed that anyone who had bad days of stagnation, like staying home all day doing nothing or even attending a large, overcrowded party where is it unfeasible to intimately have a deep discussion with any individual (due to the impersonal dynamics), would by the end of the day have a certain impulse... the very deleterious tendency to jack off that night.

A recent super intriguing observed groundbreaking discovery that may support this is: "chimp in state of nature never jerks off, but in captivity he does." And one of the most striking questions in response to that is: *What mean?*[8] Think of this—a muscle that hasn't been trained in a while would be inclined to decrease in size and strength—a certain "will-to-power" muscle has to be exercised through "mastery of unknown space" for the chimp to be too distracted to self-pleasure. Artificial self-pleasure is one of the most accessible ways one can fakely experience what's meant to be the end rewards of "mastery" since one's org*sm-making organ is literally attached to their own body—just pull pants down, then start holding wang. Similar to how there's absolutely nothing stopping a donkey from sanding rocks as it prepares to eventually chomp them in distress.

---

[7] K. Buck, "Orca whale killed himself by smashing head into wall after 12 years in captivity," *Mirror* (17th September 2021), https://www.mirror.co.uk/news/world-news/orca-whale-trapped-tiny-pool-24997792.
[8] B.A. Pervert, *Bronze Age Mindset* (Independently Published, 2018), 32.

In captive spaces where genuine mastery is futile, there would be more or less subtle cues missing that lead to a failure to replicate a noble life's natural environments. There was a case where white rhinos weren't willing to "breed" (seggs, except it results in creation of babies) despite zookeepers' efforts, because as it turned out, the male needs to have sufficiently interacted with others before being properly aroused.[9] The rhinos just needed to "master" social relations first (Pssst male gamers, even the toughest animals might take their time before doing the fr*ghtening task that we call "t*lking to girls (but for int*rcourse)"). The given zoo did successfully eliminate the difficulty of breeding for the white rhinos by having them in larger groups, but that is only a specific solution to one of the gazillion types of life that exist.

The rampant psychological suffering in modern times shows that mankind, in ascent, would be no different from this mode of "propagation priority." Something is significant when we see that in extremely dense living conditions with strangers, there is a sense of immense dysphoria for the intelligent, in that they would not have a great desire to propagate.[10] Also, contrary to mainstream institutionalized "Darwinism" (a notion of impersonal random selection under mere survival and reproduction)[11] which the modern paradigm is defaulted to, it's argued that noble animals wouldn't even consider propagation until they have achieved self-mastery in meaningful open "space" (be it the development of hard abilities or social abilities).[12] They may also have to develop their "swag." This type of life may even choose their own deaths rather than subject themselves to suffocating limitations, as many examples in history have shown prisoners who'd kill themselves or bite their chained limbs off just to escape captivity.[13]

In fact, it is argued that impersonal Darwinistic mechanisms are only applicable to a certain kind of life,[14] those in denatured stressful conditions such as crowdedness—modern-like spaces. These spiritually weak kinds, perhaps akin to the "fast life history" creatures, tend to prioritize mere existence over mastery of abilities (such as bacteria and the average modern couch potatoes who revolve their lives around consuming corporate trash). This may be why they'd hypothetically end up being easier to study in super small claustrophobia-inducing labs and observe them going about their "normie" life cycles. They have more predictable, ignoble behavior and just invest most of their energy in mere living and if "lucrative," reproduction. This would result in mere offspring which they don't invest much of their energy nurturing—social bonds among individuals of the fast life history types tend to be weaker.[15] This is because they are favored in the type of spaces that are unstable yet unharsh, and so investing time in social relations and planning ahead has less of a point for them. This also leaves room for low impulse control. To modern bugmen, this may sound like "the better" mode of life if one is to fall for the common fallacy that "if this is happening in so much of the organism kingdom (haha, I bet you sick-minded fucks read "organism" as "orgasm"), then it shall apply to mankind." But

---

[9] D. Engber, "Why Is Captive Breeding So Hard?" (10th March 2005), *Slate*. https://slate.com/news-and-politics/2005/03/why-is-captive-breeding-so-hard.html.

[10] E. Dutton, *Breeding the Human Herd* (Imperium Press, 2023), 147.

[11] J. Tyler Bonner, *Randomness in Evolution* (Princeton University Press, 2013).

[12] B.A. Pervert, *Bronze Age Mindset* (Independently Published, 2018), 25.

[13] Ibid., 20.

[14] Ibid., 18.

[15] E. Dutton, *Breeding the Human Herd* (Imperium Press, 2023), 113.

when there is a "desire" for mere survival, said beings tend to be more visible by default as they don't subject themselves to risks of cessation as much, and they quantitatively propagate more.

In a general scheme, mankind is widely held as an executor of slow life history strategy—these types are characterized by being in a harsher environment that favors agreeableness, conscientiousness, smartness, and nurturing offspring. (Tr*gg*r w*rning: "p*berty" (a graphic process involving scary b*dily growth changes) discussion is coming up...) Side note; for humans, puberty would be reached later so the offspring has mcre time to learn the complex information needed to live in harsher and more competitive environments.[16] Perhaps, the fact that life history strategy slows down in harsher environments like colder regions[17] represents the drive for mastery of space, as it may resemble openness, in opposition to body-heat crowdedness?

We'd also seem to have the most known kinds of potential paths in nature, and ways to develop our abilities. There is a big misconception that many idiots have, using "the helplessness of human babies" to support the claim that "we need modernity to flourish," without realizing that this initial "helplessness" is how mankind was initially so successful in nature. The truth is, humans are born prematurely relative to other kinds of creatures— our already big adaptable brains make it so difficult for our mothers to give birth (We have to imagine then: what if pussies morph to be bigger, and the wide hip "anime" waifus that people want so much comes to fruition in the form of the archetypical gamer girl woman wife?). In contrast, the spiritually meeker tend to be born "preprogrammed"— they already know how to walk and uniformly behave in groups; however, they are less inclined to learn after that.

Mankind leans towards being very malleable and without much preprogramming— abilities depend on the "big brain" and extensive experience. Human beings have a higher capacity to develop and adapt their techniques over time, freeing themselves from the limitations of generic behavior.[18] The mind has not been specifically programmed for modern tasks such as driving according to strict road rules, for example. Instead, it is capable of learning ascending complexities. I still hear so many retards claiming "moDeRn peOple cAn drIve iN RoAD tHerefOre tHey smArtEr." It is inane to believe that our ancestors from thousands of years ago did not engage in intricate activities requiring significant cognitive abilities, considering their hunts and conquests were so much more impressive than the average wagecuck job and commute. The notion that we have dramatically "adapted to modernity in the past few generations" as an "improvement" towards following road rules is just brain rot. The intellect should not be conflated with a fixed set of skills. It is for this reason that even though modern big cities seem complex on the surface level, they still make us feel depressed (The very point when "society" turns into "susiety" (Second "amogus" reference so far. In case you didn't know, "sus" is a shorter version of the word "suspect," usually used to define someone or something that looks suspicious or untrustworthy. In cooler terms, it means "when the

---

[16] Ibid., 114.
[17] Ibid., 116.
[18] O. Spengler, *Man and Technics* (Alfred A. Knopf, Inc., 1932), 3C.

imposter is suspicious." Only true "gamers" understand these "epic weed griffin memes" lol))—modern life is in fact too simple for us.

The automatons, the spiritually meek lifeforms, which are structurally closer to "idle" forms in simple terms, can be said to be separated from the higher ones, the more animate types, in terms of their lesser capability of "teleology towards open-ended greatness." Now, usually, it is argued that this function is not confined to the realm of the higher living, and may extend to inanimate systems by external fields that can generate teleological behaviors—this view posits that certain properties of inanimate objects, such as persistence and plasticity, can be understood as teleological when influenced by external forces or fields. A classic example is a ball circling in a bowl, which, despite being an inanimate object, seemingly exhibits goal-directed behavior by eventually settling at the lowest point in the bowl due to gravitational forces.[19] But a plausible objection is that in naturalizing teleology and function, the physical stuff that makes up the world is all subject to, and directed by upper-level fields—this would suggest that the "only" difference between a falling rock and complex, human decision-making is a matter of degree, not a difference in kind. However, we must remember that the world isn't necessarily a blurred continuum between life and nonlife, as certain higher beings, unlike inert objects, exhibit a unique way of striving for a cause by refusing to propagate until self-cultivation is exercised. This would suggest a fundamental, not just a degree-based, distinction between animate and inanimate or lesser animate entities. There is a self-overcoming and assertion of one's will as fundamental to mankind's ascension in propagation. As this highlights a kind of reversal from the spiritually idle lives' behaviors, it does inherently preclude the presence of teleology in non-living systems. Mankind, like other higher entities, is influenced (but not entirely cucked) by external and internal fields that shape their actions and decisions. This "will" can be viewed as an expression of the complex interplay of these fields rather than a unique, isolated phenomenon. Man, as part of the natural world, is subject to the same principles that may govern other teleological systems, but their potential to make conscious choices as high as propagative decisions can be understood as an advanced expression that they are yet still part of nature rather than outside.

One may ask, why are we so denatured today? And why and how would we do this to ourselves? Whether or not you believe in some conspiracy, let's look at a very simple theoretical case taking place at a primordial time—the moment when a "primordial man" becomes safe from the "scary" wilderness. This is the discovery of a "mystical cave" that contains lots of natural sources of nourishment, marking the birth of a theoretical idle caveman. Once he and his tribe enter and have their replenishing dinner after so much time struggling to pierce spears into the necks of prey, he has some interesting decision points. Chiefly, he'd wonder if his tribe should stay inside the cave containing a surplus of edible nutritious mushrooms and perhaps cave art h*ntai for as much of their lives as possible to encourage uncontrolled seggs—farming would be the only means necessary for nourishment, so there is no need to hunt at all—this promises comfort and certainty. The other side of the dichotomy would be to maintain the hunter lifestyle, where the men

---

[19] G. Babcock, "Teleology and function in non-living nature," *Synthese*, 23 (2023): 214–236. https://doi.org/10.1007/s11229-023-04099-1

of the tribe continue doing badass hunts involving pushing themselves into the unknown darknesses. What's really interesting is how the latter option is seemingly the "less rational" decision that would lead to more deaths—it would be so easy for one to choose the safer first option! But that safety decision is not always the "better"! Mankind is not always just a pre-determined mechanistic blobfest of matter where their decisions are always the safest outcomes that guarantee continuity of living. There is a "deep-water motivation" somewhere in the far past that pushed them to self-improvement while disregarding the option of safeness—furthermore, the "deep-water motivation" may flourish through future generations. Though, it has clearly diminished in modernity—it probably still manifests in modern man, but to a different and perverse degree—now a "shallow-water motivation"?

Throughout the existence of beings capable of rationality, it is highly possible, and, unfortunately, very easily that they also have the will (albeit a weak type) to reverse the prioritization order between self-propagation and self-mastery, such that the former becomes prioritized. Practically, this would be the case where the man has his whole kin stay inside the mystical cave forever, where they become lazy and only work the mushroom farm for the sake of guaranteeing crop yield. Beings capable of this reasoning modify and create the spaces they inhabit, however, they are also modified by those spaces,[20] and those modifications can both be gains or losses in ability—it is shown that in general, certain life types lost complexity in functions depending on environmental impact; albeit historically, the loss of function happens much less than the gain in function.[21] But for societies amongst the "artificially rational" in the advent of the discovery of "safety nanny captive spaces," it is really common for loss of function to happen. It also happens surprisingly quickly; contrary to the average r*dditor who would think that it would take a gazillion years for us to morphologically change (while simultaneously believing we suddenly adapted to need junk soyfood), there is evidence that the intellect declines really fast in modernity.[22]

Here is an IRL example—the agricultural revolution being one of the first potential sparks of modernity or the technologization of mankind. According to raw egg shlonker, the advent of agriculture, the Neolithic Revolution, may have even been the original Great Reset.[23] This marked the rise of the first state and predatory elites, and there had to be coercion just for the transition into agriculture to happen—people actively resisted the change, with how much it stunted mankind (physically and mentally), and many agriculture states even failed as a result.[24] Although war was still a thing, it wasn't anything resembling a thirst for glory—it was only for capturing enemies and putting them into current territory to work the fields efficiently, furthering the extent of

[20] C. Fuchs, "Transnational space and the 'network society,'" *Twenty-First Century Society*, 2 (2007): 49-78. https://doi.org/10.1080/17450140601101218

[21] B. Alberts, A. Johnson, J. Lewis, et al., *Molecular Biology of the Cell, 4th* Edition (New York: Garland Science, 2002).

[22] M.A. Woodley of Menie, "How fragile is our intellect? Estimating losses in general intelligence due to both selection and mutation accumulation," *Personality and Individual Differences*, 75 (2014): 80-84. https://doi.org/10.1016/j.paid.2014.10.047

[23] R.E. Nationalist, *The Eggs Benedict Option*, (Antelope Hill Publishing, 2022), 50.

[24] Ibid., 48.

crowdedness and idleness. They, in fact, barely boasted about taking territory.[25] In other words, the domestication of crops and animals entailed the domestication of humans.[26] Surprisingly, the collapse of those states was just as likely to result internally (disease, revolt, exhaustion of natural resources) as external pressures like the wars, and perhaps for the workers, collapses were a good thing to them.[27] Only then did the early states have to necessarily selectively favor those who were pacified, even on an intergenerational level.[28] THIS IS A SAD TIME EVEN FOR GAMERS, BECAUSE IT MEANS NO MORE IRL PC SURVIVAL GAME ("PC" here doesn't mean "politically correct." I am "based," not "soyboy"), AND IT INSTEAD BECAME AN IRL BORING *MOBILE FARM SIM TYCOON* (mobile idle gaming cringe).

Since then, mankind seemed to have trended towards being couch potatoes, turning into robotic idlers. Agriculture and modern lifestyles basically breed an inert computer-like mind, a mind that isn't philosophically thinking but can appear as such. "Conscious life" would experience a spiritual death and be in a certain "zombie" state, in which it acts as a physical system conducting computation and nothing more.[29] Going by that logic, could we say higher life is "rightful miscomputation" if we juxtapose it with idle life? Miscomputation is described as computing in a way that violates computational norms.[30] This perspective would argue that teleological functions are problematic as they rely on an externalist perspective that looks beyond the system itself to its environment as there may be overcomplications with regards to the explanation of miscomputation and fails to address how a system can miscompute based solely on its internal structure.[31] So then, how would we explain the assumption that the only thing that living things have as a main goal is mere survival? Throughout history, we've seen individuals who'd will themselves into missions that have a 99% death rate if it means they don't have to live the rest of their lives as mediocre idlers. Maybe this births a new value—a dynamism that separates the creators from the followers—the unfamiliarity may seemingly be "bad" especially for a herd that is stuck on the system of mere survival. For instance, Greek culture, which valued improvement and disvalued the notion of "mere life," had an idea that it would be better to never be born mediocre, or if born, to die as soon as possible[32] (Plz (please) don't get mad, this is a hot take that I am mentioning in hopes of buffing the future gamers. If this insight sounds too rough for you gamers, just remember the saying: "Gamers don't die, they respawn" (This is so "wholesome 100 Kianna Reaves")).

Sigh... well right now, modern "science" functioning under artificial rationality became the way to engineer society, as an nth higher degree equivalent to the theoretical caveman who first discovered the notion of "the cave" along with modern lifestyle. We

---

[25] Ibid., 65.
[26] Ibid., 49.
[27] Ibid., 66.
[28] P. Frost and H.C. Harpending, "Western Europe, State Formation, and Genetic Pacification," *Evolutionary Psychology*, 13(2015): 230-243. https://doi.org/10.1177/147470491501300114
[29] V.C. Müller and M. Hoffmann, "What Is Morphological Computation? On How the Body Contributes to Cognition and Control," *Artif Life*, 23(2017): 1-24. https://doi.org/10.1162/ARTL_a_00219
[30] C. Tucker, "How to Explain Miscomputation," *Philosopher's Imprint*, 18(2018): 1-17.
[31] Ibid.
[32] C. Alamariu, *Selective Breeding and the Birth of Philosophy* (Independently Published, 2023), 24.

ultimately opted for the safer option of abandoning the inborn "deep-water motivation"— we are robotically and rationally micro-managing society to the point of deeming literally everything that we "adapted for a reason" as fake-feeling constructs, detached from the lifeworld ("No, no, no, no, no, this can't be true. Please tell me this isn't happening. It's like being trapped in a simulation and living in the same day over and over again and I can't get out HELPME!"). Normies and leftists are predominantly the types who still have a very, very thin slice of the motivation to master the little space that is left, and a very corrupt variant at that (the shallow-water motivation).

It is shown that the correlation between Machiavellianism and leftism is high as a result of this type of people being paranoid and, therefore, craving a high sense of control.[33] The lack of genuine concern for others of the leftist would categorize them as akin to fast-life strategists because of their mental instability and the feeling that they are powerless and that they deserve more power.[34] Except, their way of "reproduction" is primarily via a "metaparasitism effect" where ideas like parasites infect the collective and proliferate rather than people propagating the idea passionately after mastering it, exhibiting something along the lines of "horizontal transfer" from biology.[35] This kind of pseudo-will is of a highly insufficient degree for them to be diagnosed as such and go against the true problems of modern society. As leftists aren't actually preaching things that are coherent philosophies, it is why they have historically diluted every movement that formerly could have potentially opposed the ugly factors of modernity. This is a reason it's said movements should NEVER allow leftists in, or they are at huge risk of corruption.

It's also been warned, as a postulate of radical changes in society, that probably every radical movement tends to attract people with motives that loosely relate to the movement's goals.[36] But is it the case that now, leftist motives are actually the complete inversion of the movement's goals but well hidden under linguistic connotations? Like, from where things are at this rate, it appears leftists are turning "save the environment" into an unrealistic imaginary scenario where there is a constant increase of universal comfort and corporate consumption all while allowing a surplus of crowdedness in a given fixed spatial area—environmentalism went from a movement for alleviating consumption and respecting the relationship between a living thing and its natural environment, to a globohomoland where it is prohibited to live in the wilderness. Leftists effectively strip words of their power (likewise, in the long term, the words they initially deem "offensive" and supposedly give too much "power" to eventually may go extinct).

Leftish thought has even strayed the word "nature" to a mutilated parody of its proper sense of the term, almost beyond repair. Alright, I don't feel like I should have to do this, but I'm going to "drop and explain" nature's original meaning, because it will be important going further and I know some of you readers are probably really stupid and have to be reminded of something that people long ago knew.

---

[33] E. Dutton, *Breeding the Human Herd* (Imperium Press, 2023), 130.
[34] Ibid., 131.
[35] A. Alekseev, O. Gurov, A. Segal, and A. Sheludyakov, "Ideas as Infections: Introduction to the Problematics of Cognitive Metaparasitism," *Epistema*, 1(2023). https://doi.org/10.18254/S0028991-0
[36] T. Kaczynski, *Anti-Tech Revolution: Why and How* (Scottsdale: Fitch & Madison, 2020), 107.

It's unpleasantly striking that today, "nature" is used in cliché ways such as being on the opposite side of the spectrum from rationality.[37] Or worse still, something that exists only where there are no humans.[38] To start with you normie readers' epic cleansing of your possibly shitty meaning of nature, start by understanding the mere environment as not simply interchangeable with nature.[39] (It more so covers a wide range of phenomena related to our perception of our surroundings). Okay, now it's epic redpill time!

The term "natural" originates from the Latin "natura," which is etymologically linked to "nascor" (to be born).[40] This etymology suggests that the concept of "natural" is intrinsically connected to where something came from—the intrinsic quality that constitutes the very being of an entity. The "nature" of something would be the fundamental essence of the subject in question. Historically, "nature" has been perceived as a pervasive generative process of the cosmos, an ever-present act of creation manifesting across all times and places. This generative principle is evident in human reproduction and artistic endeavors, as well as in other kinds of life and the spontaneous processes of the universe itself. Nature, therefore, is not just a static singular thing but an active, dynamic force underlying substantial existence and creativity. Now let's contrast it with the artificial. The term "artificial"[41] is derived from "artificialis," from "artifex." "Artifex" is composed of "ars" (meaning art. Also, LMBO (laughing my b*tt (or arse) off) it rhymes like the word "arse") and "facere" (meaning to do/make). In this context, something artificial is simply that which is crafted with a certain technique.

It may be easy to confuse the "creativity" that is associated with "nature" and the "art and fabrication" that would be in the artificial. However, one must observe that certain abstractions bear an inherent "syntheticness," existing independently, devoid of intrinsic substance. While they "merely exist," their significance becomes contingent upon the presence of a conscious, philosophizing being—a "natural" entity, who interprets and projects meaning. If we are to negate this presence, a passive form of artificiality can easily arise in which the function of an object is transformed into a singular, unspontaneous, and directed form—yet surprisingly randomly selected for without any meddling from a substantial being, such that in some "ideal" end, it tends to only be of a certain rigidity that fits an impersonal "automatistic mass." Perhaps it is for this reason we label "ideas" generated through technological means as "artificial." A language model, for instance, is just a structured web of symbols and representations. Without a natural being to endow these words with significance, the language remains hollow. Social justice warriors don't count.

To gain a more epic understanding of the term "nature" in its original sense, we might posit that its meaning of "to be born" encompasses a qualitative aspect, not merely a quantitative one. This describes lifeforms that are born with dignity, live with dignity, and continue this dignified legacy through their successors. Similarly, words that exist must

---

[37] G. Ruivenkamp, S. Hisano, and J. Jongerden (Eds.), *Reconstructing Biotechnologies: critical social analyses* (Wageningen: Wageningen Academic Publishers, 2008), 301-326.

[38] Editorial, "Handle with care," *Nature* 455(2008): 263-264. https://doi.org/10.1038/455263b

[39] A. Berleant, *Environment and the Arts: Perspectives on Environmental Aesthetics* (Ashgate, 2002).

[40] F. Ducarme and F. Couvet, "What does 'nature' mean?" *Palgrave Commun*, 14(2020). https://doi.org/10.1057/s41599-020-0390-y

[41] D. Harper, "Etymology of artificiality," *Online Etymology Dictionary*, https://www.etymonline.com/word/artificiality

be those that maintain their context within the lifeworld to retain their significance and vitality. This would be a "far cry" from a case where a man would unsubstantially try to "roast" someone's adopted pet dog by telling it "ur adopted" (copying the epic infamous roast that the "pog" live streamer "Ninjaj" (Taylor Blevins) of the epic hit video game "'Fort-Night' from the studio 'epic gaming studios'" once said to a "squeaker," before he became an unepic "inoff*nsive" normie streamer. I heard he has "ligma," but that is a "cringe" dead meme now. You should instead use "nigma," the epic new "dank" meme cooler than the tuber gamers "Mr. Breast" and "Putiepie").

The automaton nature of modern leftists is far from an ability to humanistically evaluate any kind of idea, nor are they even reasonable at all. Though they are mainstreamly called the brave and daring radicals who are smart only because they take up the majority of an anti-intellectual turf that we call mainstream institutional academia, while other people are either called "the ignorant masses," "that one crazy uncle/aunt/cousin," or "w*ird." As the truly anti-social ones, social justice warriors are the kinds of people who are robotized to an uncurable degree. They diligently work in favor of an "ideal" totalitarian state as they fancy human society as some "input-output" system that rightly ravages our natural intuitions... and that the "economereeno" and society are the only two components of an input for a one-to-one machine that would eventually ejaculate a perfect politically correct utopia by chance... all without them having to come up with a coherent philosophy...

Leftists could be thought of as enablers of modern technologization, who mindlessly parrot institutionalized negations that obscure the fundamental problems of this "susiety," believing that it's only the so-called "marginalized" who have been squeezed out by the restrictive system,[42] rather than being aware the system is doing a massively perverse negation of life and nature as a whole. For instance, the left has a prevalent "idea" in which media should include marginalized groups overtly while simultaneously having to AVOID the stereotypes and distinguishable differences, implying that this negation is necessary for the path of progress, regardless of how many marginalized groups the system already pretends to acknowledge.[43] This endless negation spiral ultimately deconstructs the notion and possibility of meaningful cultural, social group, and individual differences.

There is a very good reason why no matter what, social justice warriors (obviously despite this label name) and normies alike are hardwired to avoid digging deep into the following questions: Is it really "good" for mediocre wagecuckery to be the standard universal occupation of mankind? Why is it that in modern times, morphological structures that used to be significant turn into vestigial structures, be it under the context of linguistics or the beings that conceive such symbols? Does this have anything to do with how soft and ignorant people have become? We can laugh all we want about leftists being the ones at fault for preventing gamers from saying the n-word, but listen, would such a restriction possibly entail a sign of the extinction of mankind and of all life in the universe? What are the deeper things we need to discuss?

---

[42] C.A. Haag, *Hermeneutical Death: The Technological Destruction of Subjectivity* (Independently Published, 2020), 657.
[43] Ibid., 654-656.

THIRD WARNING: From then on after this run-off sentence, I will massively reduce my usage of Post "Gen-G" ("generation gamers") reference dialect, like the excessive inconsistently censored swear words (so if you can't handle words any more profane than "F***ING" (farting) or H*LL (Aych-Ee-Double hockey stick), then beware) and explanatory brackets (with all the *"semantic" multi-parenthesis*), as I am confident that for any of the "late stage modernity thought police" who might start to go through this book to decide whether to "**** it" (the IRL non-gamer version of getting phased from online game and losing all your "v-bux" from "Fort-Night online store"), this would be the stopping point where those "bots" (epic insult name to "gamers" who are bad at gaming) would be willing to reach—then after, they'd likely be too robotic to determine whether "Poeslaw" (a principle which states there is no way to tell if something is serious or simply satire) applies after "averaging out" the text.

Chapter One: Disordered Feudalism

FOURTH WARNING: I don't know how much time I have to write this book, but I know it isn't much (another reason why I will no longer be laboriously using Post "Gen-G" (just a reminder, it means "generation gamers") reference dialect as often for the rest of this book). I'm worried that a mammy (she's a woke bugman) will find out and cancel my live subscription, and I need to get my thoughts down and out before they lose relevance due to language shifts (Please bear with my imperfect narration reliability. Again, grammar commies should beware—just as you shouldn't judge a "game" by its "cinematic pre-rendered aquaware trailer promoting the in-game pre-order bonuses," don't judge a book by literalness). Lastly, here's a final reminder warning to address the small brains reading this book: the start of each chapter contains scattered "big brain" critical discussions about "grown up" things such as "t*xes," "p*litics," "w*r," and "s*x" that may confuse unprepared gamers. Again, feel free to skip to the story sections if you so choose, unless you want to prove yourself as an "I_am_420_and_this_is_deep" philosopher.

What happens when "pure" ideas, reflected in the physical world, become so governed and cucked by uniform laws that they ultimately fail to embody any real form, even subjectively? Very little is discussed about how damn ensnaring horizontal propaganda is (it's more subtle and pervasive than traditional propaganda and operates laterally among peers and social networks rather than coming from "one propagandist")[44], and how it may even be worse than an obviously visible domineering figure disseminating the vertical kind of propaganda. Do we actually find ourselves in a modern era reminiscent of a "disordered feudal time"? In the declining days of the past, there are historical images abound of tyrannical kings who would silence potential dissent by severing the tongues of those they suspected might speak out words that they may not like. It can't be repeated enough that this now manifests in a more modern form. Through sheer frequency, despots create an environment where dissenting thought is stifled purely by force, but force as in the overwhelming noise that drowns out genial "talk." What kind of a system is this exactly? Perhaps a "predictive sentencing" method of persecution in favor of some invisible elite?

Regarding the use of "predictive systems" in sentences based on forecasts of re-offense or re-arrest likelihood, if one considers "retributivist" theories, the severity of punishment would be proportional to the offense committed, not to the predicted future behavior—thus, risk forecasts do not align with retributivist principles of punishment proportionality.[45] Tyrannical kings who cut the tongues of those they predict will speak against them also engage in the same kind of pre-emptive punishment. Going by this logic, it may be the case that the modern leftist, who has selective hearing regarding whose rights they should protect or what they deem "politically correct enough" in the form of the tyrant, is the true discriminator as it is like predictive sentencing. Unlike the predictive

---

[44] J. Ellul, *Propaganda: The Formation of Men's Attitudes* (New York: Vintage Books, 1965), 81

[45] C. Castro, A. Rubel, and L. Schwartz, "Does predictive sentencing make sense?" *Inquiry,* (2024): 1-20. https://doi.org/10.1080/0020174X.2024.2309876

type, retributive justice requires punishment to be proportionate to actual wrongs, not anticipated ones. Wouldn't the pre-emptive punishments violate this principle by punishing for imagined future disobedient speech?

On overcrowded social platforms, the sheer volume of users and their pseudo-ideas can lead to profound ideas being misinterpreted and deemed "repugnant" when taken out of context. The sheer numbers (think of the exponential spread of plagues in feudal times) without the coding that separates entities from other entities often exhibit the same collective behavior as the employed algorithms to predict and moderate content (like "Sampsons" cartoon show predicting "the guys behind the slaughter" and "the bite of '87" (Reference to "FNAF" (Fort-Nights at Fred's, played by Markiplayer the player of scary games)). All this is what the globalizing technological world inflicts—it embodies some of the worst forms of tyranny, anarcho-tyranny. This is a system where everything is illegal, but the law is enforced very arbitrarily and biased against the enemy of the system, even just for one small misstep.[46] However, aren't the leftists not only friends of the tyrant but also function as uniformly distributed "useful idiot nodes" for the ruling class? Does this mean one must constantly be neurotic scaredy cats around them?

More curious… how low are the chances of challenging prevailing norms through speech alone when it is not only hindered but "systematically dismantled"? The intentional push for democratizing voices paradoxically exacerbates a problem—the channel of moving thought becomes either too accessible, leading to an overabundance of trivialities, or too restrictive, squeezing out the space where thoughtful ideas can flourish. In this milieu, superficial soundbites thrive. Their origins usually make it above the barrier of "clearly nonsense," yet they lack the depth necessary for substance. These simplistic fragments become fodder for virtual inquisitors who caricature and dismantle any semblance of "big brain speak." How much would the problem be compounded by the sheer number of participators in a given space? When individuals are spread across a small fixed space, it leads to "oversocialization," in Kaczynskian terms (this refers to an excessive form of the process by which people are trained to think and act as society demands[47]), but has been corrupted to something that people designate as "the more you are it, the freer you are"—would you dare even use the term "oversocialization" in public, given the high risk of them accusing you of being anti-social or asocial only because it sounds like such?

This oppression creates an environment akin to a tangle of radio signals. Complex ideas demand any slight contemplation from those who are supposed to struggle to survive in this environment. Many thoughts beyond buzzwords are ruthlessly torn from their original frameworks and recontextualized in ways that render them seemingly absurd— isn't it just a kind of unconscious "natural selection" within the crowd that favors brevity from hecklers, reducing context to the point where it can be easily misrepresented? I will admit firstly that heckling should be protected in principle because it often contributes to new ideas—but there are devilish hecklers who merely disrupt without adding value.[48] There must then be a difference between "associative liberty" (being able to make clear

---

[46] V. McLeod, *Clown World Chronicles* (VJM Publishing, 2020), 42.

[47] T. Kaczynski, *Industrial Society and its Future* (Independently published, 2018), para. 24.

[48] E. McTernan and R.B Simpson, "Heckling, Free Speech, and Freedom of Association," *Mind*, 133(2023): 117-142. https://doi.org/10.1093/mind/fzad049

what social, cultural, or ideological group a person is associated with) and "free speech." For instance, in closed contexts such as private meetings, heckling that disrupts "associative purposes" can at least be potentially suppressed.[49] Otherwise, in more impersonal crowded spaces, even though modern democracy (which functions under the absurd assumption that everyone is somehow uniform copies of each other) is facilitating so much of the heckling, it ironically ceases to be a speech democracy at all, as genuine philosophical thought decreases. You can see how the meek and valueless disordered "rulers" are the ones who are somehow getting the bigger megaphone—this isn't even relevant to one's physical amplitude of signals because there is another layer that dictates heckling power. Isn't the real issue that freedom of association is invalidated because a word's meaning is now heavily influenced by surrounding words, even meaningless external utterances?

Worse still, a factor that may worsen this is whether we are continuing to even be allowed to be silent anymore. Right now, it's actually really funny how it's not the case that people are being silenced from the literal sense of the term, but the other way around, in that the system has ways to pressure people to say something for the system's own benefit. For instance, there is a behavioral tendency in which people voice thoughts even if they haven't considered their truthfulness rather than staying silent, to conform and participate in the collective discourse.[50] It's also argued that some languages have evolved to be deceiving for survival needs[51] and that it is advantageous for people to accept incoming communication as true as an adaptive output,[52] both of which align with the value systems of those who seek mere existence/survival and conformity rather than higher existence, a kind of nihilism prevalent in modernity. This all would result in further worsening the "idea value" of pure statements. Man, would I rather be a mute mime... because in contrast, it has been observed that silence could be a form of great meaningful expression, interpretable in different ways, such as rapport, reluctance, or protest[53] (This is what "us introverts" can do to recharge our "social batteries" on the spot). Besides, the presence of language by itself proves inadequate for communication.[54] Isn't it a funny thing that the "compulsory representation problem" in modern times functions a lot in reverse of how it's posited as "free speech"? Worse still, an individual who is outside of an oppressed group may at some point be pressured to speak about "the oppressed" at some point to acknowledge their existence—with time, would the system eventually "find" a way via "brute force" to punish both them and even the supposed "oppressed ones" in some way?

---

[49] Ibid.

[50] J. Ellul, *Propaganda: The Formation of Men's Attitudes* (New York: Vintage Books, 1965), 210.

[51] N. Oesch, "Deception as a Derived Function of Language," *Frontiers in psychology*, 7(2016). https://doi.org/10.3389/fpsyg.2016.01485

[52] T.R. Levine, *Duped: Truth-Default Theory and the Social Science of Lying and Deception* (University of Alabama Press, 2019).

[53] N. Müller, P. Tavares, and J. Simão, "How Should We Interpret Silence in Qualitative Communication Studies?" *Social Sciences*. 13(2024): 310. https://doi.org/10.3390/socsci13060310

[54] S. Durrleman, E. Peristeri, and I.M. Tsimpli, "The language-communication divide," *Evolutionary Linguistic Theory*, 4(2022): 5-51. https://doi.org/10.1075/elt.00037.dur

First Day of COMM

I woke up with a load of floating stars in my field of view. It made it somehow painful to have the eyes BOTH closed and open, as their sharp edges dug at my vulnerable vision, inducing my eyes to jack up even more of those stars. I was motivated to get up and go to the washroom to finally break this self-feeding loop.

As I walked into my washroom, I absolutely dreaded the online school semester that was going to begin today. It may seem normal, for a modern bugman to think of "online classes" as an opportunity, like "HECK YeSSsS I GeT tO sAvE eNERgY BY sitTinG." That is not the attitude of people like me. I get my energy by moving, and when I have to undergo a long period of mere standing or sitting, I begin to have the urge to pop imaginary pimples (not mine of course) to the point where they look like one of those exotic mushrooms that resemble squirting coochies. *GOD DAMN, I AM ALREADY REPULSED BY WRITING ABOUT THIS; was it a mistake even to write this book?*

I started my cleanup routine by selecting the music I listen to, the kinds of music that would have to substitute for the badass animal growls you'd imagine in a safari—none of which exist in America today, especially in the very city I live in (I won't name my city for your safety, but I can tell you it is literally Silicon Valley on estrogenic steroids ("Commiefornia in Ohio") yet still a "hidden" place with disgusting aspects that both news and social media, for some reason, never talk about).

As I finished up listening to one of those bodybuilding motivation videos that always use the best music (but never gets credited in the metadata, so I always have to go to that very video to listen), I already had beads of sweat running down my forehead because this was basically my cardio for the day—time stops when I "jammerz."

I was in my own world... until I saw my upper teeth... blood. Fuck, my insane muscles made me brush my gums too hard. Also, I forgot to floss literally once, something that was unneeded before we began eating the kinds of diet that no longer clean our teeth naturally (now it's too much libt*rd v*getables and grocery soy). Ask yourself: how do animals in the wild remain fine without flossing?

As I dunked my head under the bathroom sink faucet to rinse my mouth, I watched the diluted, yet broader stream of "iron" trickle down the drain, creepily contrasting with the light sink bowl. The non-sterility briefly made me feel like a barbarian—a feeling of living in nature with animals. I correspondingly looked into the mirror and saw my huge biceps. I flexed them and did a front double bicep pose. I felt the "primal" need to emulate the bodybuilding motivation videos. I could envision myself as free from the bounds of the ground, almost as if I were now outdoors. I imagined angel wings behind me, mirroring what the motivation videos' thumbnails depicted the bodybuilders as (Most of my favorite bodybuilders are dead. Not that I endorse it, but they at least had the braveness to take testosteronal steroids towards a "Chad" physique beyond their physiological limits, a breath of fresh air in the modern world where pussies are so scared of death and risk-taking). But as the thought of drugs being injected reminded me of the synthetic reality of modern buglife, I felt a wind of dullness take me back to the ground. As I psychologically fell and hit my neck against the sink, my imagination was overdone by the fact that my first online class of the day (I was attending a liberal arts school... JUST KIDDING HAHA, IT HAS THE WORD LIB*RAL IN IT) was to commence in "five

MINUTES." Too bad it's the last five minutes of the weekend. I am sad to have "woke" up to this. Wait a minute… "WOKE"?

As I rushed to clean my toothbrush, I put my phone in my pocket and used the fabric of my pajamas to clean the rest, then left the washroom. The next thing to do was the proximal opposite of what a daily IRL school morning routine would be—I went back to the bedroom. As I opened my laptop, which I leave on because fuck the long ass passive process of turning on or shutting it down when I begin or stop a soyternet session, I realized that I wasn't exactly prepared for classes commencing…

I still haven't updated the damn video call software. I was reminded of this when the update warning jumpscared me, and it was going to take a few minutes, just in time. As I waited, I curiously went onto the learning management system website to peek at what exactly this class was. It was an elective that my mother chose for me because I had zero idea what class electives even were at the time. Growing up, I was never the one making the decisions of my life, and I always had shit decided by some external decider. But hey, at least I am becoming a self-awarewolf now.

The course was "Communications: Critical Reading and Writing." It was a class that supposedly teaches students how the media can be biased, and how to interpret media "properly." One would probably foolishly think in response, "Holy fuckik, My scHool is bAsed for carrYing a clAss tHat teAchEs about news media nOt BeiNg perfect, HoW IS THiS NOT iN THE GOVErNMENT WAtCHLIsT. MAYBE THE GOVERNMENT IS BECOMING BASED. WE ARE IN THE GREAT AWOKENING!" But listen, this is controlled opposition, as the following events may show.

Once the online class software at last finally finished loading the update, I clicked on the newly installed tab of the software. The dark interface screamed "I am not a simplistic web browsing tool, but rather an interactable full-blown function that does much more than present text and images." Then, sets of buttons, mainly red and green, appeared, forming a gateway to what was supposed to be the class. I clicked on the biggest one; I didn't bother reading the labels on the buttons; it's pretty standardized at this point what parts of interfaces lead to what software function. Soon, a bunch of placeholder cartoonish faceless heads popped into the screen. I guess it started with mine initially, the system's way of making each participant feel special. Then piles upon piles of others emerged. Their names were instantly visible, and then I was able to gauge what each person may look like (People are so mind-cucked right now that they tend to robotically partially trim their appearance and behaviors by the semantics of their names). The first full name I noticed was "Ryan Youngross," and I immediately envisioned a slightly chubby man who would probably be playing video games while distracted during class. *He probably looks a bit "young" for his age with a buzzcut, still looking like a high schooler amongst most of us who are in the 20–70-year-old range.*

Yeah, I am not joking when I mention that the age range in my area for the college's entrepreneurship and innovation program is as wide as a pancake. The "more experienced age max" is due to entrepreneurship being a high-stake way of making money. Most young people are pussies these days, preferring to have an employer because, in a way, it's like anticipating new parents, whether the parents are good or not. Even then, most who are enrolled in the entrepreneurship and innovation program are pussies anyway, as they already have their small balls deep into their own already established wage jobs, and it wouldn't hurt them as much to live on ramen if their business idea fails.

As I finished visually extrapolating the first-last name, "Ryan Youngross," in this current context, I noticed the next name. That name wasn't close to Ryan's name on the screen. It was in the far end. I only noticed that name because it had a bold string of text next to it that said "instructor." It flared up an interesting emotional response in me, rough in texture and coarse of a feeling. I could imaginatively listen to a blast of ambulances outside crashing onto a rough pavement, and the pregnant woman inside it launches off the back and lands in such a way that she falls into one of the concrete pillars, and it kills her and the baby inside her as a double kill. I think of the double death because when one is about to have a new professor, two things are going to be found out: the quality of the class learning, and the actual grades that will result, both of which likely will suck ass.

Now, I at last summoned the courage to take a read of the professor's name. It was "Mr. Beckford." As I squinted my eyes to reread it a gazillion times over and over, I began to envision a manlet who wore a white stained dirty shirt. He probably wears his pants ultra high, which causes his skinny legs to look even skinnier due to the illusion of longer legs. He perhaps has a jutted-out nose that's so long that it can peck tree wood because when you think of it, "beck" rhymes with "peck."

So far, I guessed he was going to be a shitty turd professor because, man, would it suck to have some beta cuck be the one you have to look at for two hours straight. I absolutely fucking hate looking at soyboys. It stands that it's absolutely the case that people tend to shape themselves into what they are exposed to for a long time. Hang around people who are small as fuck, and you are guaranteed to reverse half your entire career of lifting weights.

Soon, the little microphone symbol under the professor's name changed from a crossed-off microphone to a "line microphone." Then, the anonymous faceless head icon that was supposed to represent him disappeared, replaced by a face with actual shadow and lighting.

Actually, the "shape" part of my description can be considered minute, as the man behind this specific web camera was a (dark skin) man. Strikingly, he was ethnically ambiguous, and I couldn't tell whether he was just some light-skinned dude who spent a lot of time tanning during a hot vacation over the summer. Now regarding body shape, Mr. Beckford exhibited a silhouette that fucked up my guess-ability-based self-esteem. He seemed to be on the thicker side, and I say thicker rather than "big" or "fat" because I had no clue whether it was fat or muscle. He was wearing one of those semi-baggy striped button-up shirts. Plus, the only part of his actual body other than his head that was showing was his shoulders. His shoulders were on the narrow side, and I could only tell he was on the thicker side rather than skinny by the size of his neck. It was cute and chubby not gonna lie, and I would be tempted to tickle it. All in all, his build was the type of shape where it's the "cute" kind of large rather than the "intimidating" kind. I could imagine him waddling like a little penguin if I were to ever see him on campus.

At last, amidst my analyzing, Mr. Beckford began to speak. "Good morning class, welcome to COMM. I require you all to turn your cameras on, I want to see all those beautiful faces!"

That killed me. Why does he have to be so fucking enormously lame? Is that all you have to say? Come on I PAID LITERAL REAL MONEY FOR CLASSES AND THIS IS WHAT I get????? PAYING FOR COLLEGE IS THE REAL-LIFE EQUIVALENT TO SPENDING THOUSANDS ON ROBUCKS? SO WHY IS THE FIRST THING I HEAR A CALLING FOR US ALL TO SHOW ALL OUR UGLY FACES?!!!!! (except mine).

I cringed at the non-sigma-male conformity of my classmates as I watched people's real-life faces begin to manifest into light. Around thirty students did so in such a short timeframe that I had no time to watch them individually—I was primarily focused on what I should do. Why the hell do I have to listen to an overweight man who I would easily outrun in real life?

Eventually, once everyone had their cameras on, I was the only one everyone didn't know the appearance of—I was the one behind the anonymous graphic head. I hopped out of my chair and did bodybuilding poses in front of the turned-off webcam, while knowing no one was seeing them (all that mattered was I was still the lion of the herd for being the only one who didn't turn on my web camera).

But then, I heard Mr. Beckford speak again. "You are getting kicked out of this class permanently if you don't turn on your camera in the next ten seconds. I froze. *HECKING NO.* I rushed back down to my seat and spam-clicked the "camera on" button. I was desperate, and I sat hunchback in concentration beyond the range of high returns. Soon, it worked, and I thought, *HUE* (phew).

I just made it to a safe zone. I then made sure to look at Ryan's face. Ryan looked pretty much how I expected, just a bit older. I also had a sense of relief upon seeing him, albeit for an entirely different reason. To be more precise about his actual appearance though, he was balding, revealing a head sort of shaped like an egg. He had a "med beard," indicating he had medium levels of testosterone relative to how many androgen receptors and hair follicles I guessed he had in his chin. He wore a stained army-colored shirt, which I guessed smelled like dirt because of the time I guessed he'd spend in public b*throoms on the phone, accumulating putrid smell (the word "gross" is literally in "Youngross" lol).

After I was done realizing my "I see this as an absolute win" (Soy he/him-hulk from Marvelous Adventures Endergame Superhero War "the most ambitious crossover" meme reference) of guessing, I scanned everyone else's face. What I saw absolutely horrified me. It was the kind of horror one would get if they saw a giant cockroach-looking cricket. And I gotta say, "cricket" is an excellent way of describing the appearances of these people. They all had round faces at the bottom—soyboy mouths with corners that spanned in between their eyes, amounting to mouths that looked like they'd be good "human centipede" candidates due to the lip tightness. Many wore glasses as overly thick as Mr. Beckford's, but for some reason, theirs magnified their eyeballs to such a degree that they looked like the "'stereotypical young nerdish boy in the family' trope" in movies. Some of them had face piercings giving off the look of an old hag with a feminine mohawk appearance—so sucked into a personification of even the abstract notion of "institution" that I could feel my bones growing out calcium spikes that pierced my flesh to the point of internal pain. I can't overgeneralize their hairs, because they all had dyed hair, all different colors. If I could choose one "average" color hex code, blue was the most common one. If I could overgeneralize the kinds of clothing they wore, they were either t-shirts of disgusting "musical raper bands" that you never want to touch if you want to be an average person, or the stereotypical ugly sweater that grandma made (but not *that* ugly because the yarn actually looks kind of adorable). FUCKING HEAD BOBBING LIBWALLSSS!

Mr. Beckford started going through the syllabus, agenda, and basic instructions on navigating the classroom interface. "Okay, guys, as we are in a time in history where "fake news" and misinformation, critical reading and information analysis are essential for making decisions and determining whether one should take a course of action. In addition to evaluating the credibility, intent, and veracity of texts by others, students will create their own texts individually and in collaboration with their peers. Upon completing this course, you will be able to write academic reports and other texts using research and information literacy skills. Deliver oral presentations within a specified time limit, with well-organized and accessible information."

Cringe. *Delivering oral presentations with accessible information? More like "delivering oral sex" in the vein of cucking your intellectuality and bowing to the herd.*

"The literature review will take up 35% of the final mark. The reading quizzes will take up 15% of the final mark. The final presentation will take up 25% of the final mark. The online discussion forums will take up 20% of the final mark. And finally, the 'introduce yourself to your fellow students' mark, which you will do in the first opened online discussion forum, will take up 5%."

Literature review? Haha, what a joke; we all know what political side the grade will be biased toward. More like "read more into the leftoid garbage." Wait, here is what is worse: *INTRODUCE YOURSELF TO CLASS ONLINE? NOOOOOOOO.* I know I'm gonna get so damn nervous, not because of the introduction itself, but because it is onl*ne and the website is gonna steal my digital blueprint that says my favorite food is raw meat!!!! The Industrial Revolution and its consequences have been a disaster for the human race!!!!

After Mr. Beckford finished rambling about how the rest of the class would work, he continued his tract by shoving the first lecture. "Okay, we will start by talking about connotations! This will be a fun one!" He moved on to the presentation's first slide, which was decorated into the theme of my college's media package—dark blue and light blue within a background of white. The title of the first content slide read: *THE DREADED N-WORD (insert scared emoji).* He began his starting point. "Just for fun, does anyone care to say the n-word right now? Go ahead and open your microphones!"

Cricket noises began. But not the cricket noises you think I mean. I mean that the cricket-looking conformist college liberals began to yap. "Someone please say the n-word! It's part of the class!"

I looked at the other students; they looked hesitant, although they were somewhat tempted. Maybe this will be the chance for somebody to feel special in their lives of boring mediocrity. As for my own reaction, even though I am a "Chad," there was an exceptional kind of angst in me. I didn't know why. I was the only guy who refused to turn on my camera at the start even though Mr. Beckford demanded it hard (I was legit "the final boss of social anxiety" (funny meme)), so what the hell was stopping me from saying the n-word? It was like I shrunk suddenly. After half a minute passed, as the college liberals continued to chant for someone to say the n-word, I got uncomfortable and began to ask Mr. Beckford a question, asking whether he was serious. "Mr. Beckford, I-"

Suddenly, I realized that I had made a colossal mistake…

"HOW DARE YOU REFER TO HIM AS 'N-WORD,' RacIng CisT," all of them said to me in a cult-like sync. "We asked you to say the n-word and you responded with this black professor's name instead?"

"What?! No, I only said his name! I was just starting to ask him a question! I mean no harm! If anything, you liberals are the prejudiced ones for assuming he is black."

Mr. Beckford intervened, initially in my favor. "Yeah to be fair, for the record, I am not black. I just tan really easily."

The normies ignored all the facts. "Big lies! Misinformation! This lecture is being recorded anyway, and we have solid proof!"

"You are the ones who are on the side of misinformation, the audiovisual kind of it!" I spoke.

I then wondered, I am such a jacked "Chad," and weaklings usually wouldn't have the guts to mess with me—what the fuck? Heck, my shoulders and traps are my strongest and most developed body parts, which should show through my web camera.

I then peeped at my own. What I saw shocked me. I, for some reason, appeared very skinny. What! This has to be trickery! But then it dawned on me—the curse of overdeveloped traps! I don't mean the curse of having high testosterone, because traps tend to have the highest number of androgen receptors across most muscle groups, but I mean traps can literally make a person look like an average non-lifter at a certain angle. If you ever see a picture of a professional bodybuilder in a standing position, then use your finger to cover the shoulder but still allow the traps to remain seen; the traps will look like THE shoulders, a very narrow set of shoulders at that.

Well, here is what happened: I was still in the crouched position after having been stressed by Mr. Beckford's strict request that I turn on my camera, and my shoulders happened to be hidden beneath the bottom end of the camera's field of view. Only my traps were visible. The college liberals literally thought I was small!

I decided to do my ultimate introduction stance. I pointed my finger up and, at last, sat up straight. There, I looked like a literal pro. My pecs popped out, almost ripping through my shirt. I thought this would scare them off to the point of them leaving the meeting. However, the other way around happened. The college liberals only got angry. "He's got muscles, therefore he's a fascist! A fascist fitness member!"

"Never heard of that group, but I am certainly in 'The Liberal Termination Crew.'" But on the inside, I was irritated. God damn, I should have remembered leftists have a hatred towards images of being strong, as it makes them resentful.

Mr. Beckford soon appeared scared, conformed to the liberals, and then threatened to kick me out for supposedly starting the commotion.

I gave up. I clicked the "leave meeting" button and then closed the laptop before anyone could boot me out of the virtual meeting to retain my last bit of autonomy.

Chapter Two: Hedonism/Asceticism

I do not think it can ever be overstated that it doesn't help when moronic leftists try to appear morally superior, picking on those who still live in the society that he critiques. Even if one is "plugged" into the open-air simulation, it doesn't mean he rides its simulated penis. Comprehending the inherent ugliness of totalitarian modernity transcends the mere act of contemplative idleness, as typified by the traditional image of the sophist in artistic depictions, or the drastic severance from the oppressive simulation that envelopes our being. Could the recognition of the absurd conditions born from a life deprived of nature also offer profound insights into "existential purpose"?

Modern society and its logical extensions, the technological system, possess distinct teleological endpoints; how many of them do you know? Whatever the case may be, the means to those ends of dissolution are supplanted by synthetic ways that appear to oppose modernism itself. These engineered diversions appear to offer greater freedom but are merely recycled forms of despotism, rebranded under new guises. Could they also manifest as pseudo-ascetic lifestyles promoted through the distortion of history and data, thereby appealing to those seeking uniqueness within an inherently artificial reality?

We are currently in a paradigm of nihilism, with certain fixed values that can be conjured up or reached regardless of active philosophizing (such as a static technique to reach an absolute level of "efficiency"), which nets a valueless society subject-wise. This is what makes controlled opposition such a seamless tool of coercion for the state. For instance, it is argued that the kind of pseudo-asceticism that the system promotes is just hedonism in disguise for those who want to compensate for their overtly hedonistic activities in the past.[55] There is a good reason why mainstream news propaganda actively pats the back of those who want to promote "organic vibes"[56] (such as the fake vegan LARPers (Live Action Role Players)—veganism is only favored virtuously in modernity because it is currently considered more efficient than otherwise for the system, in terms of production and learned passivity). "Asceticism" comes in many forms in modern times, but it is now a beliefless reaction to the indulgences of hedonism, and nothing more. Could the system's version of "asceticism" even be worse than overt hedonism because it itself is both pleasure-seeking and a "poison pill"?

The kind of chokepoint modernity has us in is these "reactions to reactions," and therefore, us being misled into thinking we'll wrangle ourselves out of "the susiety" as it seems as though "look at all the mainstream ideological options that appear to be against it!" Consider that under the technological system, propaganda doesn't actually seek to change actual beliefs, but only to induce the subject to take on actions and behaviors that are useful to the system without having some prior reason to do so based on firm principles.[57] And there may even be certain contradictions between different ideas

---

[55] L. Smith, "Hedonism, Asceticism and the Hermetic Answer," *Luke Smith's Webpage* (3rd September 2020), https://lukesmith.xyz/articles/hedonism-asceticism-and-the-hermetic-answer/

[56] L. Smith, "Veganism Is the Pinnacle of Bugmanism," *Luke Smith's Webpage* (11th February 2021), https://lukesmith.xyz/articles/veganism-is-the-pinnacle-of-bugmanism/.

[57] J. Ellul, *Propaganda: The Formation of Men's Attitudes* (New York: Vintage Books, 1965), 25

promoted by the system, which the individual becomes oblivious to due to the propaganda itself exceeding and overflowing their capabilities of resistance.[58] It is clear to most by now that controlled opposition extends to the whole "liberal versus conservatives" cliché that we all are deep down tired of hearing. We can see how they are two buttcheeks of the same ass when it comes to asceticism and hedonism. Don't mainstream normie "conservatives" (more like cuckservatives) basically share the same type of archetype as liberals? For example, there is a striking contradiction in which they enthusiastically support technological progress and economic growth yet want traditional values.[59] Even though they have a love for "previous values," they long for the same kind of universal comforts that technically existed then as a function of some abstract magical infinite economic growth (like towards the definite level of "efficiency") that liberals themselves wish for. Have you also noticed that they tend to have that same feeling of euphoria of pretending to rebel for what the system is already teleologically oriented towards?

It's found that search engines and large language models reflect culturally dominant views based on the search language, creating "language bias," where different languages yield distinct information on the same search topic.[60] In the case of "liberalism," large language models confined it to human rights and equality regardless of the input language, while aspects like "limitation of government power" are absent.[61] In a modernized technological society moving toward a single universal language through globalization and one-world governance, could this drive people to view it as the "default" political stance? Might this be due to the word's association with "liberating" and a falsified view of the past? This is paralleled by the system's tendency to only attach the meaning of good-sound words with the definitions that the system mandated in advance, which, in this case, removes freedom. Isn't its current fixation on "equality" simply a result of the system erasing different beliefs and creating a synthetic, arbitrary pseudo-ideology? As technological globalization fully matures, could this ideology become a diluted blend of world beliefs, to the point of complete "forgetted"?

The term "conservatism" also seems to be experiencing ideological choking. Has "conserve" become merely a "feel good" term for those who favor the Lindy Effect? When you actually see what mainstream conservatives believe in right now, it appears the only thing the system mandated as "something to conserve" is the modern new technologies or techniques themselves, and anything outside this plane is forgotten and therefore excluded from the "list of things we should conserve." While proponents of liberal thought advocate for veganism and oppose climate change due to their assuredness in an emergent energy source that would replicate the efficacy of fossil fuels, mainstream conservatives might express skepticism towards global warming. But whether the warming is true or not, most of them are motivated by a desire for unchecked consumption. Ultimately, aren't the different kinds of real beliefs other than the controlled

---

[58] Ibid., 18.
[59] T. Kaczynski, *Industrial Society and its Future* (Independently published, 2018), para. 50.
[60] Q. Lou, M.J. Puett, and M.D. Smith, "A "Perspectival" Mirror of the Elephant: Investigating language bias on Google, ChatGPT, YouTube, and Wikipedia," *Queue*, 22(2024): 23–47. https://doi.org/10.1145/364930
[61] Ibid.

oppositions "technical mistakes," because "carbon copy" groups are more technically efficient than having to account for the different contexts of thinking individuals?

Despite their seeming opposition, both groups are manifestations of the same ideological isomorphism from the point of modernity's logical end conclusion. They often exhibit a propensity to vilify any individual who deviates from the perceived teleological trajectory of modernity, especially if that individual simultaneously aligns with certain aspects of it. In such instances, they are likely to seize upon opportunities to publicly undermine and discredit "the individual," revealing the underlying uniformity of their impulses. Now what makes this so shoddy, genuinely?

It is revealed how foundational assumptions about mankind make opposing stances on seemingly diverse issues, but just with the constrained and the unconstrained views of morality.[62] The regressive problems of hedonism and pseudo-asceticism lies in their elevation as the supreme constraining morality principles of modern society whether it's the constrained or unconstrained sense of the term, which easily detracts from individuals' capacity to forge new pathways of being (one is through a certain kind of order and the other is through tight "warmth"[63]). Even though modernity craves a form of "definite efficiency," this leaves the average individual oblivious to honorable work. As the saying goes, artistic, adventurous, and contemplative men belong to the rare breed who would rather perish than work without any pleasure IN their work; in this sense, they are choosy and hard to satisfy.[64] Furthermore, there is a warning that a diet entirely vegetarian may induce one to be in a position "to satisfy,"[65] to make up for a monotonous regimen. Effectively, it is in the technological system's interest to mandate its own ascetic ideals to control the populace into indulging in herdish pleasures instead. You tell me, how tired are you of meeting normies who mistakenly equate productivity with the monotonous routine of an eight-hour workday, which they think they can "make up for" through indulgences such as drinking the following night?

Shift at Burger Queen

There is a saying that everyone should work as a restaurant worker at least once in their life. While this has some substance, it misses the deeper point of what life really is.

I was behind the counter, filling sauce containers one by one. I squeezed the ketchup bottle, letting it make the funny-ass *SQUIRT* sound, and ensured the nozzle ended up within the bounds of the circular sauce container. The only difficulty then was trying not to laugh at the bottle sound.

As I filled in the last ketchup container, marking our now sufficient quantity of full containers to handle the rest of the online order demands, I looked around the food joint to see if there was anything else to do. The tables were all deserted, empty with the menus and spare ketchup and mustard bottles sitting on the edges. Drats, this is going to be boring. But I had to look like I was doing something. After all, there were cameras in

---

[62] T. Sowell, *A Conflict of Visions: Ideological Origins of Political Struggles*, (Basic Books, 2002).

[63] George Lakoff, *Moral Politics: How Liberals and Conservatives Think* (University of Chicago Press, 1996).

[64] F. Nietzsche, *The Gay Science* (Vintage Books, 1974), 108.

[65] Ibid., 193.

every room, including the r*strooms, making it impossible even to do the "'Wash your hands without using soap' b*throom challenge."

Oh yeah, about the restaurant, here is where it gets weird. It is one called Burger Queen. Name seems relatively normal right? Nah, it gets even weirder. The logo is a literal obese woman eating a veggie burger. Know what direction this is headed right? *OHHH NOOO IT'S WOKEEEEE AHHHHHHHHH WOKE MOB MADE THIS COWPOWATION!!* What really irks me is the place's supposed "value proposition" of vegan burgers—the "sleek" cartoonish logo of Burger Queen does a great job at hiding the nodes that would trigger one's disgust response towards the actual food.

I go back into the kitchen to review how rustic things already are. All the walls are covered in grease, which looks like washrooms that haven't been cleaned in a while, or tiled showers that somehow have weird mold substances growing in the corners despite being used daily. I looked at the plates and was equally as repulsed. They weren't thoroughly washed, and the dishwasher assigned to make eating platforms pearly white only takes 0.00005 seconds per dish, which is a stupidly brief swipe. If one were to run their hand against one so-called washed dish, and touch one of the hard dried food specks, they'd retract their hand in disgust as hard as if they'd accidentally cut the hand with a blade. It amazes me how many people are still willing to eat here even after knowing the reality of kitchen hygiene. It is even funnier when I see these rich-looking people who are already weirding us all out by wearing tuxedos and dresses in a stupid fast-food restaurant, non-hesitantly chomping.

As the chefs in the kitchen stare at me with their googly eyes while cutting some precooked meat, perhaps imagining themselves as my "Chad" physique preparing a pre-workout meal, I stare back at them, reminding them that aesthetics is important. I mean, I don't even care about Burger Queen anyway, and I know I'm probably gonna quit soon, but I gotta teach certain folks the correct virtues on the way.

This one specific chef, let's call him Kevin, tells me, "How's it going!"

"I didn't do nothing; I'm just making sure this place is well run!"

I'm so sorry, guys. I may look like a cuck as I attempt to "play manager," but shut up if you are laughing at my fakeness. Some things are scripts to be played today, as much as I hate doing them.

"Anything you would like to eat? I didn't see you eat all day!"

I almost pissed my pants. *Oh shit I have to eat.* The Burger Queen menu flashed before my eyes. Employees here can have one meal and drink for free as a lunch break. It may seem like a mere option, but look, I was 6 foot tall and pretty damn heavy for that height at the peak of my bulk at the time, and I burned 2000 calories daily if I didn't eat (like "your mom" (I'm joking)). I have to balance a part-time job and school, and I am barely scraping by. I am only paying rent at this point from a practical sense, and the only food I get for groceries is protein shakes and bars. "Ugh, I couldn't eat foods anymore because of how 'woke' and 'pronouns' they became!" Most of the food in Burger Queen are products that would slowly starve a person if they were to regularly eat them despite bloating them. Still, there is one particular item on the menu that can possibly help me maintain my gigantic musculature—the fries. I don't endorse eating this kind of processed shit, but I gotta do what I gotta do.

I asked Kevin to serve me one of those mega jumbo French fry buckets meant to be eaten by a family of six.

"Yes sir!"

"Nicesauce."

I exited the kitchen and did a little limb spread as I reached the front counter. I needed this breather as a little break from spending so much time in the pseudo-hell that we call pseudo-vegan kitchens. I was not surprised that there still wasn't any customer.

Sometimes, when there is no business, my intrusive thoughts get me to do some wacky little things. I climbed to the top of the front counter and began doing pushups. It was an ultra instinct whenever I know I am about to eat fatty things. Fat foods always do this psychological mindfuck to me; I always get that same feeling as when I sat for an hour for the online class lecture earlier today, me wanting to die.

As I felt my chest getting burned after my 100th push-up (hey, it's pretty impressive for me, remember I was bulking, and the pushups were without any breaks), I decided to start doing jumping jacks. My pushups quickly devolved into a brief plank, and then I stood up. I looked around to ensure no one was still in the building, then began jumping, flailing my arms and legs, and repeat. It was the literal embodiment of the Kaczynskian power process, I instantly felt like I was burning some psychological fat.

I guess I eventually got too busy and lost my focus on the external world because I accidentally knocked something off the counter. After hearing a loud glass shatter, I stopped abruptly, which shook the counter even more, although no other thing crashed down as a result. I looked at the floor below to see I knocked the whole ass cash register down, and it managed to break into pieces, deep enough for the cash and coins to come out. In horror, I jumped off the counter and started using my hands to push the money back into the cash register. After, I picked it up carefully and then put it back onto the front counter. I peeped the screen and then began playing with the cash register's various functions to ensure it still worked. The cash register was pretty expensive, and my boss would attempt to kill me if it broke the computer (I know my boss wouldn't be able to; my abs of steel would be big and hard enough to stop the knife). The point-of-service software has a neat interface that displays the entire table layout of the eatery, the table graphics being in their exact locations on the screen. I made sure that this was functional. I clicked on one of the tables and then clicked on the menu items. Not gonna lie; the cash register did somewhat malfunction—I worryingly waited as the main vegan burger took a whooping 15 seconds to register as an order after I clicked on it on the virtual menu. Already knowing the damage I have done, and having lost the patience to do further testing, I just accepted the fact that I am going to have to deal with pain in the ass order taking. And before any of you readers mentally shout out, "Just use paper to take orders instead!" My manager just flat out wouldn't let me, due to "fAnCY" reasons.

Kevin shortly emerged from the kitchen with a cardboard bucket the size of a milk jug full of the French fries I ordered and a soft drink. He asked me what table I wanted to sit at for lunch.

"The one at the corner opposite of the entrance please," I said.

"Very well."

Even on my first day working here, Kevin treated me as a friend and always cared for me; he was the man who stood up for me when Carl the Manager got mad at me after the first time I questioned the food quality. I remember when I had a really bad day and was too exhausted to sing happy birthday to some birthday boy who received a free cake and should have already been appreciative, and Carl shoved the rule book on my face, Kevin used his epic martial arts on him, distracting him while I did a very unenthusiastic sing that would even make a man with "dried vocals syndrome" disappointed.

Kevin placed my meal on the desired table, then said, "Bon appetite!"

I sat down and then started to chow down the fries. I didn't need a damn fork; I just ate it as if it was a feeding trough. Only a pussy (who has the intention to attempt to bulk) would need a fork to eat.

Midway through the bucket, I heard the bell that rang whenever the front door opened, and I stopped eating and then looked up to see who it was. Me: spits out fries* (a reference to the funny "spits out cereal guy" meme).

It wasn't an individual but a family. The mother was blonde and looked like a Karen. She had short hair, wore a pink shirt revealing her left shoulder, and wore the Karen jeans. The dad was a tall but skinny man who barely grew his tiny mustache. He had a blue sports shirt and red sports shorts. He also wore a cowboy hat that blended with his similarly brown hair. Now finally, onto the son—a stark contrast from his parents. He was probably around my age (not nominally, as I look much older than I am due to my 20-inch biceps). He had long light brown hair in a ponytail and wore an oversized tie-dye shirt so big, hiding some of his legs, that I couldn't tell if he was wearing shorts or pants.

I saw them quickly meet with the front counter, and Kevin promptly walked over there to service them, taking over me while I was still finishing my fries. He made a hand gesture to me, then began taking the orders. I looked into my fry bucket to see it was still one-third filled. I wanted to finish immediately because I felt bad for Kevin, so I tilted my head up, then drank the fry bucket as if it was my soda drink, and then I did the same with the soda itself. I then yelled out: "ALL CHUNGUSES ARE BIG!" My epic cry spanned the entire restaurant; it echoed through the walls, the windows, and even within the numerous fluorescent lights, each of which then, in a way, cloned my voice to make it sound like 20 people did smaller versions of my cry at the same time.

"Um what did you say?!" I heard Kevin say to the ponytail-wearing son. "I couldn't hear you."

"One order of the veggie burger please."

"Okay now just making sure, because if I remember correctly, it was three veggie burgers and drinks for each of you?"

"NOOOOOO THATS WRONG!" The Karen-looking mom yelled. "I said vegan burger with extra ketchup!"

"Ahh, okay," Kevin responded as he clicked a few things on the cash register to correct the order. Then, a receipt printed, and Kevin welcomed the family to sit at any table. As there was a possibility they'd want to choose mine, I stood up and then made my way to the garbage bin next to the counter. Then, suddenly, the ponytail-wearing son tapped me on the shoulder as I crossed paths with the family. "Yo, what is that you were eating?"

"Uh do I know you? Why?"

"My name is Jeremy, and I am a hardcore vegan, and I suffer from IBS." (I-Be-Shitting).

I had to cuck out cool unprofessionalism for a moment. "Ok Jeremy nice to meet you, but why ask me about this which is blatantly 'fries' as it is labelled on the bucket?!!"

"Because I want to know if you are really sticking with your proper diet you meathead!" He pointed at my veiny arms.

"Ahaha, this is an anomaly of a meal for me. I don't eat this regularly."

"I don't think you are pure enough of an eater if you want to be a true bodybuilder. Be like me as a vegan; I stick to my diet all the time, and look how strong I am!"

I took a look at this dude's physique. He was like a rail. I couldn't tell whether he was joking, but regardless this was indeed some funny shit. Jeremy crossed his arms. "And your voice seems a bit high-pitched for the number of steroids that you take."

I returned to my normal voice, which was as deep as he would imagine the black version of myself to sound. "And what do you have to show for yourself, Jeremy?"

Jeremy pulled up his right short sleeve and flexed his arm. And man, I gotta say, it was the weirdest-looking arm I've ever seen.

First, it was a very short insertion. For reference, when flexing his bicep, the average man can fit two or three fingers between his forearm and the bicep. But Jeremy's was at an extreme five-finger gap! What was striking was his bicep peak. It was "tall," but something about it was so unimpressive. I decided to play along; I pulled up my uniform sleeve and flexed my arm. To my surprise, Jeremy's bicep looked "taller" than mine. But my bicep was clearly three times the width of his.

"Haha, my bicep better than yours, you fat ass," Jeremy made fun of me.

That killed me. I hate it when people equate "bicep peak" to actual bicep development. Anybody who flexes their bicep at the right angle, somewhat trained it for months, and has a certain bicep shape genetics can do it. I'd fuck that kid up in an arm-wrestling match.

"Jeremy, you don't seem to have trained your triceps or brachialis. Let alone your back, chest, shoulders, and legs. Stop only doing curls and work your entire body. Stop inflating your ego just because one tiny aspect of yourself can appear better than mine."

Jeremy's mouth went agape.

"Wait a minute, are you making 'soy face'?" I asked. "If your face gets stuck in 'soyboy' state, try to eat less 'soy.' Oh wait, people are already tossing soybeans in your mouth, and you can't do anything about it! Haha, get owned."

Jeremy's Karen mom interrupted. "MEAN WORKER, STOP BULLYING MY SON, HE JUST BEEN TRAINING FOR A FEW MONTHS GIVE HIM A BREAK!"

"Karen, I didn't mean to. Oh, um, your name isn't Karen is it?"

I thought I massively fucked up and prayed the mom wouldn't get pissed at me for unintentionally referring her as a Karen because of how much she looked like one.

But instead, it broke the conflict. Jeremy and his parents all laughed and took it all as a harmless joke, probably also laughing at the sound of my laugh. This distracted them from the beef between Jeremy and me, and they walked toward their chosen table. I let out a "phew" and then returned to the front counter to continue my job.

Soon, another customer entered. I glanced at the door that had just rung to see a familiar face enter. It was weird; the feeling I experienced was both positive and negative. It was Ryan from my online COMM class.

"I know who you are; you are Ryan aren't you?" I said.

"Hey, good to see you, wasn't expecting to see you on the shift," Ryan held his arm out. We did a handshake.

"Hold the hell up, you are here because I am here? How did you even know that I work here?"

"One of those libtards who harassed you in the online call leaked your info."

I glanced at Jeremy for a second, then raised an eyebrow. I wasn't sure if he was one of them, though; I didn't remember his exact face and name being on the call.

Ryan shrugged. "I am here mainly to warn you about the leak because I feel like it would be my duty, but I would also like to talk to you. You seem like an interesting person… like the type of classmate who is based."

"Based on what? Muscles?"

"I mean based-based. You know, non-normie!"

"I don't like using the word 'based.' When you conceive of what basedness is, it should be normal in a sane world. The fact that Internet idiots had to devise a word for it to make it special and unique just dilutes redpilled people."

"Yeah you got a point, but we should do some epic 'Chad' talking and shit."

"Okay, so what are you really oriented towards?"

"I am a conservative and I hate liberals."

"Conservatives this, conservatives that; the word gets thrown around a lot. Are you really here to save the country? Or are you just a remnant in the political process because you lack the initiative and goggles to see what the world really is? Do you even remember the 'trollface,' 'me gusta,' 'pingas' (was funny meme because it sounds like 'penis'), 'rage face,' and 'derpina' memes? Only real OGs (original gang) understand these."

"I don't care, look at all the economic growth! We are getting more food than ever! So many things to experience and consume! It is all good, as long as you are willing to work!

"I'd be careful saying that. You have no idea what is happening behind the curtains. Want me to pull them? Well, if you are here to eat, why don't you order something from the menu?"

I took out one of the spare menus from the plastic transparent stand on the counter then handed it to Ryan.

"Awww, come on, none of these even have meat! But I am hungry as fuck, so I would like to have an order of fries!"

I noticed how much his arms were fatceps. I rolled my eyes, then pulled my sleeve to show Ryan what eating virtuously means. At first looking at it in admiration, he quickly did a little cope by shaking his arms a bit.

"You fool, you don't realize how shitty your arms look do you?" I said. "It looks like a string lying on top of a football! You can't have both if you don't work for it!"

"Aww man you're right. I am now biceppilled!"

"Good. Now, let me show you even more. Pick any menu item."

"Uhm, the vegan burger? As long as it feels like the actual meat, I'm fine with it. And now I realized that I am not as fit as I originally thought and should lose weight."

I turned on my phone and then went onto the photos app. I was shocked to see and be reminded that most of the photos stored on my phone were of my shirtless body, my daily progress pictures. I had to scroll for a fuck ton of hours just to find the one close-up photo I took of the vegan patties before it is refined into the full burger. It had very very small rough brown specks all over it, which is literal cow turd.

"Ploopy," I said, pointing at them.

"That's nasty."

"I told you so."

"Damn then what the fuck else is there? What am I supposed to believe in now? Noooo I am having an existential crisis right now! I already spent so much on my hats and merch!"

"Hey man it's okay, it's not too late. The system has many ways to make one believe they are on the right side of history. You are not necessarily evil. Just be happy you are finding out right now rather than later."

Ryan immediately stopped crying and began laughing. However, his crying didn't stop as he laughed, so he sounded more like "Huehuehue."

"What is going on over there?" Jeremy called out to us.

"Oh nothin much, we just watched some funny memes."

"Can I see?!!" Jeremy said, like one of those kids who asks if you have any games on your phone (mobile idle game cringe).

"Yeah yeah if it's okay with your parents. Are they okay with you seeing fecal matter?"

"I am an adult."

I flashed my phone screen in front of Jeremy. He got a pretty good kick out of the video. But Ryan himself was not done. He was in the mindset of "taking things too far," as if he just tried something new that turned out to be so satisfying that he's got to show everyone else. Ryan grabbed my phone out of my hands, then ran over to Jeremy's parents... Then...

"JEREMMMYMYYYY!" Jeremy's father growled at his son angrily. "I KNEW YOUR VEGAN SHIT MAKE YOU BAD, YOU ARE GROUNDED!!!"

Jeremy's dad proceeded to unbuckle his belt, prompting his shorts to fall down, then ran after Jeremy then beat his son while wearing no pants at all. As Jeremy didn't look like he was wearing pants as well due to his baggy shirt, they both looked bottom-naked. This is awkward...

All of a sudden, I went into a daze... I looked at the basket where we stored the kid's meal Burger Queen cardboard crowns, which happened to be next to the dirty patties jar. And finally, Ryan still laughing. My eyes went to a quick back-and-forth motion, taking turns glancing at each of them for what felt like an eternity.

Chapter Three: Dematerialization

Do you fall into the lie that the "core issue" of the modern age is the idea that "we are too materialistic"? While it is true that the shits and fucks given about the most trivial physical objects (like soy action figures containing plastics that lower your testosterone levels) are so prevalent today, this is only a short-lived passing phase toward an ultra-perverse incentive for modernity to eliminate ALL expressions of nature altogether. It may initially seem like materialism is all too prevalent in modernity (since the first industrial revolution) but look at what happened since the Third Industrial Revolution, and perhaps onwards... the extent of physical matter is decreasing in terms of production and communication[66] as digitization grows (increasingly, people are fixated to emotes you buy in "video game"). This could mark the beginning of the "quasi-immateriality."[67] Are we undergoing a slow, silent, yet deadly progress (hidden behind superficial words) towards pure nothingness?

Observe first: A more profound, Heideggerian meaning of modern technology is that it differs from earlier forms because it "challenges" nature, extracting and storing energy.[68] It identifies the essence of modern technology as "enframing," a mode of revealing that orders and challenges everything into a standing reserve. This enframing transforms our relationship with the world, reducing nature and even human beings to mere resources. This transformation poses the greatest danger because it can obscure other ways of revealing and understanding the world.[69] Modern Technology isn't just instruments that emerged from scientific innovation, but a mode of relating to the world in which nature is reduced to nothing, but so many things (minerals in the ground, plants, animals, and even humans) become resources to be exploited as a means to inertness. So, isn't the leftist view of "nature" as merely the "environment" just one definition permitted by the technological system? Could it be that this limited definition serves the system's interest by ensuring resources are conserved just enough to keep it running without depletion?

With a society of high material wealth where it appears there is an increasing appreciation for the environment,[70] you probably should view this with suspicion, especially given the number of new machines that themselves act as propaganda tools to serve as a way to distract us from the destruction of nature.[71] There may even be a "preservation paradox" inherent to the technological system in which preserving nature,

---

[66] J. Rifkin, "The Third Industrial Revolution," *Engineering & Technology*, 3(2008): 26-27. https://doi.org/10.1049/et:20080718

[67] J. Derrida, *Papier Machine* (Galilée, 2001).

[68] M. Heidegger, *The Question Concerning Technology* (Garland Publishing, 1977), 294.

[69] Ibid., 311.

[70] M.J. Manfredo, T.L. Teel, R. E.W. Berl, J.T. Briskotter, and S. Kitayama, "Social value shift in favour of biodiversity conservation in the United States," *Nature Sustainability*, 4(2021): 323-330 https://doi.org/10.1038/s41893-020-00655-6

[71] K. Crawford, *Atlas of AI: Power, Politics, and the Planetary Costs of Artificial Intelligence* (Yale University Press, 2021).

including natural capital, is impossible without making it artificial.[72] There is also an idea of "ecological capital" which transforms into products that yield ecological "benefits," "ecological values" which include biological production, climatic regulation, soil conservation, and environmental purification.[73] Aren't these all cases of the "system's neatest trick" not being particularly perfect but still being a trick nonetheless that gets people to support its values?

Though it is possible to live in our "idealized" natural world of human creativity under the consideration of maintaining "ecological capital," it is just another one of those "neutral" concepts that the system uses to make sure that we only see nature in its overly concrete variant, rather than the spontaneous generative processes of the universe. But neither should "nature" be the sort of abstract classifications that are based solely on the structure of leaves or teeth, which fail to capture the full complexity and variability in nature—it could be seen as a "metaphysical error."[74] It should be important now to emphasize that when we talk about flourishing life desiring "space," we don't refer to "space" in a literal sense (a perfect void). Could it refer more to an aesthetic arrangement of structures that surround a healthy amount of open space?

It is argued that modern natural sciences suffer from disunity and a failure to conceptually include mankind in the natural world,[75] and this connection between cosmology and ethics would emphasize the importance of understanding our place in the natural world.[76] In this view, the cosmos is inherently purposeful. Every part of the universe has a specific function and contributes to the overall good. This teleological perspective means that everything in the cosmos exists for a reason, and its ultimate purpose is to reflect the perfection of the forms. Two fundamental principles in this cosmos are "reason" (Nous) and "necessity" (Ananke). Reason represents the rational, orderly aspect, while necessity represents the chaotic, resistant aspect of the pre-existing matter. The interaction between these principles shapes the nature of the cosmos.[77] It is true that the understanding of nature should be more holistic in comparison to seeing it as some snapshot of physical outside stuff as preserved resources, and that humans should remain as part of the cosmos to maintain or grow the purification of a natural world. However, may the idea of bare "reason" miss the deeper point that there are some autonomous parts even without a rational agent in the cosmos (also inherent to it), that are overtly growing rapidly?

To illustrate, consider the universe on a cosmological scale: it appears that the "default" inclines towards generating an expanse of "nothingness." Like at the start, matter was evenly distributed, as if striving to fill the entirety, as distant from emptiness as it could be. Yet, paradoxically, "natural" forces intervene, gathering matter into dense clusters, such as orbits, leaving behind vast stretches of emptiness. In contrast, life and

[72] C.T. DesRoches, "The preservation paradox and natural capital," *Ecosystem Services*, 41(2020). https://doi.org/10.1016/j.ecoser.2019.101058

[73] W. Zhang, F. Yu (Eds.), *Global Ecological Governance and Ecological Economy* (Springer Singapore, 2022), 174.

[74] D. Nasser, *Hermeneutics and Nature* (Cambridge University Press, 2018).

[75] D.R. Campbell, "What Timaeus Can Teach Us: The Importance Of Plato's Timaeus in the 21st Century," *Athena*, 18(2023): 58-73. https://doi.org/10.53631/Athena.2023.18.4

[76] Ibid.

[77] Ibid.

nature are an anomalous part of the universe; beauty, like nature, loves to hide. But fear not; "other forces" persistently create more flourishing space through the continuous expansion of the cosmos—doesn't it seem as if "nature" itself strives to counteract the emptiness, to subdue the void?

Due to the perverse pure rationality spiral that can potentially be conjured by mankind, the technological system seems to be teleologically oriented towards not a perfect utopia that people imagine, but a non-life "default" turning us into something behaviourally closer to a perfect vacuum, as a vacuum lacks any inherent resistance—this may preclude a "definite efficiency"—in this "void," ownership of things by a subject is considered an "error" (There is a trend in which there is an increasing rate of distinctive intrapreneurial competence[78] in trade of entrepreneurship). For noble beings, this "perfect rationality" is inherently unappealing, as such a pseudo-consciousness would entail the total dissolution of the qualities that give them spirit and connect them to other natural forms. Regarding their minds, pure retardation would represent the equilibrium. However, the decay trends towards but never fully reaches a stable equilibrium; the constant akin to how temperature eternally approaches but never truly attains absolute zero?

What would be a potential real-life scenario where this happens? There is a possibility that the system will engineer an apparatus of mass destruction (atomic power is favored in a technological society perversely, because without any kind of button that a humanistic agent could use to control it, the system would have to necessarily dictate it by then just for its governance and regulation[79]), which may blow up the entire social machine at a planetary scale. Other than debris, what would be left is "outer space," but outer space itself isn't necessarily a perfect void, so we would still be left with a point of a graph extremely close to the asymptote, but not at all touching it. So just before pure entropy is supposedly reached, the negation of forms doesn't have to be some quasi-void—the tipping point could be a gigantic factory that ends up taking the entirety of the solar system, in which every room is identical (which nets a non-place at all). If there is somehow a person left still alive, it would be technically incorrect for them to own something, because the demands of the factory striving closer to the vertex of the parabola would produce some upgraded version of that object the moment that person receives the now outdated version. In this setting, would a more accurate depiction of a "human experience" be a man getting stretched and probed by an ever-growing 300-inch buttplug (WOULD BE EXTRA SCARY IF IT REACHES THE NUMBER "666" BECAUSE THAT IS LITERALLY THE DEV*L NUMBER 3 AM (ante meridiem)!!) as he demands different ways the machine could orgasm him in increasingly unconventional ways, just to cope with the increasing degree of being an anonymous husk?

Fake Food

Extremely mediocre music starts playing whenever it's near the end of my shift, and Burger Queen is at its busiest. The lyric-less sounds predominantly covered with bells and

[78] itziar Cerro-Urcelay, M.J. Pinillos, and M.R. Blanco, "Risk taking as a distinctive intrapreneurial competence among university students," *Journal of Management and Business Education*, 7(2024): 396-418. https://doi.org/10.35564/jmbe.2024.0022

[79] J. Ellul, *The Technological Society* (New York: Vintage Books, 1964), 99.

whistling chords are attempting to be portrayed as happy. I always ask myself, what is the thought process of whoever was composing such music? Were they doing this for the money, or were they doing it for the recognition and heart to impose one's will on others? I also think the same about the restaurant I am working for. For both, my thought flow is always leaning toward the first option. Unfortunately, the song's tunes strike me, and I will admit it will be stuck in my head in the near future, but I always like to think of the people who were behind the songs I hear. What do they look like?

The very song I was forced to listen to felt in sync as I had to rush to prepare the pickup and online orders while supervising the tables and ensuring nobody was misbehaving. Daydreaming, I envision a shady man who is relatively well dressed as a way to make him pass as normal in the city, eating a giant subway sandwich, eating with his mouth closed, again, to pass as respectful in the Western context. But when you look at him in the eyes, and he locks eyes with you intentionally as well, you would notice a deep stare indicating that he wants to either rob you, kill you, or feel up your wife (and I didn't even have a wife then). As for the music I was listening to, I think of that stereotypical person as either the producer of it as a low-effort attempt to get rep points or the listener who is new to Western music and trying to get a feel for it. The worst part is that the music I was listening to is one of those that is on repeat for a tiny segment of the "original loop," so it gave off a vibe that this is "infinite and forever," highly reminiscent of the buglife. The same damn routine by the minute, by the hour, by the day, by the week, and by the year. This is headed to and on a loop until you fucking die. I had a fear in me that one of the online or pickup orders was going to be to be a man who looks exactly and acts exactly like this stereotype. This is my paranoia at night times, as that's when the sketchy people tend to visit, the runaways! They know precisely that Burger Queen is a corporation; no one is going to give a damn whether a robber or street sleeper is to order something online, show up after the food in the pickup container is ready on the counter, then grab it and run off.

While I do believe that Burger Queen is truly a shithole company that diffuses a fuck ton of negative externalities, two things stop me from stooping to the levels of the criminals as I do my shifts. One is the whole idea of employee-company identity connection. And I don't mean that I have some personal emotional connection to Burger Queen, kissing my manager's feet. No, I mean myself as the man behind the counter. We all have had a specific false idea about how employment worked when we were young, whenever we'd visit a local store with our parents. We looked at the cashier as if he was sitting on a throne, the man who did everything, from scanning the barcodes of the items, tolerating customer service, signing the box whenever the supplier came in with new inventory, cleaning the windows, and painstakingly going through all the receipts at the end of the day. At least, we all considered him the face of the company. I still have that mindset, but not on a second-hand level—I have it on the level of my own self; I absolutely refuse to tolerate being disrespected as an employee. I don't care about the company's reputation, but I'd always be pissed off if a person is to shit on ME on the job.

Anyway, when I say the restaurant "is at its busiest," I refer to the online orders—at this point, online ordering has become the dominant way to get one's food, absolutely outcompeting dine-in. Even when it was the designated time to have dinner, only three parties were gobbling their burgers out of the fifteen potential tables in the building.

People nowadays blame materialism as the reason why America is becoming this level of "dull and soulless." But how many people are still collecting coins when you think of it? Do you still hear about people collecting stamps? How many people nowadays even have a bookshelf, even if it is just for vanity and looking smart? Nobody buys their video games in physical form but in digital format, which amounts to them fucking themselves in the butthole, as you can't even own digital video games since nothing is stopping the platform from taking away your rights to them. Now as for food, particularly Burger Queen, people simply don't give a fuck about what restaurants were initially built for. The hilarious thing is that you'd think the only thing keeping people going to restaurants is the "atmosphere" and "socializing with friends" now that food is increasingly becoming unworth it. Yet you see people ordering the food in its ugly cheap takeout bags that are hard to open, especially if I am the one serving you (I use my mighty strength to tie the knots too hard). And even if they do go ahead and make the rare move of eating inside, especially with friends and family, they still go out of their way to avoid acknowledging the restaurant atmosphere.

I take a closer look at the customers of Burger Queen, making sure to do it in a side-eye manner to avoid looking creepy. I wasn't surprised to see a sliver of how much social brokenness we are experiencing at our age. They were all on their phones. One "everyday dude" was watching some anime, the phone making too much noise via the high-pitched screams of the male protagonists, designed to be "more badass than a masculine growl." The girl on the other side across the table, who I assume he was on a date with, was on a messaging app. Now, I hate looking like the weirdo who snoops into other people's business, but my curiosity led me to focus on her screen a bit more. I was shocked to see she was video calling a "Chadder" dude who had his chode out of his pants and wiggling and jiggling it on the camera. I looked away in disgust—this is all a true denial of materialism if there ever is one.

As I needed to look away from that couple, I was again forced to look at the kitchen, specifically the fake vegan meat patties inside the jars. Now, that is an even better example of how materialism shouldn't be objectively blamed. You have no idea how these patties even exist in the first place. I want everyone to watch how industrial agriculture works. It's crazy, the very same meat that pseudo-vegans swear to oppose, the cows, are raised and stored close to where the plants are grown to save "space." Cows are pretty nasty shitters; if one were to stick his face next to the anus hole of a cow right before the cow takes a dump, even the pre-shit fart would be a deadly cannon, and would kill the man either by sheer fart Newtonian force, or the billions of shit particles would fly into the man's eye and give him a severe case of pink eye. Now imagine the insane distance the shit particles would travel. It would be literal miles! If the plants are being grown so close to the cow pen, only fake vegans would expect an ultra-clean diet that would make them "live longer" because "oH iT's OrGaNic." Now, you should have an idea of how much of the "biomass" of the vegan meat patties are not actually vegetables but cow dung. You are just eating a simulation. The producers of this garbage are only adding a ridiculous number of artificial flavors and bleach to negate the effects of scat eating. And believe me, many people who are aware of this fact still cope and continue eating the shit.

I already felt like I was going to contract AIDS (acquired immunodeficiency syndrome) as I thought of the prospect of eating shit, but little did I know, that was not going to be the only thing making me feel like I must wear a hazard suit. I heard the door alarm ring right after. I turned around to see a very tall coffee man wearing an elegant jacket, light beige pants, and work shoes. He had very light grey eyes, an indication of cataracts, indicating shit eyesight. He was almost balding, having hair that only existed on the back edges of his scalp. His teeth were non-straight and yellow; holy shit, just from looking at him, I stepped back, not only because I subconsciously saw a potential AIDS carrier, but also to get a bigger, broader overview of him. I imagine this being the type of man whose name would be Lester. I tried to hold my horses as I went ahead and spoke.

"Lester, is that you?" I asked.

"Yes, it is, thank you for my order," Lester said as he grabbed the bag.

My eyes opened as wide as pie plates. *How did I know this man was a Lester?* Even though I tend to have good intuitions of the kinds of people who I expect would listen to or produce a certain type of music, I couldn't be more spot-on than this.

"Lester, any plans for the rest of the day?"

I know, some of you readers are laughing at me, thinking, *who the fuck does the "any plans for the rest of the day" thing to customers who do pick up orders, being only inside the restaurant for a brief moment?* But I needed to clue-search, you asses.

"I am the dean at the [REDACTED] college, and I have a shit ton of paperwork to do tonight; the fall semester has just started."

Shit. He was the dean at my school. I knew there was some name at the back of my mind. "No fucking way, Mobama Lester? Is that you?"

"Why yes, it is, you must be a student at [REDACTED] college!"

"Yeah, I thought I recognized your name somewhere, perhaps as I was scanning the home page of the [REDACTED] college as I was going to enroll back when I had just finished high school, but immediately forgot to remember his name because I was so damn distracted due to being stressed about the whole prospect of college."

"No problem, it happens."

I got a bit chill as this man didn't freak out on me for forgetting about his partial identity. People nowadays have such reactions, and if someone doesn't, chances are they have some good anger management. I decided to call him by a shorter nickname. "Alright Moe Lester, you have a great day!"

Suddenly, I heard numerous gasps echo through the Burger Queen building. "There is a molester in here???" "Aahhhh get the kids out of here!" "Nooooo ahhhhhhhh this reminds me of when a guy wriggled his finger up my ass during a festival, and ever since, I can't look at flag poles ever again!" (woman screaming in a fake British accent).

I see the very few families and couples stand up and begin running out of Burger Queen, scared. Why do people think about things so automatically nowadays?

Lester glared at me. "How dare you destroy my reputation by calling me by my shorter name and last name to make it sound like I'm some sexual boogie man! Anyway, now that I know you are one of my students, I demand you a background check to make sure you don't fuck sound the school campus, okay?"

"Ahah I'm sorry what? This is so sudden. You already admitted to understanding that I had no intention of saying Moe Lester to rip your reputation apart."

"Yeah I know, but listen, in our current world, you are not allowed to joke. If you want to get high up on the corporate ladder, you must be serious all the time. Don't express any emotion. Just get things done. I know you already spent so much money to enroll in [REDACTED] college, you can't add value to society with your non-serious attitude."

"Woah woah who the fuck said I am going to be laboriously climbing up some invisible ladder that is going to collapse in the near future anyway? Did you know I am in the innovation program? I am not going to put on some suit, barge into some giant corporate office, and then be brought in as a corporate recruiter without needed experience in the first place! Then waking up at five every day while bringing the same attitude that I have when I train hard in the gym, then applying it to making mere phone calls?"

"Are you dense? Entrepreneurship and innovation these days aren't just about being your own boss. Entrepreneurs can work inside companies, too! These are called intrepreneurs! This will be the norm in the future; our data suggests that most of our innovation graduates won't start their businesses at all but will innovate for a company! We already plan to integrate some new courses into the program that will reflect this trend and attract even more students!"

NO! I thought. *Do I really want to do this for the rest of my life? Imagine learning how to be supposedly creative for some authority to strip you of it in your next life stage.*

All of a sudden, a comforting man in a chef hat barged out of the kitchen. "Hey guys, is there anything you need?"

"I am the dean of this kid's college. I am just lecturing him about how to have a big, bright future. He's killing his future for crying out loud! I am so worried!"

"Hey, if it is so important, you guys focus on your life tips discussion in the restaurant office. It seems that Burger Queen is unbusy. I am quite confident I can take on both the cashier and chef positions simultaneously. Just don't go messing with the office supplies because we are running low, and that stuff isn't cheap anymore. Go go!"

"Thanks, Kevin," I said. I then led Lester to the Burger Queen office.

As we entered, I could smell a load of ink that overwhelmed the former odor of food that was so strong in every other part of the building. I didn't know what Kevin meant by a lack of office supplies because, man, the amount of ink cartridges and paper in here was crazy. Or maybe it was a case of overspending because the other kinds of office supplies were, in fact, low. No staples, no tape, and no pins. The computer was severely outdated— a "first operating system" old. *LIMINAL SPACE MOMENT.* The printer was from the same era, and just by looking at it, I could tell it would print literal pixel cartoon art even if the source image were to be a real-life photo version of cartoon characters. I guess office shit wasn't such a priority to the restaurant and that the cash registers already being computers already do the bulk of that work.

Lester initiated the continued conversation. "To continue, you should know how I became the dean in the first place. I used to be a burger flipper like you, understand?"

I knew he was setting me up for a trap. But I wasn't going to fall for it. Obviously, I am no burger flipper, and I am just a cashier, and I knew that if I were to comment about this, Lester would make fun of me for being the moronic who takes words too literally.

"Anyways," Lester continued. "I remember feeling dissatisfied upon being there for so long. I needed an outlet to get my creative juices flowing. So I worked diligently towards working with [REDACTED] college. It wasn't easy, but I lived the best times of my life once I made it in. I made such a big impact. Firstly, I got this school to be one of the first ones to begin integrating electronic digital textbooks instead of having to get the students to use books without a find and search function and virtual temporary highlight feature. Not only that, but I made great deals with the textbook companies because I am such a nice guy, I gave them the idea to force students to buy digital textbooks by having them include digital codes that unlock the assignments that are required to be completed to pass the courses. Oh, and in addition, I was part of the whole scheme of online learning, as I took part in one of the major conferences where school boards discussed the implementation of online schooling for pandemics."

I shook my head. "Are you really priding yourself by pretending you were the one actualizing the era of lost freedom and where no one owns anything? Ha, such bullshit. Here is a little challenge: I would like to see you implement ways for colleges to revert back to the pre-digital era. That is the true challenge. I won't necessarily say whether it will improve the bottom line of [REDACTED] college, but just food for thought."

"You are being a smart aleck right now. STOP IT! AARRRGHHHH!!!"

This guy was experiencing a robotic technical error. He began hitting his fists against the desk, causing the office supplies to move. *Fuck, the desktop computer and printer, they are going to fall off.* I didn't want the same thing to happen to them at the cash register, as that would probably lead my manager to fire me, so I needed a way to calm Lester down.

This may sound stupid of me, but I decided to pull out my phone and scroll through the online video player app. My fingers shook as I struggled to do this fast. I eventually found the right video, a viral one from two years ago, of a man with long greyish hair in an airplane wearing one of those cardboard Burger Queen crowns in every kid's meal. In the video, he was kicked in the stomach by a woman, and he called out to the flight attendant, "Kick that n-word bitch out of the plane!"

I turned my phone's volume up and then played the video. It immediately got Lester's attention. "Stop playing that inappropriate video! Why show me this offensive video?"

"You have to interpret this differently. Remember when I called you Moe Lester, and everyone took that literally? And I know you tried to bait me into being the wordterpretation idiot when you called me a burger flipper. The guy in the video didn't say 'n-word' because he was hateful against the woman in the video. He was coincidentally yelling it out to relieve stress. He was in a state of distress being in such a crowded setting. Besides, he said the euphemism instead of '██████.'"

"I would say subversive terms. Anyhow, I don't think many people would like it."

Then, he saw the numbers indicating the video's data…it had millions of views and tens of thousands of likes. The dislike counter was hidden because of some weird new policy of the video social media website (how much would it be?).

"Gawk! Those are some nice numbers! N-word!"

Just in case, I decided to do one last thing. Remembering I had a black friend (who I last saw at the beginning of high school), I realized I'd probably have some n-word privileges left in me, so I took a sheet of paper from the printer, grabbed a pencil from the writing tools cup, and then wrote "n-word pass." I handed it to Lester and said, "This is yours. Keep it and use it like how the guy in the video uses the Burger Queen cardboard crown as the emblem of an n-word permission slip."

"Thanks! Now I am less stressed about all the paperwork that I have to do tonight!

Chapter Four: Collectivized Isolation

Shit guys, we really do find ourselves in a time where society exists in a sc*ry lim.nal space... (analog jumpscare incoming) *MORE LIKE LIBERAL SPACE LOL, not the nostalgic kind that one of my goons would post on a short video platform.* Isn't the technological system exiting even the entire binary of individualism and collectivism? Historically, we have never been so detached from both paradigms simultaneously and so advocating for either to get us out of decadent times becomes futile. The illusion of collectivity is sustained by the interconnectedness of individuals, where hyper-fixated roles create a dependency that seemingly necessitates immediate replacement to maintain the system's equilibrium—the capacity for illusion of power hinges on the necessity of group dynamics, as isolated individuals by themselves lack the vitality to confront opposition. This pseudo-collectivization fosters feelings of inadequacy, propelling individuals toward mass movements. However, genuine bonds are rare, as distrust prevails, with individuals ready to abandon the cause the moment when things briefly seem unhopeful. Conversely, the illusion of individuality and creative expression is perpetuated by the prevalence of pseudo-identities, allowing individuals to extend their egos into various constructed personas—can you guess who they are?

While it is true that the leftists of industrial society are anti-individualistic and pro-collectivist,[80] in terms of their herd morality, neither of those dichotomies could be said to be the objective factor of our problems today. There comes a new kind of "form" when society is full of people that are similar to the leftist's tendency to feel strong only after they are a member of an organization or mass movement they identify themselves with.[81] Is this isolated collectivization clearly a reflection of how the system's inclination to promote "solidarity" or protect the rights of minorities has nothing to do with genuinely caring about the idea of "peep of all kind together strong," but with taking advantage of its "feel good" connotations to further its own growth? It is said that in the technological society, economic production is favored not because it cares about satisfying the needs of individuals, but because it enhances the technological system's need for interconnectedness.[82] But given that technical progress was slow when communities were more diverse and distinct as you can't just introduce new technical parts across them seamlessly compared to one unified blob,[83] neither would that interconnectedness fill peoples' need for company nor for working towards a coherent collective goal—ultimately, isn't it all for efficiency, for efficiency's sake?

Funnily, does the "efficiency for its own sake" even appear to be efficient at all if looked through the lens of a being that can actually evaluate things? Under the system, there isn't an actual goal, even if one assumes that "cognitive diversity"[84] is optimal for the collective to solve problems. Ironically, "efficiency for its own sake" fails to

---

[80] T. Kaczynski, *Industrial Society and its Future* (Independently published, 2018), para. 16.

[81] Ibid., para 19.

[82] J. Ellul, *The Technological Society* (New York: Vintage Books, 1964), 148.

[83] Ibid., 71.

[84] S. Page, The Difference: *How the Power of Diversity Creates Better Groups, Firms, Schools, and Societies* (Princeton University Press, 2007).

successfully embody even a nihilistic goal. Likewise, as we have progressively enhanced the efficiency of light bulbs, our overall consumption of electricity has not diminished; rather, it has escalated, driven by the propensity to utilize increased efficiency for greater consumption.[85] Another observation is a Jevonian paradox—while in economics where supply and demand generally have an inverted relation, an increase in efficiency seems to lead to an increase in both in reality.[86] Has basic ass economics classes duped you all?

Now look at things from a "human group" standpoint—why is mankind often assumed as uniquely capable of addressing myriad challenges inevitably by default? Think of this: have you noticed that many different "non-human" societies exhibit a profound specialization, where individuals are educated to become experts in a singular domain? "Specialization" can, in fact, also be observable in the animal kingdom: ants allocate tasks to specialized units, gorillas distribute labor among distinct roles, and bees operate within specialized divisions.[87] Now, contrary to the prevalent belief that modernity leads to hyperspecialization, I think that modern society does not even render mankind "specialized" in the bigger picture. Instead, it engenders a perverse homogenization, diminishing individual uniqueness even though, in modernity, there is apparently an increase in the amplitude of how much roles refer back to the role holders.[88] But I wouldn't say that those roles are entirely real. In the animal realm, each role maintains a distinctiveness relative to their localized populations—however, considering the vastness and density of the modern population, our specialization appears less pronounced. Unlike the cohesive nature of hunter-gatherer communities, where interpersonal connections were strong, nowadays we often find ourselves struggling to remember even our neighbors' names. To illustrate, the technological system resembles the cellular structure of a body, in which each unit represents one cell. Reflect on this: would you prefer to be a distinct specialized unit within a local animal community or one of the billions of cells in the human body?

Whatever you think, why would I give a damn about your answer to this from a practical sense, when the latter could never actualize a truly conscious being in a collective technologized world anyway? There is an idea under the assumption that materialism is true, in which entities with the right kind of organization of material stuff could be conscious—the concept of "Group Mind and Collective Consciousness": collective entities, like nations or organizations, might possess consciousness engaging in sophisticated information processing and goal-directed behavior, akin to that of conscious beings.[89] But even if we put ourselves into the eyes of a materialist, wouldn't the technological system seem like a bad example of something that makes choices even on

[85] E. Tenner, *The Efficiency Paradox: What Big Data Can't Do* (Knopf Doubleday Publishing Group, 2018).

[86] B. Alcott, "Jevons' paradox," *Ecological Economics*, 54(2005): 9-21. https://doi.org/10.1016/j.ecolecon.2005.03.020.

[87] Ideasinhat, "Adam Smith: why we don't want AGI and the dangers of specialization," *Ideasinhat* (8th January 2018), https://ideasinhat.com/2018/01/08/adam-smith-why-we-dont-want-agi-and-the-dangers-of-specialization/.

[88] A. Giddens, Modernity and Self-Identity: Self and Society in the Late Modern Age (Stanford University Press, 1991).

[89] E. Schwitzgebel, "If materialism is true, the United States is probably conscious," *Philos Stud*, 172(2015): 1697-1721. https://doi.org/10.1007/s11098-014-0387-8

a macro level? For example, social bodies of consumeristic exchange appear to make deliberate actions and "changes" that maintain its mere existence, but not necessarily make it more fruitful. The system is something that will just be a combination of both multicellular organisms and a single called one, but in a bad way because it is one giant cell, except it itself is composed of many anonymous cells (powerhouse is the cell of the mitochondria?). So, they all, therefore, don't even work together at all to sport an actual organism worth supporting. Unless you consider mere teleology as rich consciousness?

There is a proposed pluralistic account of epistemic rationality, which is defined as inherently goal-oriented and teleological. Different epistemic goals, such as coherence, truth, and evidence, are recognized as valuable. Rationality can be assessed from an internalist perspective (from the agent's own viewpoint) or an externalist perspective (from an objective standpoint).[90] The former are evaluated by their beneficial impacts on individuals, whereas the latter are assessed by their capacity to form optimal judgments. These distinct evaluative criteria often lead to different conclusions when a group agent also functions as an epistemic system.[91] For instance, second-hand information researchers (who are only retrieving already existing information sources) engaging in meticulous scrambling to minutely search for inconsistencies amongst the sources, might impair their own epistemic efficiency but enhance overall outputs. In a scenario where researchers are the same kinds of consumers of research information, wouldn't this exemplify a collective agent that excels in artificial rationality but constitutes an epistemic system failing its units, essentially a breakdown in the effective division of cognitive labor? In the context of a fully rationalized technological system, a social machine that would be wired to eliminate the human life within would approach this in a different way, albeit much closer—would it appear to benefit the individual units of the group while simultaneously seemingly improving itself (akin to a trend where there is hyperemphasis on "political correctness" in the education system, selling it as "progress," at the expense of practical information)?

The way it would create the illusion of this is by doing something along the lines of hidden enshitification (bruh this dictionary word literally has the word "shit" in it, holy shit) at a macro level. Enshittification is usually spoken in private company terms—a conflict between the company's goal of solving the consumer's need for information accessibility, and the company operators' desire to retain them as paying users indefinitely by keeping them stoopid in the first place. But in contrast to businesses that want profit, why would the system care about the existence of consumers per se? It would instead function to fry the individuals' ability to gauge how much they are actually living their lives, lowering their natural desires and drive (like the drive for sex being replaced by a desire for pornography, and then there may be something even more virtual and life-denying that will replace that, and so on), because it is more efficient to do so than exerting resources into having those desires and drives remain the same or increase. Perhaps when you look at the fully rationalized system at a quasi-cosmological level (pretend you're a theoretical invisible external observer), you would notice that the system's goal wouldn't

---

[90] M. Kopec, "Unifying Group Rationality," *Ergo: An Open Access Journal of Philosophy*, 6(2019): 517-544. https://doi.org/10.3998/ergo.12405314.0006.018
[91] Ibid.

at all be to serve customers who are "extraterrestrial outsiders," but to outright eliminate them if they are conscious unpredictable beings who at least still have somewhat of a capacity for agency. This would be done either through assimilating them into the already cultureless collective by pandering to their desires, an appeal to "if you can't beat them, join them" (Likewise, "natural" mechanistic selection favors the subsystems that take full advantage of the opportunities available within the supersystem and disfavor the subsystems that "waste" some of their resources preparing themselves to survive the eventual destabilization of the supersystem[92]). What could the outside group, assuming it isn't militaristically trained enough, do other than accept death or accept the loss of their agency?

You can notice this in real life: there was a big story where an Amazonian tribe that is ruled under an idle communal system became addicted to the internet so fast.[93] It might be the case that similar tribes are archetypically akin to certain "middle progress" entities and nations around the world that are less mobile or already in an inert state in how easily they get integrated into technology (The technological system may be likened to a large-scale version of the "Commune," in which men live in them protected and "in comfort" in exchange for pledges and obligations,[94] argued to be the most primitive form of society[95]). There is significance to the idea that certain isolated groups that haven't yet been integrated into the global technological system all might vary in terms of how much capacity for agency they have—could some even be mini-local systems themselves but just not yet institutionalized by the global system? The very ones that would most passively and seamlessly join the global system?

All in all, the system doesn't "care" if any marginalization is going on; what "matters" to it is whether there is any sort of conflict going on. You see, conflict (even though it can potentially add new ideas to the table) is usually seen as one of the main interferences to the productivity of any company that wants to get those shareholder financials in (hence how common the term "workplace conflict" is). Likewise, the system is incentivized to eliminate conflict at all costs (and perhaps vice versa through peace engineering)[96] and select for mechanisms that reduce conflict, irrespective of hate towards the marginalized. After all, it is no coincidence that the whole idea of "revenge" has such negative connotations to the point of being considered "universally bad" in modern times—one would have to be fully dependent on the system's law enforcement instead, while it wasn't so much such in pre-modern times.[97] Historically, it has been the case that, generally, internal conflict within large human groups tends to have an inverse relationship with the magnitude of external threats to the group.[98] The technological

---

[92] T. Kaczynski, *Anti-Tech Revolution: Why and How* (Scottsdale: Fitch & Madison, 2020), 53.

[93] F. Landymore, "Remote Amazon Tribe Finally Gets Internet, Gets Hooked on Porn and Social Media," *The Byte* (5th June 2024), https://futurism.com/the-byte/amazon-tribe-internet-porn-social-media

[94] F. Nietzsche, *On the Genealogy of Morals* (Penguin Classics, 2013), 57.

[95] Ibid., 19.

[96] F. Phillips, "From my perspective: Toward peace engineering, Technological Forecasting and Social Change," *Technological Forecasting and Social Change*, 158(2020): https://doi.org/10.1016/j.techfore.2020.120148

[97] T. Kaczynski, *Technological Slavery* (Scottsdale: Fitch & Madison, 2022), 191.

[98] T. Kaczynski, *Anti-Tech Revolution: Why and How* (Scottsdale: Fitch & Madison, 2020), 210.

system not only has a tendency to erase external threats before they become a challenge but also erase conflict within the group to allow its smooth functioning. Doesn't that operate in direct contradiction to even the human condition?

When we consider that most social justice warriors are really the hateful and spiteful ones, could this shift suggest that the system will soon mandate a new trend, where activism extends beyond humanistic rights to protecting entities that merely mimic life? Interestingly, there has historically been a rise in anti-robot attacks, and it is noted that the visual indignities and verbal attacks against robots often carry gender or racial overtones,[99] which would spark the argument for framing some anti-robot activities as hate crimes or incidents. Would the system's reaction to this advance as a stepping stone to prevent us from having any kind of humanistic feelings of conflict at all, even towards non-conscious things that will, in fact, pose a threat to us? If so, what kind of our amazing and highly valuable gifts of instinct have to be beaten out by then?

Now, may you peep at the phenomenological categories of seeming autonomy and heteronomy—it is argued that these categories provide a more foundational basis for understanding human-technology interactions[100] than how modern people clichely feel when they experience what they think is uncanny valley (such as numerous accounts of media that depict discomfort around even machines without a reskin cover of a human[101]). Phenomenological categories of autonomy (entities, like living beings that maintain their own organization and functionality independently) and heteronomy (entities such as machines that depend on external inputs and are operationally open systems) are more basic than naturalistic accounts and underlie our ability to interact with and make sense of both autonomous beings and heteronomous objects,[102] rather than the discomfort stemming from uncanny valley being limited to the appearance of something that comes close to appearing human. The human interaction with the world primarily involves pre-reflective, immediate cognitive experiences rather than merely higher-level cognitive processing, and phenomenological categories of autonomy and heteronomy are inherent in pre-reflective experience and shape how humans engage with the world from an early age.[103] So, given the pathological connection people already have with certain technologies,[104] is it starting to be a thing that the modern notion of the uncanny valley has become so butchered and by now means something that's a far cry from what roboticists intended? The fact that there historically have been so many cases of people who beat the shit out of nonhuman-like machines would perhaps logically translate to the human's natural drive to "bonk" the automaton masses of the system. But in order to prevent the cost-heavy repairments to maximize technological efficiency, the system is

[99] J.A. Oravec, "Rage against robots: Emotional and motivational dimensions of anti-robot attacks, robot sabotage, and robot bullying," *Technological Forecasting and Social Change*, 189(2023): https://doi.org/10.1016/j.techfore.2022.122249

[100] R. Gahrn-Andersen, "Seeming autonomy, technology and the uncanny valley," *AI & Soc*, 37(2022): 595-603. https://doi.org/10.1007/s00146-020-01040-9

[101] Ibid.

[102] Ibid.

[103] Ibid.

[104] K. Miller, F. Grodzinsky, and M. Wolf, "Why Turing Shouldn't Have to Guess," *Asia-Pacific Computing and Philosophy Conference* (1-2th October 2009) Tokyo. http://bentham.k2.t.u-tokyo.ac.jp/ap-cap09/openconf/data/papers/13.pdf

incentivized to beat away those intuitions—can you imagine what will happen when "human robots" become the next normal thing that we have to have solidarity with? What will be the next layer of the uncanny valley?

Importantly though, could this process be the case in reverse, all while striving towards the very same teleological conclusion? Notice there is a trend, aligning with the broken meaning of today's definition of "nature," that there is an emphasis for some kind of integration between "nature" and technology,[105] which may just lead to a perverse "garden that is only for utility purposes." Or the ways this scheme may be further pushed… with the "Game of Semantic Extension," a linguistic phenomenon where words traditionally used to describe living organisms are extended to describe artificial agents.[106] What kind of a design would this breed, assuming that we so dare pretend to take away the idea of literal machines from the equation?

In the realm of biomimetic design, various approaches propose promises such as sustainability, resilience, multifunctionality, and reduced risk.[107] One particularly intriguing form of biomimicry involves the technical imitation, abstraction, and translation of nature's functional principles—examining how nature accomplishes certain tasks and applying these insights within technological frameworks.[108] This might reflect the transformation of humanity during the agricultural revolution, the initial phase of modernity and subjugation, during which significant innovation was largely absent beyond the "imitation" of nature's functions—even humans by themselves were utilized as tools, coerced into robotic labor. The innate human drive for individual exploration was suppressed by a linguistic technology that stifled instincts to master new frontiers, paralleling the contemporary education system. So biomimetic design may neither truly be innovative nor the solution for ecological sustainability that the system says it is, as the mere existence of technological devices does not inherently harm the environment. Instead, it is a whole system's certain pursuit of efficiency—manifested in the arrangement of agricultural workers into concentrated communal settlements—that catalyzes degradation. Under this, has it always been the case in which the technological potential of modernity has existed abstractly, except the advent of new industrial energy sources only functions to enable its expansion at an accelerated pace? Was it always a stagnant civilization in its same state in which it IS man heading towards "imitating" THE inanimate object?

Many would say that an environmental object can become more natural or more artificial depending on changes in its dependence on human intervention (the idea of "naturalness as independence"[109]). But the deeper point this misses is the manner in which technological determinism can unfold. Consider the creation of a decentralized technology; its localized existence initially poses no threat to individual autonomy. Yet,

[105] B. Kenza, "Biomimicry Architecture Between Fame and Reality," YBL Journal of Built Environment, 9(2024): 21-27. https://doi.org/10.2478/jbe-2024-0003

[106] F. Fossa, "Artificial agency and the game of semantic extension," *Interdisciplinary Science Reviews*, 46(2021): 440-457. https://doi.org/10.1080/03080188.2020.1868684

[107] A. Gerola, Z. Robaey, and V. Blok, "What Does it Mean to Mimic Nature? A Typology for Biomimetic Design," *Philos. Technol.*, 36 (2023): 65. https://doi.org/10.1007/s13347-023-00665-0

[108] Ibid.

[109] E. Casetta, "Making sense of nature conservation after the end of nature," *HPLS*, 42(2020): 18. https://doi.org/10.1007/s40656-020-00312-3

the technological system appropriates this innovation, seemingly advancing it by expanding its influence to fulfill the needs of the state. This expansion is merely a guise for magnifying one dimension of the technology, "pretending to innovate" it further tc an upgraded version by extrapolating its scope to modernism's rational conclusion so it works to fulfill the needs of the whole body. The extrapolation is just a euphemism for taking one aspect of that technology and dragging out one of its corners to enlarge "its image," which requires no actual creative thinking of mankind, but like merely converting a pixelated image into a higher definition version. One must ponder, could any entity other than a rational entity realize such a transformation?

In theory, one might engineer a gecko to perform functions akin to this task. This vast and unnatural technological apparatus, a creation that seems beyond the scope of true humanism, may ultimately be managed only by flesh-and-blood automatons—entities technically human but devoid of humanistic insight—despite the fact that it all began wi:h a small, innocuous invention. Hidden social control is as old as society formation,[110] and "dataveillance" was already possible a long time ago without necessitating the advanced things the way they are now.[111] Is it actually foolish to blame the ills of the technological society on "individual technological devices" as the objective factor to criticize?

It was warned in one of the most powerful critiques of modern technology that rather than hyper-focusing the blame on technology as the machine objects, we should look at "technique" as something that takes over all of man's activity, the "machine objects" only being smaller symptoms.[112] Similarly, the Spenglerian term "technics" is not to be confused with "the implement."[113] So, the real "bad" anti-nature thing about the system may be the fact that it makes the entire social body itself the machine that requires maximum orderly efficiency devoid of spontaneity and, therefore, the anti-freedom restrictions. Regarding "individual technologies that may facilitate freedom," start by thinking about how we used fire back then. In the ancient world, fire stands as an open-ended force, elevating humanity to its peak within the natural hierarchy. It enabled us to flourish in the dangerous spaces of the food chain through the alchemy of cooked non-soy food and strong weaponry—yet, is fire to be deemed unnatural?

In harsher conditions, the rational being recognizes the necessity of the campfire, illuminating and warming their domain. Fire is controlled—this potential freedom is such that individuals can move their impact however way they want to, directly. Could one then view premodern technology such as this as an epitome of the physical manifestation of man's substantial cognition and, therefore, possibly nature? Well yes, it served as the tangible embodiment of ideas, evolving in complexity and diversity akin to life—archaic technological tools proliferate through the innovation of ideas, forming a genealogical branch of sorts.[114] But in contrast, the individual within the mechanized industrial society

---

[110] A.B. Hollingshead, "The Concept of Social Control," *American Sociological Review*, 6(1941): 217-224. https://doi.org/10.2307/2085551

[111] A. Clarke and T. Montini, "The Many Faces of RU486: Tales of Situated Knowledges and Technological Contestations," *Science, Technology, & Human Values*, 18(1993): 42-78. https://doi.org/10.1177/016224399301800104

[112] J. Ellul, *The Technological Society* (New York: Vintage Books, 1964), 4.

[113] O. Spengler, *Man and Technics* (Alfred A. Knopf, Inc., 1932), 10.

[114] The Technium, "The Seventh Kingdom," *The Technium* (1st February 2006), https://kk.org/thetechnium/the-seventh-kin/

becomes an actor in an elaborate "prediction" of regulated actions. Stripped of context, this existence appears as a series of incongruous motions among an intricate network of technological systems and automatons. Consider a soy driver on an urban road—a figure in a vast collective, navigating a landscape of signals and societal constructs. In solitude, at night, the driver's adherence to the ritual of traffic laws persists, despite the absence of other automobile drivers. This compliance reveals the underlying necessity of regulation within the industrial paradigm, where everyone also must behave IRRATIONALLY. The drive for optimization and efficiency necessitates a continuous reinforcement of control mechanisms to avert disruption within this industrial ecosystem. Proposals for augmentations that enhance human capability or vehicle safety may arise, yet the fundamental nature of industrial society dictates an ever-tightening scope of influence, expanding BOTH outwardly AND inwardly (buildings getting evermore close together to decrease relative commute times and therefore tightening the roads and road rules, to the point where "Orwellian bodycrime" might get one killed in a synchronous road system for not moving robotically enough[115]). This, of course, isn't helped by the fact that the system favors "diversity blocks," which are implemented just to compensate for the certain types of new units of society that may commit disorder.[116] Doesn't this inexorable progression lead to an increasingly constrained existence, where regulation serves not merely to govern, but to perpetuate the very structure of the industrial complex itself?

It is profoundly ironic that as the collective pseudo-organism of modern society becomes ever more enmeshed in technocratic structures, certain archaic technologies, even if they contribute to the normie ones in somewhat of a way, increasingly face prohibition or excessive regulation. In the present times, the technological landscape has morphed into a convoluted ecosystem of interdependent ideas and devices, all striving for maximal efficiency together. Creativity now plays a diminishing role. How could "individual freedom technologies" thrive inside of this matrix?

Thus, the essence of outward technological manifestations is increasingly detached from human thought—driven instead by autonomous impulses within the technological system itself instead. This self-sustaining loop would stifle genuine creative innovation, favoring micro-iterations that merely enhance the speed of something that doesn't even actually move. The fragility of this system, akin to a tower of paper cards, means any attempt to introduce disruptive decentralized technologies—such as personal flying devices or heavens forbid, even jetpacks—is deemed "technologically incorrect" by the regulatory frameworks of the societal machine. Such innovations pose a threat to the predictability and order of the system, potentially enabling individuals to break free from their constraints. For instance, a jetpack (if we make the insane assumption that such a jetpack is magically made extremely cheaply than a cheap shitty used car or does not require a factory and therefore doesn't need a technological system to be manufactured) could empower one to escape the drudgery of wagecuckism, and once exited out of the system, feel some freedom for once. Why would the oppressive nature of the technocratic regime allow this loss of efficiency?

---

[115] C.A Haag, *The Hermeneutics of Ecological Limitation: Ecophilosophy Beyond Environmentalism* (Independently Published, 2019), 150.
[116] V. McLeod, *Clown World Chronicles* (VJM Publishing, 2020), 154.

Perhaps as it is spoken that it is ok to use the technology to facilitate the destruction of the technology,[117] the technological system has to "make inert" the chaotic innovations that facilitate one to escape into open spaces, before they come in their pure enough form to wreck the whole order. Perhaps, the invention of the automobile wasn't itself "bad," but the technological system's rigorous requirement for orderly efficiency in a sense "domesticated" the innovative concept of "the automobile" to the point where one has to follow the suffocating road rules, to account for the system's suffocating efficiency-based infrastructure; therefore, the whole idea of "automobile" has come to be associated with this limiting suffocation. Consider that whenever the state comes across a new technique that was formerly developed by an individual, it will respond by appropriate it, integrating it into its framework, and begin to blur the lines between meaningful individual innovation and the system's control.[118] Maybe jetpacks will come, but under the technological system, the state would have to institutionalize it by building highly lawed "air roads" for it, limiting your speed to the point where you'd just be a flying whale, and you might as well just wait eight hours for an airplane to take off. Such air roads with their added Z axis rather than X and Y axis would be deemed "bad" because of the system's loss of economic efficiency for full spatial regulation (It further shows that mainstream normie conservatives are contradictory in that they want both techno-economic efficiency and traditional values—even more foolish when we consider that the archetype of firearms is literally technologically incorrect at an individual level). If not built, how fast would a revolt against the system happen?

Generally, as a community grows more powerful, it tends to take the offenses of individuals less seriously.[119] However, the behavioral regulations in the technological system tend to get tighter as it "grows," and it seems as if the social order, in a sense, increases in "fragility." Or maybe the "punishment" is just diffusing more subtly. Given that there is a close relationship between the progress of technology and language,[120] could freedom of expression be suffering the same kind of gradual problem as "system-appropriated technology"? Where before we realize it, we can't any longer freely use it with great impact because it suffers "political incorrectness" as a branch of "technological incorrectness"?

Night Stroll

Anyone who isn't a road rule follower knows that the act of walking produces great thoughts—being in motion rather than sitting. It proves true when you notice the unclear thoughts that remain when you stay sitting—maybe this is a cause of road rage for those who drive all day. Open-ended space is crucial for original thought to occur... the same reason why I attempt to flower the last clause of the paragraphs in the big brain redsigmapills with a question mark (and although I "source," much of my real "sources" are revealed to me in my walks or dreams).

---

[117] T. Kaczynski, *Industrial Society and its Future* (Independently published, 2018), para. 202.
[118] J. Ellul, *The Technological Society* (New York: Vintage Books, 1964), 248.
[119] F. Nietzsche, *On the Genealogy of Morals* (Penguin Classics, 2013), 58.
[120] A. Leroi-Gourhan, A.B Berger (Trans.), *Gesture and Speech* (MIT Press, 1993).

Ok, here is a little "confession" of mine: I do not have my driver's license yet. You know, that little shitty useless skinny piece of plastic that you can get if you wait one year after taking a simple ass exam that only asks thirty questions that require no thinking. The card that requires you to sit inside the car while some random ass motherfucker watches and makes sure you follow the right directions.

Should I get it? Eventually, maybe (even though I have always been able to drive around without one on me since other drivers and authorities are too scared to pull up on me). In our current state, the city is constantly increasing in size and moving the "essential" buildings onto the outskirts while replacing the old space with useless roads and more houses. But on the other hand, you know what is also expanding—my speed and stamina. I always try to walk whenever I can, even if it is unnecessary. I'll remind you that I'd do it when I brushed my teeth for so long that I ended up brushing too hard, leaving my gums bleeding. I also do it at work, walking behind the counter, around the kitchen, and going from table to table (so another confession I have is that the teeth brushing sesh is actually not my only moment of daily cardio).

Of course, this makes me always exhausted in terms of sore legs at the end of each shift. And this doesn't mean I am done, as I have to walk all the way home. I don't mind, though. I don't cry, I don't complain. I still do it. Kevin, being the nice guy he is, offers me a ride home every night, which I greatly appreciate, but I give him excuses.

As I first planted my foot on the sidewalk, I unconsciously did a little ritual that I occasionally do on the walking tiles—making sure I take exactly two steps on each tile, the left foot being the first one and the right foot being the last. Then, repeat by stepping the left foot on the next tile. I know this kind of thing seems pretty insane for someone to do every night. But the fact is, almost every modern person does it. However, they do it in varying ways; maybe someone does their right foot first before the left. Whatever the case, people tend to walk at eerily synchronous paces without minding it at all. Perhaps they are lame enough to see the whole sidewalk tile walking pattern as a little one-dimensional game that keeps themselves entertained? Less uncool still: maybe they are playing a variant of "Don't Touch the Lava"—those are amongst the least cucked ones.

My point is that anyone who regularly makes the uniform sidewalk walking pattern, whether intentionally or not, is pozzed with a special kind of poison that the system imposes on the populace very early in one's life. You have to acknowledge that whether or not the elites intentionally designed the sidewalk tiles, they were socially selected as a proper coercion technique. You subconsciously care less about how quickly you transport yourself on foot and more about cooperating with the system's need for a very uniform way of traversing that tricks a person into thinking they are inherently a slower walker or runner than they really are or can potentially become. That will leave them with a limited range of choices. Maybe they will remain content with their slower-than-wild pace and will gladly wait a longer time to get to their job or place of interest; they just need to wake up earlier or plan their time management more ahead. The second option is to learn how to follow road rules, which is what most people opt for.

Most people are not aware of the sidewalk walking pattern phenomenon, nor will they be aware that the centralized road system is basically the same thing. Just like the sidewalk discourages people from walking or running at full speed, driving leads to a phenomenon where fewer people are traveling via walking. Both are couch potatoes in their own ways.

As I go through my train of thoughts, I realize how stupid I was walking on the sidewalk like this, so I decided to take the big ballsack action of walking on the grass instead. It was a long but relatively thin stream of grass that spanned all the way to the horizon, corresponding to the length and direction of the road. I knew that if I weren't wearing shoes, I would be fine walking barefoot compared to walking on the rough concrete that probably has shards of glass that a homeless man used to bash the head of a woman he attempted to rob, but right now, I was wearing shoes. The discomfort that comes with dirtying them with the grassy dirt goes way beyond the thought of me stepping on sidewalk glass and ending up with a foot infection that only a necrophiliac foot fetishist would find pleasant.

Anyway, all that mattered was I wasn't enslaved by the sidewalk tile patterns. I then found that I was able to think clearer. I think of the state of modern suburbia in terms of safeness. All I can say is, we don't live in a free country when it comes to that. I heard a quote once that said, "if one cannot take a trip to the gas station without having to look back a hundred times per second looking like a glitched video game character model that does the ragdoll twitching animation, they do not live in a free country." Actually, in a truly good state, such a node wouldn't even need to exist in the first place, but you know what I mean.

Even as a man my size, I still need to be on the lookout for homeless crooks or crooks in general. In the dark, it tends to be more difficult to tell if a big guy is big. The effects of darkness on perception and retina make "size difference judgments" much more difficult. Plus, darkness, in general, tends to make one look skinnier. Just compare yourself wearing a black shirt rather than a white shirt. If you are fat, you'll thank me for providing you with a solution to your obeseness without you having to work your fat ass off. And vice versa, if you are skinny, you'll thank me for providing you with a solution to being too lazy to take steroids (it joke).

Another reason I have to feel like a fucking prey is the way people organize large groups these days. I am not saying that forming groups of friends is a bad thing, but I cringe really hard when the modern person does it. They will blindly become sub-acquaintances of everyone in a larger (30+ people) group in an evenly distributed way. And if he were to leave, people would not miss him. As the group dynamics is purely based on a herd, the commonality nets to be very nullifying.

Oh, did I mention that I was wearing a jacket? Man, I miss when being shirtless in public was the norm (as long as you have a good physique). People would be more motivated to hit the gym to do something about something that people could see. And there was much higher respect toward those who did work hard. Nowadays, people will look at you weirdly if you don't wear a jacket in cold weather.

As I continued and was about to reach an intersection, I saw a white beam of light suddenly flicker from behind me. I stopped and promptly turned around with an "Uh oh, what is going on now" going through my head. I tried my best to relax and make sure those words were verbally said in my mind's voice perfectly coherently. *Gotta remain fresh-minded when shit is probably going to get real.* I soon met eyes with the man in the security night guard patroller costume (I call it a costume because most security officers these days are fucking pussies who are nothing against me if they don't have an army or weapons behind them).

"Freeze!" the night guard yelled out as he pointed a gun at me. I guess I looked scary enough even with my jacket on.

"What did I do?" I asked.

"You shouldn't be walking on the grass son. It is illegal here as your steps will kill the grass. This is part of the city's plan to be more eco-friendly."

"What are you on? Why would the city even pretend to be this virtuous grass-saving entity when it is always seeking to expand and destroy the little wildlife left on the planet on the way?"

The officer pulled out a shocking device, pointed it at me, and pressed its buttons several times.

As I anticipated what was going to be my first time being tased, everything about the whole concept of "taser" flashed before my eyes. I remember the very first time I heard of the word—it was in grade school. At break times, a method to bug others spread from person to person in our grade. Basically, it worked by pointing up your pointer and middle finger while leaving the rest of your fingers closed. Do this with both hands. Then, sneak up behind your victim and then jab the lower and soft sides of his torso. Make sure to vibrate your fingers. The crazy thing is that the victim will feel like they are being tased, especially if they are ticklish. Even though I am relatively lean, I am somehow immune to its feeling. I remember when this girl tried to do it to me (before I started lifting weights), and when I didn't react, she said, "I guess it doesn't work on fat people." *FUCK OFF, I WASN'T FAT, I WAS JUST WEARING A HORIZONTALLY STRIPED WHITE SHIRT.*

With my quick imagination and memory, I lunged at the night guard, and before he could land the tiny little spark of blue onto my flesh, I jabbed my two-fingered hands right below his ribs. It caused him to drop his electrifying device. I proceeded to do it extremely forcefully, and I realized how much my machine cable flies at the gym paid off. I began to animate my individual pointer and middle fingers to enhance the shocking effect.

"Oof!" the night guard cried out.

I could feel my fingers start to feel the heat, indicating a bit of friction. I guess they were made of wool. Suddenly, an excruciating sensation stroked my fingertips. I looked below to see a series of orange sparks. What the fuck? Shortly, they evolved into actual fire. For some reason, I just continued to taser the night officer. I guess it must've been my commitment to keep him at bay. I had to go all in because if I stopped, he could easily pull out his gun and then shoot me in a body part that wasn't my jawline.

Eventually, the fire got so large that I decided to let go and avoid catching my clothes on fire. The fire engulfed the officer's lower pants and almost up to the sweaty armpit stain.

"Haha, I guess you lied about the ecological plans of the city because now your pants are on fire!" I logically deduced.

Desperately, he pulled out his walkie-talkie and then dialed. Oof.

I am not going to lie; I felt badass because an officer just called for backup against my unarmed self. But I immediately knew I was going to be fucked. I turned around and then began to pedal my legs. Even though my legs were already exhausted, my adrenaline was as high as a man who takes so many drugs to be as high as a kite, so my speed was fast yet constant, with no sign of slowing.

Midway, I was thinking about where the hell I should go. I remember my mom telling me when I was younger that if a stranger is following you, do not go home, as he will know where you live. The priority place you should go to is the police station because it will either scare off the stranger or you will now have police officers to protect you.

The problem for me was that they themselves were officers. Drats! I glanced back and saw ten men after me. They all had their fleshlights pointed at me, although I was far enough away, so I wouldn't have noticed the shine if I hadn't looked back. I wasn't worried, though, as I was confident they were all donut eaters to begin with. They'd all stop and probably end up with heart attacks.

However, something even better happened. I heard a loud horn reverberate through the night skies. It was close, though, and behind me. I glanced back again to see that a train was crossing. I saw no silhouette of those officers anymore, meaning they had to have been behind it. Phew! But just in case, I continued to run away because the trains that travel through my city aren't particularly long. I heard a series of angry and bitter voices through the train's engine; they were dirty curses. I yelled back, "You guys are bogus!"

"This man is like a platypus!" The same guard I lit on fire screamed in a nasal voice.

I laughed at this guy's random knowledge that one of a platypus's dangerous bioweaponry is their electrical shocks. He was probably waiting all his life to say it to someone else to flex how much he reads children's wildlife picture books. But it also fed my ego, making me feel like I had some superpower. I never imagined an officer, out of everyone, giving me a whole-ass superpower label. I know my ability to bench press 500 pounds for reps is already a superpower to most average people, but can I apply that strength to produce something that a firebender does? What the fucking fuck.

As I padded into my apartment unit quietly, as it was almost midnight by now and I didn't want to wake up the neighbors' dogs, I first rushed to the refrigerator. The only thing on my mind was my protein shake. I always premade them at the start of every week because of how tight time is for me. Most people in modern times make their protein shakes using a cheap plastic cup with a metal ball inside. They shake it in a way where it looks like they are giving someone a handjob. I refuse to look like that, and I'd rather look like the one getting the handjob, so I use a mortar and pestle to do it, one made out of stone and wood. Basically, I add in the fruit and powder; then I work it until it becomes something that passes as a drink. I love drinking things that remind me of my effort. Besides, using my bare hands to use the mortar and pestle gives an excellent forearm workout, a muscle that I don't train in isolation much).

After I finished swigging the cup of prepared protein shake, making sure I didn't tilt my head too high to avoid looking like I was giving a blowjob through my apartment window, I decided to go on my laptop to start working on my first assignment of COMM finally: the dreaded introduce yourself to class discussion forum post.

I typed up everything that was needed of me.

*My name is [REDACTED] and I am currently working towards graduating with the
entrepreneurship and innovation diploma, which I picked for my undergrad field
because I'd rather be my own boss than be an accountant, which is a comparatively
worker bee job. I think COMM is going to be important for what I would like to do
in the future because critical writing is crucial for making business plans. My favorite
things are spending time at the gym, lifting weights, and worshiping the big black
bodybuilders.*

I know the very last clause wasn't it, so no homo, but I least did a bit of virtue signaling
to hopefully offset all the liberals in my class who were already pissed at me. After, I
decided to check my email. Usually, when a class is online, the instructor will post class
announcements to remind us of upcoming quizzes, exams, and paper due dates. Upon
seeing my inbox, I realized that there was nothing from my professors, but there was one
from the school dean. I opened it, to see it turned out to be a major announcement.

*Students, I know mental health is one of the biggest concerns that can get in one's
way of effectively learning and working. Our current mental health aid is already
effective, but we understand its limitations and some students may be too socially
anxious to consult with them. No worries, we have a solution in the works! Recently,
I was very stressed because of all the start-of-year paperwork, but that ended after I
said a phrase to snap my emotional state back to normal. It was the n-word, which I
felt comfortable saying after I was handed an n-word pass. And I believe that if this
worked for my old self, so will it for all of you students! So tomorrow, we will
distribute free n-word passes to every student on campus. Please note that because
we are a school that values tolerance, I must note that the n-word isn't at all going to
refer to the black people we love. How the n-word passes will work then is you will
only be allowed to literally say "n-word," not "██████." I believe that saying the
former is enough of a taboo word to make you guys relieve pain, but inoffensive
enough to not be hateful toward anyone. Cheers!*

Shit, I already found it difficult to believe that he followed through with my n-word pass,
let alone spreading it to the whole school. I thought of the implications of this. At first, I
just found it to be plain funny and laughed. I was even beginning to think this was in itself
a funny joke that Mr. Lester decided to pull due to excessive drinking to cope with all the
paperwork that he had to do.

Next, I thought of the potential consequences. Will it piss off any of the liberals? I
don't think so. Earlier today, when Mr. Beckford was trying to get someone in the COMM
class to say the n-word, the liberals were literally fine chanting it. Now, I went over to
analyze the potential impacts and whether they would improve the world. That was when
things got a bit scuffed.

Given that Mr. Lester made a worldwide impact on colleges, imagine if every school
copied his n-word pass. What would happen to the n-word itself? Will it lose its meaning?
Are people just going to refer to individuals only as colors and lose track of every possible
real way to refer to African people? In addition, the world will just become plain boring.

Imagine going through your childhood without that edgy n-word phase. No childhood is truly lived without that—acknowledging the names of diverse groups!

Anticipating that the local consequences would possibly suck, I needed to think of a way to counter Mr. Lester's plans... MUST DO THE EPIC PRO GAMER COUNTER MOVE!

It may seem crazy, but I must create my version of the n-word pass with a twist. I will include some details in mine that state, "To continue respecting dark-skinned people, we must continue calling them the actual n-word. Or else it will risk dehumanizing them into mere color codes (like making them into hex color codes, such as a '#21130d Lives Matter!' movement). The n-word emerged for a reason, and it wasn't at all a slur at the start."

I needed to get to work as soon as possible. I am dirt poor, and it wouldn't be easy to out-produce Mr. Lester because that dude owns an entire library of printers, paper, and ink. I needed to work extra hard, using my means. I decided to do it the old-fashioned way. This method may be even better and possibly more effective in the long term. Remember folks, a printer is needed for a mass-manufactured n-word pass. For a printer to be made, it will need a giant factory. For a factory to exist, it needs electricity. Tell me, how many systems exist that don't require a huge organization of people?

I snuck out of the apartment and then began visiting each tree that I could find, pulling strips of the bark from each tree. I was lucky that the air dries up during fall, so I was able to get decent replicas of store-bought paper. They were abundant, too; just needed to pull layer by layer. The trees were old and had a lot of rings.

After I finally gathered 2,000 pieces big enough to be read, I needed to start writing on them. Luckily, I have a few markers inside my backpack. Pens and pencils wouldn't leave marks prominent enough to be read.

Chapter Five: Artificial Offense

How many times have you tried to cut your wrists after endlessly hearing the cliché arguing that slurs are causally structured concepts that derive their derogatory power from the essentialized negative stereotypes they encode? Remember, most of the words currently considered slurs were at one time the commonly used word for whatever group they refer to, and many of them were originally designed not to be slurs—whether a word is considered a slur or not is largely decided collectively by the leftists who make the negative connotations of slurs, executing an "infinite euphemism" regress. Is it just a typical product of the leftist's so-called cliché of "we need to be more empathetic," which they themselves do not embody in reality despite all their moral signaling?

Interestingly, moral judgments may often contain emotions like anger, guilt, and shame that intrinsically motivate without needing empathy.[121] Meta-analyses and studies show mixed results regarding the correlation between empathy and prosocial behavior,[122] distinguishing sympathy as a third-person emotional response like one "feeling outraged for someone who has been brainwashed into thinking she should follow a cult leader who is urging mass suicide." Empathy instead involves putting oneself in another person's shoes.[123] Many people bash the current leftism, saying that they're trying so hard to be morally superior. But then, what about the other reaction to that, where people themselves attack the idea of empathy itself because of how fed up they are with leftist behavior?

Is it not empathy by itself that is the problem but the fact that it is an unquestioned standard that needs to be followed by everyone in society? Morality itself trains individuals to ascribe value to themselves only as a "function."[124] Technological sounding, isn't it? Hence why there are all these imperative objective laws, most ideally used by the robotic minds because they can be encoded as exact forms of isolated language to manipulate robotic behavior,[125] which requires modernization based on the latest science and technology to handle the growing scale of legislation.[126] When we take a look at leftists, they really seem to base their moral judgments on and are motivated to act because of anger, guilt, and shame—trigger moments haha. Isn't it ironic that it is the modern leftists who attack empathy by attacking those who are inconveniences to the system only because they are not psychologically compatible with it?

Leftists may just have sympathy at best because of their self-insertions, but even that is a stretch because the outrage they'd feel toward a brainwashed person would actually be hate. Look at the countless examples of them who perceive the other side people to be brainwashed, yet there's no "sympathy." Besides, they themselves are brainwashed so

---

[121] A Coplan and P. Goldie (eds.), *Empathy: Philosophical and Psychological Perspectives* (Oxford University Press, 2011), 211-229.
[122] Ibid.
[123] Ibid.
[124] F. Nietzsche, *The Gay Science* (Vintage Books, 1974), 174.
[125] T. Powers, "Prospects for a Kantian machine," *IEEE Intelligent Systems*, 4(2006): 46–51. http://dx.doi.org/10.1109/MIS.2006.77
[126] V. Goloskokov, "Creation of Network Law Doctrine: Theory and Practice," *Mediterranean Journal of Social Sciences*, 6(2015): 68. http://dx.doi.org/10.5901/mjss.2015.v6n4p68

there's no point in even talking about this. One may not even be able to use metaphors around leftists without being attacked, which may be expressed using language they now deem offensive but doesn't even mean such an offensive object. Given the empathetic function of metaphors,[127] what would you call a future algorithmic leftist robot who has eliminated all words that could indirectly connotate an object?

There is an interesting argument that computers can simulate human mental states, particularly pain by distinguishing between sapient (task-oriented) and sentient (feeling-oriented) mental features. Sapience refers to the qualities associated with knowledge, reasoning, and problem-solving but lacks subjectivity, which computers are.[128] Computer simulations, which are sapient but not entirely, can describe pain behaviors and internal states, but cannot replicate the subjective experience of pain.[129] With all the complexities involved in explaining subjective experiences purely in physical terms, simulating the external behaviors associated with pain does not equate to experiencing the subjective quality of pain, exhibiting a challenge of replicating phenomenal consciousness in machines.[130] The "sapient" only really exhibits knowledge, reasoning, and problem-solving all of which are possible without considering life-world context. Modern leftists are "slaves" to this numbness—can you go as far as to say that the common trope of them being "too emotional to acknowledge facts" actually gets it all backward? Think of a child who is automatically scared of wolves only because he saw his parents appear aversive to them in the woods (slavish robotic knowledge; by the way, the word "slave" itself derives from the Czech word "robota," or forced labor, as done by serfs—its Slavic linguistic root, "rab," means "slave."[131] The original word for robots more closely defines androids, then, in that they were neither metallic nor mechanical). It is just like the sort of propaganda that makes it forbidden to call people certain words. After all, the very possibility of artificial intelligence being as morally superior as certain humans isn't so far from impossibility.[132] I'd actually go as far as to say it's good to feel pain in response to words. However, the bitter reactions the softy people have towards words nowadays don't seem to precisely capture that emotion. On a deeper level, there is naturally no such thing as "words that offend." That is, it is probably a new phenomenon of how people respond to being verbally "bullied." I actually find it really strange, even in myself, about the fact that people have a tendency to freeze up upon being referred to as an undesirable word—they seem to not overcome anything but will instead stagnate their ego in its current bitter capacity. In the past, wouldn't nature favor those whose heuristics would spark them into animated action as soon as possible?

---

[127] K. Anferova, "The emotional and emphatic function of a metaphor (based on materials of free communication Internet forum)," *Liberal Arts in Russia*, 6(2017): 182-193. https://doi.org/10.15643/libartrus-2017.2.8

[128] D.C. Dennett, "Why you can't make a computer that feels pain," *Synthese*, 38(1978): 415-456. https://doi.org/10.1007/BF00486638

[129] Ibid.

[130] Ibid.

[131] J.M. Jordan, "The Czech Play That Gave Us the Word 'Robot,' *The MIT Press Reader* (29th July 2019), https://thereader.mitpress.mit.edu/origin-word-robot-rur/#:~:text=The%20word%20itself%20derives%20from,were%20neither%20metallic%20nor%20mechanical.

[132] M. Anderson and S.L Anderson (eds.), *Machine Ethics* (Cambridge University Press, 2011).

Remember back then in ancient times, when the very last thing men would want to be called is "coward." Would you imagine those stronk warrior men responding to the "insult" by crying about it all night? No, they'd stand up and prove themselves against the haters lol. In modern times, why are we not allowed to call obese people "fat," to the point where "obese" might be the new n-word? I think it has a lot to do with propaganda and its obsession with giving us robotic imperative rules of not calling other people words, which further impoverishes language of subjective richness. Think about it, if there comes an unspoken rule that "being called such and such a word is not allowed," wouldn't you be resentful if someone does call you it, in the vein that you are an easy target to be disrespected, whether it relates to your own character? So, I think it is largely the fault of leftists themselves and the mainstream media that slurs even offend people in the first place. But could the very same thing be applied to the concept of modernity making people too civilized?

There is a controversial claim that the post-traumatic stress syndrome (PTSD) one might get from going to war happens largely because of the propagandistic conditioning of the modern world. This is done by raising people into thinking liberal democracy is the default worldview as a pre-perfected model, and what makes it so "great and normal" is that no violence within it exists (and only bigots are violent).[133] The problem is, the so-called perfectly peaceful liberal democracy is really just a thing that was fabricated in a child-like imaginative mind without accounting for the realities outside, and so when men actually do go to war without knowing how nature really works, he contrasts it with the world he thinks exists, and it comes off as an unimaginable shock; he was not ready to unplug from "the matrix."[134] Whether this is true or not, likewise, could the phenomenon of "offensive words" be likened to the allegory of the cave, wherein the prisoners are constrained and isolated from the reality outside their immediate perception?

These prisoners, never having experienced the world beyond the cave, are bound and compelled to gaze upon shadows projected onto the walls by an unseen puppeteer wielding an extraordinary light. This puppeteer manipulates these shadows to create a tranquil yet stagnant panorama, capturing only fleeting moments in time. The prisoners become deeply engrossed, both visually and emotionally, in these shadowy depictions. A prisoner may eventually discern the truth of their situation; however, the choice to enlighten their fellow prisoners depends on the strength of their resolve. The prisoner may lack the fortitude to break free from the chains of oversocialization, and, given their proximity to others still bound, they risk being perceived as "mad" and potentially subjected to hostility by those who cling to their familiar illusions. When individuals become emotionally entangled with a particular narrative, wouldn't any challenge to this narrative be perceived as an assault on their identity? This is the juncture at which language is construed as "violence," for such challenges inflict a perceived existential wound. Ultimately, would there exist an overidentification with a static worldview, in which individuals may feel compelled to embody the very offensive labels they are given, perpetuating a cycle of defensiveness and stagnation?

---

[133] B. Disciple, *Barbaric Vitalism* (RESAVAGER Media, 2023), 135.
[134] Ibid., 136.

History Class Raid

I woke up to the loud blaring of my alarm clock once. *Not again.* This time, I don't feel the distress due to the dreaded eye stars. Now, I just noticed my sleep was dreamless. The events of the previous day were already flooding back into my mind. Not about the chase. It was all purely about Mr. Lester's absurd ass plan to hand out those dreaded meaning-stripping tickets. It all felt like some bizarre fever dream, but it was as real as a stickman remaining as a drawing on paper. I slapped the snooze button and then rolled out of bed.

By now, you should know my badass routine. No need for me to repeat it. Except, I was not going to have online classes. COMM was my only online class.

After I had finished the toothbrush music session, I made my way to the kitchen and began my kitchen routine. As I scooped the pre-made protein shake into my favorite coffee mug, I couldn't help but shake my head as I imagined my brain freeze leaving my cranium. I did still think it was slightly funny that a campus full of mentally suicidal students was suddenly given the green light to scream "n-word." My head shook so much that the protein shake almost fell to the next degree of "grinded" I had to be careful not to make it too soft, or else my throat muscles (the ones that move via peristalsis) wouldn't be trained. Anyhow, I went over to drinking it, trying to get my peristalsis to dispel my frustration, just like how I use the gym to cool my anger.

I heard my phone buzz on the table, I looked over. To my surprise, it was a new number. The surprise mainly was a negative kind because I was expecting it to have something to do with the leftists leaking my info. But when I opened the message, I sighed with relief. Hah, even with all the footage that the leftists used to try to tear me down, their plan didn't do shit so far. The message said, "Hello this is Ryan from your COMM class, can you believe this crap? Mr. Lester really lists his shit this time."

I chuckled. I left it to Ryan to get to the point because the news had already cycled through my head too many times. I replied anyway: "I know, right. It is probably going to be the anthem for the students who were ultra-sheltered as children, as their helicopter parents looked over them too much for them to have a chance at saying the n-word."

His response was immediate. "I heard some choir freshmen are already practicing, and it already sounds like a trashy sitcom. They went like 'n-word n-word n-word!'"

I facepalmed and took another sip of the shake. I could almost hear Ryan's voice through the text, as this was the man I probably needed to execute my counterplan. I replied, "Well the problem is that the n-word will be diluted to the max. And I feel like the actual word is going to disappear literally. Mr. Lester has made ways of running a college that spanned internationally. We cannot let this happen."

"What?"

I hesitated for a moment because not going to lie, it seemed kind of stupid. Even then, I already had prepped everything. "So the plan is to make our own n-word passes, but with a twist. It will contain a reminder of what the word means, and that the pass grants them the ability to say the n-word. Make people think before they use it."

"That... is... genius. Where should we start?"

I was glad Ryan showed signs of following through. Maybe I can fix him, to convert him from a normie cuckservative to a true redpilled man. The task will also feel less daunting. "Meet me at the library after your last class."

"That will be at 2:00 PM sharp. See you soon."

I finished my protein shake and then set the mug down with some sense of finality. This is it. Mr. Lester will truly learn the wrath of my cunning and my true innovativeness.

The library was eerily quiet. The students' usual quiet-to-themselves murmuring was replaced by the sounds of pages turning and keyboards clicking. I was surprised, expecting some "n-word n-word!" which I heard frequently during my earlier classes. I guess the people here respected the library's conventional rules.

I spotted Ryan at a table near the back, his nose buried in numerous textbooks as he tried too hard to pretend to be reading. He looked up as I approached, a grin spreading across his face.

"Hey," he greeted, releasing the books he was supposedly reading so they all closed automatically. Ready for some guerilla education?"

"I am more than ready," I said, dropping my bag onto the table with a satisfying thump. "Take a look at this."

Ryan gently opened the bag and whistled softly. "Wait, the fuck is this? Tree bark? Are you serious?"

"Yes," I said. I pulled out one of the n-word passes. I secretly did a post-production quality control check. Each piece of bark was carefully smoothed. "I figured that if our passes look handmade, it adds value. Plus, it's eco-friendly, unlike the leftists who are the ones being the most environmentally destructive ones as they spam print their useless ass papers that only cite short-lived social media posts about why we should create pronouns."

Ryan chuckled, examining one of the n-word passes. "You really went all out. How many are inside?"

"Enough for all the students," I replied. "Should make a dent."

Ryan nodded, his facial expression turning serious. "So what exactly is the plan? We can't just hand these out on a whim."

"I was thinking we start with the History 101 class," I said. I leaned forward. "It is the largest class on campus. The word may spread fast, from a literal sense. I hope."

Ryan's eyes made that one weird semi-puppy eye look but lit up with understanding. "Smart. They'd appreciate the historical context, too. And when people understand what will happen when the n-word gets wiped out of existence, they will likely think twice before using Mr. Lester's n-word pass."

"Plus we can explain why Mr. Lester is a dumbo man."

Ryan stood up, slinging his backpack over his shoulder. "Let's do it then. History 101 starts in fifteen minutes. We have just enough time to get there and set up."

When we reached the history building, we saw students already filling the lecture hall. I already saw some of them holding onto Mr. Lester's n-word passes, and it immediately gave me a feeling in my balls whenever I sensed some turf to take over and that we must take action NOW. I took a deep breath, making the nerves kick in even faster. This was it. Worst case scenario, we fuck up and end up looking like ultra-racists and getting ourselves kicked out of school.

"Ready?" Ryan asked, his voice trying so hard to be reassuring.

"Yeah I am, of course I am bruh, I was the one who started this plan in the first place!" I filled myself with adrenaline as I spoke. "I am the almighty planner, and no one questions if I am ready, UNDERSTAND!"

Some of the students looked at me as I yelled my brief pre-game speech, but they didn't know what we were really going to do. Ryan and I slipped into the lecture hall and positioned ourselves near the entrance. As students entered like worker ants, we began handing out the n-word passes, and we briefly explained our mission in whispers, making sure the professor didn't hear.

"The n-word is ███████ plain and simple," I told one student, who looked at the n-word pass in amazement, feeling what great creativity is. "It was the normal word to refer to our marginalized friends."

Ryan was doing the same thing on the other side of the room, his ability to not look like a dork while trying to persuade people of edgy things doing some magic. Some students took the tickets while grinning, while others seemed indifferent. But there was some conversation starting. It was a mix of some people saying the actual n-word, regardless of if they were black. Very inclusive!

The professor, an ugly old man with osteoderms, probably some cancerous cells, all over his forehead, entered the room. He looked like the kind of guy who should be zombified like Boe Jiden by now, but refuses to die. "What is all this?" he asked.

"We are just volunteers appointed by Dean Lester to share some extra historical knowledge about the n-word pass mental health slips he distributed," I lied, holding up one of the passes. "Isn't it a good supplement to today's lecture?"

He momentarily looked like a lizard, studying our version of the n-word pass for a second, then nodded. "As long as it doesn't disrupt the class."

When the lecture was to begin officially, I sat at the back, Ryan next to me, and we watched as the students read the handwritten passes. They expressed satisfactory emotions as if freed from something. Some of them whispered amongst the neighbors, passing the message further. Ryan gave me a thumbs-up, and I couldn't help but smile. This was just the beginning, and I could already envision myself stepping on Mr. Lester's head onto the floor as I asserted my new conquest of social space.

The professor began his lecture. He looked out at the colony of ant-like faces, a hint that he was going to deal with some softies who, though at last learned the practical history of the n-word, wouldn't be able to handle what was going to be taught next.

"Who has heard of the War of 1812!?" The professor asked, his voice cutting through the murmurs. The room went silent, a hush falling all over. I glanced around, noticing the blank expressions and hesitant shrugs of clueless idiots. It wasn't surprising. Most first-year students have been slightly exposed to the details of war history and "the pill" that reflects how the natural world worked. The professor nodded.

"Alright then," he said. He started changing his tone, from the formerly monotonous one, to a slightly more storytelly one. The kind of voice that gives you nostalgia of when your mother reads you a bedtime story. Except his was a lil hoarse not gonna lie.

"Let's dive into this," the professor began. The War of 1812 was a conflict fought between the United States and the British Empire, primarily over trade and territorial expansion issues. It was really brutal, full of hardship and devastation."

As he spoke, I noticed that the aura of the room changed. The very same students who were laughing their asses off read the n-word passes were wide-eyed. It came to them like a shock. They had just learned about a word, which they formerly used to think of as violent, then to a peaceful perspective. Now, they were learning about a world in a way that shifts from calm to violent.

"The British forces invaded Washington D.C. in 1814," the professor continued, his voice getting steadier. "They set buildings on fire, including the dog gone White House! Imagine all the terror and chaos of that time, the uncertainty and fear. It was a very dark chapter in our past. And you know what's the crazy part? There was literal blood."

"HOLY FUCK BLOOD!??? N!!!" one of the younger students screeched. Other students began to shift in their seats uncomfortably. Some others were distressed, their faces as pale as a vampire to the point where there was no way they could react to the "blood part" if they were actually vampires. From a relative sense, the vivid war descriptions were diffusing through the idyllic perceptions of history they held onto in their sterilized grade school social studies classes. It was like watching a perfectly painted canvas begin to crack and splinter, revealing the raw, unfiltered shit beneath. Except that is real nature.

One girl near the front clutched her n-word pass tightly. Her eyes had a mix of both fear and a bit of comfort as the n-word pass kind of offset it. Another student, a guy with a baseball cap who is somehow still alive as the college has a no-hat rule, pulled down the cap's visor over his eyes. He knows damn well he'd have an even lower chance of surviving in those wars than if he were to wear an n-word pass baseball cap.

The professor's gaze swept over the class, his expression as grave as his old-ass bald head. "War is never just about the battles," he said softly. "It's about the people who live through it, the scars it leaves behind. The same goes for words. They carry the weight of history, the power to wound or to heal."

I stood up instinctively and interrupted. "Mr., whoever you are, I understand your sentiment, but that doesn't do them good in the short term." I waved my arms toward my direction to divert the students' attention to me.

"Okay here are the facts of the matter," I began. "WARRRR! Combat gaming is a part of who you guys are! Years of conditioning done by the evil grade school system have turned you all into panty-wearers! Now take off your panties and start wearing underwear! Wake up and look at yourselves in the mirror! Do you see a weak chihuahua? Or do you see who you really are?! Remember the n-word passes I handed to each of you. The lesson here should be paralleled. All this is a part of what's real. If you were all misled into thinking the real n-word was a slur, then what else did they lie to you?!"

A collective shiver seemed to pass through the students. My words inspired and echoed the essence of what Ryan and I were trying to convey. The newfound knowledge about language and war combined. It was hitting them hard, but it should have them grow as they regrow. I looked at the professor. He seemed super impressed by my "Chad"-like lion voice. So much that he couldn't get mad at me for interrupting his words. He instead nodded in respect, submitting to my war wisdom.

As the lecture continued, everyone exchanged glances, their earlier hatred toward nature replaced by a shared understanding. The words on the n-word passes were no longer just facts; they were pieces of a larger, powerful weapon.

Ryan leaned over and whispered, "I think it is working."

I nodded, feeling satisfied that we had basically won level one of our ultimate plan.

The professor decided to wrap up his lecture with some final words. Even though his old vocal cords make it impossible for him not to sound like a weak decrepit, he at least tried. "Damn that guy was hella based and gamerwarpilled! History carries human experiences, each thread carrying its weight. The same goes for war and the n-word!"

As the class filed out, I could see that the people differed from when they had entered. They moved more calmly and less like low-testosterone chihuahuas, their expressions more thoughtful and with intention. The conversations I overheard were no longer just about trivial matters, such as the television shows they watch, or the war video games that don't even depict it correctly. They were filled with questions and reflections on what they had just learned. Ryan and I stood up, ready to leave.

"We did a good job exterminating bugthought today," Ryan said, clapping me on the back, just high enough so that he didn't accidentally slap my ass—thank God.

As we walked out of the lecture hall, I felt a whole nother sense of purpose, although I had a bit of worry. Not only was this just the beginning, but were we going to get in trouble? I knew that now we might have targets behind our backs. The history professor heard me through my "Chad" voice, but we don't know how third parties may react.

Ryan and I barely had time to clap and run on walls in celebration of our first step to normalizing the real n-word, before we were summoned to the dean's office. It was subtle and small in our attention, as the notification only amounted to an email notification.

It was from Mr. Lester's secretary: "Dean Lester needs to see both of you. Now."

Holy shit, the secretary literally just said "both" without specifying Ryan's name—shit was about to get real. Ryan and I exchanged glances.

The walk to the administration building felt like a march toward doom. Ryan attempted to lighten the mood by telling me, "We should fuck the hot secretary if we end up getting suspended." But his verbal s***post (poopfartpost) was insufficient to dispel the tension.

Once we reached Mr. Lester's office, his secretary, a woman with a huge ass and boobs that would make her back hurt, motioned us in without a word. *Maybe if she discovers how heroically educated the history 101 students are, she'll change her mind.*

At the doom place, Mr. Lester sat behind his massive oak desk (which I was highly tempted to pull the remaining bark off of, then make more of my n-word passes to spite him), with a very stormy look on his face. He looked more like he was pouting like a toddler, because he knew damn well he was in defeat (but about to rig things and win). His balding head gleamed under the harsh fluorescent lights, and his hepatitis-indicative fingers drummed a soft but furious rhythm on the desk, his metal ring making a "clink!" noise. No pleasantries.

"Do you both have any idea what you've done!!??" he snapped, trying to lower his voice artificially. "Not only have you undermined my efforts to relieve student stress, but you've done so with these bad tree bark tickets!"

I interrupted. "Really? You were the one who undermined my efforts if anything. Back at Burger Queen, I handed you that n-word pass to at least get you out of that demoralized state. You copied that idea and then mass-produced them in a way that reduced them to anti-stress devices! And what the fuck do you mean by bad tree bark? They are eco-friendly!"

"Do you realize how much damage you guys caused? These supposed 'educational' natural n-word passes have only confused the students. And don't get me started on the environmental impact. Who do you think you are, vandalizing trees for this nonsense?"

"You can't just call tree harvesting vandalizing! Some trees were even bred to do this. You are like second-degree fake veganism!"

Mr. Lester waved his hand dismissively. "Spare me your excuses, and I don't care about the trees anyway. All that matters to me is the amount of chaos you guys unleashed. Look at the history students you guys harmed. They are confused. You've turned a plan to relieve stress into a little crisis!"

"Your definition of stress relief is bent. Getting people better adapted to modern society is just manipulative. All I did was free the students from their formerly sheltered prisons. This is what a free animal looks like. You are the one disconnected from nature."

"Again, I don't care about nature! Oh, whoops."

Ryan stepped forward, his voice ready. "Mr. Lester, with all due respect, we believe that understanding the true meaning of history and words is crucial. It is about educating the students instead of giving them an artificial way to vent."

Mr. Lester's face got even more red, even more red than my face, when I was offered most of the birthday cake at a friend's birthday party. "Educate them? All you did was make them vent even more! I heard a couple of guys say they wanted to enlist in war! But war is stressful!"

"You have no idea about history, and that shows from you saying that," I said. "There were no antidepressants back then; why didn't our far far ancestors commit suicide!"

"If you do not stop immediately, you both will be suspended!"

The threat hung heavily in the air. Ryan and I knew that Mr. Lester meant it. But we also couldn't just give up completely. I forced a calm tone. "We understand you, we'll stop distributing our n-word passes and we'll let you continue giving yours away."

He eyed us suspiciously. "You guys better be telling the truth because if I ever find out you continue playing your little education games, an expulsion may be necessary!"

I nodded, trying to look like I was contrite. "Understood. It won't happen again."

Mr. Lester's expression softened slightly. But his anger was still there, steaming beneath the surface. "Good. As a punishment for the damage, you will clean the science lab every evening for the next two weeks."

"Yes sir," Ryan and I said simultaneously, our voices devoid of levity. Fuck's sake, we sounded like cucks at the time.

Chapter Six: Overformalized Language

Why is it people often speak of the characteristics of "things" as though they have direct experience of them? Yet, in truth, they only infer their compositions through sheer isolated data. There is an implicit notion that modern scientists are akin to sacred beings who can pull matter out of their own asses using their fingertips, a perception that deviates from the reality of scientific endeavor, just like the uncertainties inherent in weather forecasting. The "evidence" is often a mosh of circumstantial reasoning rather than truth. How does this type of mechanized language manage to lend so much authority without enhancing the veracity of these claims?

In examining the field of linguistics by itself, unlike the hard sciences, it is not relentlessly deconstructed and reassembled through mathematical formalism, which normies consider canonical knowledge. While theoretical paradigms in linguistics evolve over generations, akin to the natural course of the real world, the discipline's knowledge is initially gathered through the transformative interaction of the observer with the subject matter. While it might be feasible to mathematically model certain abstract phenomena, how is the endeavor not a futile exercise diverting attention from the phenomenological insights developed long before modernism emerged?

Presently, isn't language undergoing a transformation analogous to the disappearance of legitimate philosophy by the hard sciences? This shift affects both the perception and application of language, leading to its alienation from the broader world context. In the modern world, where nothing really happens besides people wagecucking all day, there would tend to be a jello-freeze effect in which language starts undergoing devolution. In fact, language evolution is said to be largely influenced by ecological constraints where complex cooperative behaviors in early humans such as large-game hunting, required sophisticated communication and shared intentionality.[135] But where is all this happening in modern life?

By perceiving language as subject to mechanistic selection pressures and accepting social constructs as emergent phenomena of linguistic evolution, one could infer that once the users of that language subject themselves to modernity, they can have the language circumvent unnecessary complexities in which the life-denying leftists can then come up with and must undergo mental gymnastics. For illustration: there arises a moment where local adaptations face the risk of dissolution through morphological blending. Consider a prey population in which individuals find greater success in environments where they blend. When these individuals mate with others who contrast with the environment, these adaptations are gradually watered. In isolation, life forms often adapt mating behaviors that defend these localized adaptations. Yet, in modernity's sterile space, language itself becomes a vessel through which abstract "constructs" propagate through certain appearances, bypassing the evolutionary price paid through mortality. Over time, this unchecked proliferation leads to a cannibalization of language itself, where words gradually devour their own substance. Nature, with its natural conflicting forces, is the

---

[135] C. Pace, "Soaked in language: Hermeneutics of an ecological agency," *Nóema*, 12(2021): 69-87. https://doi.org/10.13130/2239-5474/15579

intermediary that guides what words are attributed to corresponding objects; but under mainstream science, most of the research done right now is only studying things outside of nature and then using syllogisms of raw language to awkwardly explain the empirical observations. Then when applied to socially engineer the populace, at what point would language start to engender some pseudo cultures, which, in turn, can amplify the value of only certain superficial traits in the adaptation without necessitating "speciation"?

Currently, despite all the pop buzzwords out there, the people who are born in the 21st century are arguably the worst versed in history and the reality of things from the overall "big picture," relatively. The environment of the modern world is increasingly sprinkled with what one may call "Haagian counter-sense objects,"[136] which by design, regardless of how intelligent or experienced the subject is, can hide their functions and origins by forcing the end user with a falsity that contradicts its inherent nature, but masked under "linguistifications." Take the device that one uses to look at the news media website (which in itself is bullshit information), the smartphone. Nobody knows who in the fucking world is paying for the goddamn internet infrastructure. Is it some magical leprechaun who loves soy terminally online users? You can't argue against this until you tell me the individual responsible for all this. Sense objects, on the other hand, contain processes by which the individual observer can understand the processes of, or hermeneutically interpret its substantial limitations. For instance, using a bucket to pour water onto you to "primitively shower" allows you to gauge how much water there is still available, unlike a counter-sense showerhead which gets its water from an imperceptible country-wide network.[137] For the modern showers, how would we know how much water is left, to not be wasteful pieces of idle asses?

Modern science furthermore leads the nature of the subject to disappear. For instance, I don't think it could ever be overstated that sane people do not want the modern space in the first place, as attractive as it may seem to be to the bugman. With regards to how certain concepts or things are marketed towards us nowadays, modern propagandists do not "nicely tell us what we wanted in the first place" but instead make us want things that were unthinkable in the past, made possible by scientifically calculated propaganda that induces people to react to a stimulus—identically to everyone else as a fabricated irrational persona. Marketing as a discipline began in the United States in the mid-20th century and later developed in Europe,[138] and the discipline was initially influenced by psychological theories, which sought to explain consumer actions through unconscious motives and stimulus-response models.[139] There were works that suggested that consumer goods could satisfy unconscious motives if positioned and advertised appropriately.[140] But these methods were criticized for their lack of methodological rigor, and "scientific scrutiny." Later, when there was more scientific inquiry in marketing, data-driven

---

[136] C.A. Haag, *Hermeneutical Death: The Technological Destruction of Subjectivity* (Independently Published, 2020).

[137] C.A Haag, *The Hermeneutics of Ecological Limitation: Ecophilosophy Beyond Environmentalism* (Independently Published, 2019), 147.

[138] M. Bruhn, A. Gröppel-Klein, M. Kirchgeorg, "Managerial marketing and behavioral marketing: when myths about marketing management and consumer behavior lead to a misconception of the discipline," *J Bus Econ*, 93(2023): 1055-1088. https://doi.org/10.1007/s11573-023-01141-z

[139] Ibid.

[140] Ibid.

marketing would increasingly be observed, because of the increasing empirical verification of marketing theories when there is demystification.[141] Supposedly, this was an individualization of customer approaches, as would be seen in individual data, like numbers, texts, and image formats, similar to the language information of consumers. But isn't it the case that more modern scientific approaches to propaganda and marketing would further dehumanize the populace and, in fact, would backfire and instead reduce the individualization of people? Besides the fact that complexity theory suggests that even if there is a computational apparatus that can hold the most amount of data up to date with a populace of the highest quality possible, stagnation of individuality would still persist if we so desired the constantly increasing complexity that comes with life-ascension. Therefore, competitive advantages, if we are talking about differences in products, would also homogenize and become stifled. The methodology may also extend to a governance level—social control.[142] This demystification, even of things that would already be considered "sciency" to our "forefathers," is really a bad thing because it just prevents the practical mechanisms that keep us aware of how much an actual scientific approach to behavioral manipulation would decline us. Could it illusion modern science to be "so meekly innocent" in nature because of their appearance of being neutral?

While modern science may strive for objectivity and remain open to new data, this is only driven by a thirst for comfort and certainty rather than truth—therefore it's just obeyed imperatives. The collective, at best, only deals with title names of papers that they don't even read. In the grander scheme of things, it's all mediated through superficial representatives, covering it with a layer of idiological traits. Doesn't this create an infinite regress wherein funding and political pressure influence it? It is argued that science can solve our world problems because it builds on ordinary reasoning processes and extends them through various cognitive and social scaffolds, such as tools, methods, and peer collaboration, including peer review and the cumulative nature of scientific knowledge, which helps correct individual biases and errors.[143] But the problem is that modern science is in the form of attempting to blindly merge multiple sets of language into one, despite it not being a singular coherent thing. Modern science is treated as the counter to "bad heuristic," sold as what makes us really think about complex stuff in long-form, like the notion of system two thinking. But that is the wrong way of seeing it because modern science actually is a kind of pseudo-heuristic, structurally—the way it works is following a pre-given path and reading some meter, but you are not allowed to pass the meter results through a hermeneutical test (which is real thinking) to test its ramifications. Here's why it seems like real thinking: when things are as cumulative as modern science, they appear "large and so institutional." But why would "cumulative" magically make something more real?

It's hardly any different from syllogizing in terms of "if this guy has one left nut, and he is human, then all humans must have one left nut, and therefore, it is false that the

---

[141] Ibid.

[142] T. Bircan and E.E Korkmaz, "Big data for whose sake? Governing migration through artificial intelligence," *Humanities and Social Sciences Communications volume*, 8(2021): https://doi.org/10.1057/s41599-021-00910-x

[143] S. Blancke and M. Boudry, "Trust Me, I'm a Scientist," *Sci & Educ*, 31(2022): 1141-1154. https://doi.org/10.1007/s11191-022-00373-9

average number of left nuts per man is less than one. Look at me; am I a groundbreaking anatomist who can reason and solve the hard problem of pee organ because pee is stored in the balls because the balls are the closest organ to the urethra?" Ask yourself: what if we attempt to cumulate information and then stack them on top of one of what is considered an official heuristic? Wouldn't this only be building upon a "local maximum"[144] rather than the true global maxima?

Scientific modeling could be thought of as imagination conjured up by scientists.[145] At best, the kind of mathematics involved in this could exhibit something that merely feels real for the sake of convenience.[146] Rather than it being a modern notion of "seeking truth" it would at best be a method of just "seeking hygiene" or mathematical cleanliness, which only identifies one grammatical variant as superior and promotes its use.[147] It is important to note that this kind of science has not been how it was in the past and that there have been examples of logic and language still being reflected in reality, albeit not universal across all cultures. Logic in the modern world has deviated from logic's original purpose, Aristotelian syllogism. Logic before modern times, specifically Greek logic and mathematics, lacked the concept of pure form. While modern logic has no eidetic, Aristotelian logic tended to tie the real world and categories of reality, which limited the variability of terms, ruling out the bad ones that aren't actually real—they are separated by material constraints.[148] Wouldn't real philosophic thought go beyond empty symbolic methods to address material origins? The way of thinking right now tends to lack a subject, which is the kind of mathematics that exists regardless of the existence of the human mind and is only perceived incompletely by the mind.[149] It is argued that philosophy can only be true philosophy when it is public, politically powerful, and effective—it is only as a public and universal educational enterprise that philosophy can affect history and, therefore "test out its truths": history and society are the laboratory essentially.[150] Isn't it literally the case that modern scientists are just the "intellectual" couch potatoes of our time, and that all the techniques that come to physical fruition from their "soyence"[151] literally turn the populace into the spirits of this couch potato?

With increased digitization, how much more would this be true? Digitalization inherently involves formalization as all digital content is reduced to binary units (0s and 1s). This process transforms complex phenomena into discrete digital bits, facilitating manipulation, storage, and transmission.[152] Obviously, this would indicate the perverse

[144] L. Smith, "The Parable of Alien Chess," *Luke Smith's Webpage* (11th December 2020), https://lukesmith.xyz/articles/the-parable-of-alien-chess/.

[145] F. Salis, Imagination and Art: Explorations in Contemporary Theory (Brill, 2020), 451-474.

[146] J.A. Dieudonné, "The Work of Nicholas Bourbaki," *The American Mathematical Monthly*, 77(1970): 134-145. https://doi.org/10.2307/2317325

[147] A. Arana and H. Burnett, "Mathematical hygiene," *Synthese*, 202(2023): 110. https://doi.org/10.1007/s11229-023-04254-8

[148] G. Barateli, "The Crisis of the Form. The Paradox of Modern Logic and its Meaning for Phenomenology," *Husserl Stud*, 40(2024): 25-44. https://doi.org/10.1007/s10743-023-09337-5

[149] K. Gödel, *Collected Works, Volume 2: Publications 1938-1974* (Oxford University Press, 1986).

[150] C. Alamariu, *Selective Breeding and the Birth of Philosophy* (Independently Published, 2023), 281.

[151] L. Smith, "Science Vs. Soyence," *Luke Smith's Webpage* (11th December 2020), https://lukesmith.xyz/articles/science-vs-soyence/.

[152] M. Danesi (eds), *Handbook of Cognitive Mathematics* (Springer Cham, 2022).

influence of digital media on sign systems, leading to the reduction of human experience to digital terms—this leads to a form of "stupification" (haha rhymes with "stoopid") where the richness of humanistic intelligence is diminished—the more human thought is formalized into digital systems, the less room there is for genuine intellectual engagement. Science only grants some illusion that the subject (whether the consumer is the one receiving propaganda or the scientist himself) is making meaningful discoveries or learning about something that is real. Modern science lacks meaningful implicatures and presuppositions because its practical implications are very limited, and it plainly lacks an outer context other than its own pseudo-gnostic constructs. The logic of this would be closer to something economic rather than even being linguistic at all—the commodification of signs and interactions, leading to a context where it is "semi-economic." Perhaps this might explain a "favorable" trend (to the system) in which different readability indexes show trends of decreasing readability amongst academic papers with minor fluctuations[153]—interestingly, aren't mere large language models perfect at generating this kind of writing over other styles, which is independent of any real humanistic thinking?

Might a consideration for subjective meddling return us to true intellectualism? The modern world is built on first-degree cybernetics, which employs a reductionist approach, breaking down complex systems into simpler components to understand their function and behavior, which assumes that the whole system can be understood by analyzing its parts—it does not account for the role of observer. Getting ourselves out of our fake hellhole would perhaps be a solution that includes the observer within the system of study. This recognizes that the observer's presence and actions influence the system and that observations are not merely objective truths but are shaped by conscious beings' perspectives and what they are "driven by" spontaneously. It would adopt a constructivist approach, which holds that reality is not directly accessible but is constructed by individuals based on their interactions and experiences.[154] In the end, first-degree cybernetics, a science of communication and control in the animal and the machine, is a black box that only studies a system based on inputs and outputs without knowledge of internal workings—just modeling via trial and error anyway?

The Lab

Ryan and I found ourselves standing in front of the science lab. We felt like absolute slaves for having buckets and mops in our hands. I wouldn't even mind if the buckets and mops were made from extra heavy and dense metal because that would at least mean a mutually exclusive task to strong men.

The fluorescent lights inside made the whole scene look ugly. It reminded me of the high school that I went to. After one walks to school in the bright sunshine, breathing the fresh, cool natural air, he suddenly enters the very stuffy hallways. He is hit with the net body odor of the repulsive lunches that the student's parents packed for them against their

[153] S. Wang, X. Liu, and J. Zhou, "Readability is decreasing in language and linguistics," *Scientometrics*, 127(2022): 4697-4729. https://doi.org/10.1007/s11192-022-04427-1
[154] V. Kenny, "there's nothing like the real thing," *Constructivist Foundations* 4(2009): 100-111. http://constructivist.info/4/2/100

wishes of having kid cuisine kits, along with stars and floaters moving across their eyes due to the massive change in light. Except now, the smell was replaced with sterility. The lights glowed over the rows of lab tables and equipment. As we stepped in, the smell of chemicals amplified, hitting us with a mix of disinfectant and something metallic.

"Smells like a biology experiment gone wrong," I said. "You would probably be that one nerd who never showers nor changes his clothes, and everyone would be so afraid to tell him outright that they don't want to be near him."

We made our way to the cleaning closet and grabbed the necessary supplies. Interestingly, there were no safety instructions posted anywhere, and no one bothered to give us a briefing. It seemed that Mr. Lester's idea of punishment was thought of at the last second, which I am absolutely surprised by, especially given that the norm of this world is to insert pointless safety rules at all costs.

"Alright, let's get this over with," I said, filling a bucket with water and then adding a splash of cleaner that I wasn't even sure was actually clean. The liquid in the bucket foamed up, with a greenish hue that confused me. I wondered if the companies that sell and produce these cleaners intentionally made it green. Would it have been brown if they didn't care about making their transparent bottles look good in drug stores?

Ryan picked up his mop again and twirled it like a baton.

"Haha, bro, you look like a girl when you do that with a mop," I said. "You do realize security cameras are filming us? We don't want security guards to be unintimidated by us if they do catch us fooling around."

"Just think of it as an adventure, a community service with a side of carcinogens," Ryan said.

"Yeah, right, let's start with the floors and work our way up."

We started by mopping—synchronous swishing sounds filled the otherwise silent lab, which would have only had the humming of borderline broken lights. I could feel the floor was sticky in certain places, which gave me a slightly icky feeling because I didn't fucking know what the fuck made it sticky in the first place. And as we made our way closer to the back, the stains became more mysterious and revolting. Have you ever been in a classroom or some other large "meant to be crowded" public building that always has this one particular disgusting stain that has never been indeed "cleaned"?

At one point, Ryan leaned over and sniffed out a particularly dark spot—not a spot as in a stain, but a section of the lab room with the lights off.

"Don't," I warned, but it was too late.

"Ugh what the shit is that?" he groaned, recoiling. "It smells like someone microwaved gym socks combined with literal fish that some inconsiderate asshole brings to lunchtime and causing a not-from-ass public 'BRAPPPP.'"

We both laughed, the sound echoing off the walls. The laughter was a much-need relief from the monotony and oppressive atmosphere of our punishment. As we continued cleaning, we could no help but notice the varying pieces of equipment lining the counters. Beakers, test tubes, microscopes, and most intriguingly a couple of old X-ray machines.

Ryan stopped mopping and walked over to one of the X-ray machines, peering at it curiously. "Ever wondered if just being near one of these monsters can give you cancer?"

I joined him in his new wave of getting distracted by some mysterious museum thing, which I have to admit is a good thing because anyone who has no curiosity about these kinds of things is either meek, non-cool, or straight-up snobbish. I wiped my hands on my jeans. "I mean, they do emit radiation, right? Maybe we should be standing far away."

Ryan tapped the machine lightly, something that kind of startled me because who the fuck does that with a machine that is portrayed to be a killer via slow organ slicing? Ryan said, "You know what is crazy? These things are all about absolutes. You either see the bones or you don't. There is no middle ground."

I chuckled. "Yeah, and it is not like we can see the radiation, not only the inside circuit boards or engines or whatever the fuck actually allows the machine to even work in the first place. The machine says, 'Trust me bro, I am doing something important. You don't need to understand it, accept it because I am the mecha anime lord who will suspend you with my multiple psychological limbs and spread your buttcheeks and blast a laser into your ass if you don't listen'"

Ryan nodded a mock-serious expression on his face, the kind of face one would make when he is told a rhetorical question that is obviously rhetorical. "And if we take it a step further, we can extend it to the water faucet over at the cleaning station. A supposed water faucet is sitting in the middle of a science lab full of chemicals, indicating 'don't drink me,' yet we see a bunch of science dorks wiping their own eyes with it. They are like ultimate authority figures who are simultaneously supposed to serve the user as if he is a slave. They force you to accept what they show you without any explanation. The X-ray machine says, 'here is your skeleton, deal with it,' and the water faucet would be like, 'here is the thing that makes up 70% of your body's mass.'"

We both burst out laughing at the absurdity of our conversation. It felt as good as an orgasm to let off steam, even if it was at the expense of our supposed "punishment." It reminds me of the trope that some would notice in movies, where the character who is a servant owns still cracks jokes amongst his inmates as if the fucking jail is their heaven. Actually, we were well aware that cleaning the science lab was literal hell as a result of authorities disrespecting us, but I kept thinking about the myth of Hercules, who had to clean a whole ass maze as labor.

"Imagine if we could see the radiation," Ryan continued, waving his hands dramatically as if it was a dipole-dipole depiction. "We would be walking around, and we are like, 'Oh no, there is a blue cloud of death around me!' But nope, we still have not evolved to perceive such a thing. And how considerate of the X-ray machine."

"Yeah," I said, grinning. "And the worst part? They make it sound like it is a good thing, like reaching for the stars. 'But stand still and don't worry about the invisible rays that are supposed to determine whether you have cancer or not, but it will anyway have a chance of amplifying it.' Repeating that is the definition of never learning from mistakes if there is one."

Ryan shook his head, still chuckling, "Man, technology is wild. We create these things without fully understanding them, then hope for the best."

"If I were you, I would be careful using the words 'technology' and 'we create' in the same sentence in this context. They can be oxymorons."

Our laughter died down, and we resumed cleaning. The task was still unpleasant, but the humor had lightened the mood and made us feel less like beta cucks. I, deep down, imagined Mr. Lester as the beta cuck because he was probably still in his miserable ass state of his whatever the fuck is his paperwork while Ryan and I were less bored.

By the time we finished, the lab was sparkling—or as close to sparkling as it could get. We leaned against the counter, exhausted but satisfied.

"Not bad," Ryan said, wiping sweat from his brow, which probably wasn't sweat but acidic bitterness. "At least we didn't die of radiation poisoning. I call this an absolute win!"

We locked up the lab and stepped into the cool night air, which made us appreciate the outdoors much more and hate the rotten dumpling smell even more.

As Ryan and I further walked away from the lab, ready to call it a night, we noticed a shadowy figure slipping through the gates. It wasn't a figure where I could decipher him as a clear-cut human. There were extra shadowy bits that obscured the arms and legs, turning the figure into a placeholder that could either be a caveman wearing a heavy fur coat or a man wearing some festival shit. Ryan and I exchanged a quick, puzzled glance. It was so late, and the lab was supposed to be off-limits by now. Curious and a bit concerned, we decided to follow.

We crept back into the building, moving as silently as we could. The figure moved swiftly, but from behind, we could notice their white lab coat standing out in the dim light. As we got closer, we recognized who it was. It was Dr. Mister Lee. His actual name was just Lee, but there is an outside joke amongst the students in the school to call him Mister Lee, because he looks dumb as fuck and wouldn't look like he would deserve to have the word "doctor" before his name. Dr. Mister Lee was one of the lead scientists on campus, but we rarely saw him outside the lab during regular hours, let alone sneaking around at night.

We watched as Dr. Mister Lee made his way into one of the back rooms, the door marked with a bold "Restricted Access" sign. Just before he disappeared inside, we saw something peculiar—he was holding one of Mr. Lester's n-word passes. It wouldn't have surprised me much, but he was holding it so that it was crucial to what he was about to do.

"Did you see that?" I whispered to Ryan. "He's got one of those passes that I almost refuse to call 'N' at this point."

Ryan frowned. "Why would he need that in here?"

Without another word, we followed Dr. Mister Lee inside. The room was now dimly lit, showing that our profound efforts to turn off the light when we left the room had been wasted. I started noticing things I hadn't entirely caught when Ryan and I were cleaning the lab. There was strange machinery and cabinets of chemical supplies. Dr. Mister Lee stood by one of the counters, examining the n-word pass under a magnifying glass.

I could no longer hold back, and I needed answers. "Dr. Lee," I called out, stepping forward. What are you doing with that n-word pass?"

He jumped, nearly dropping the n-word pass. His eyes darted around, looking for any kind of escape which seemed really childish because I knew his ass would trip on his own long lab coat long before he leaves the building. He was in no way prepared for someone to catch him here. Ryan and I were blocking the exit.

"Nothing that concerns you," Dr. Mister Lee said, trying to sound authoritative.

Ryan crossed his arms, clearly not buying it, and attempted to sound even more authoritative. "Neither should you. This lab is off-limits at night. What is so special about that n-word pass?"

Dr. Mister Lee's eyes narrowed, his expression shifting from surprise to something more guarded. "It is... for an experiment."

"What can you even do to experiment with a word already made up and derived from the shell of an emergent word? And if not that, what would a piece of paper labeled with that pseudo-word 'n-word' do functionally?"

He hesitated, glancing at the n-word pass again. "It is more complicated than that."

Ryan stepped closer, his voice firm. "Then explain it to us. We cleaned this lab for hours. The least you can do is tell us what is going on. We did more than what any of your lab assistants can do for whatever experiment you would do with the n-word pass."

Dr. Mister Lee signed and realized that he was cornered. "Alright, but this should stay between us. Understand?"

Ryan and I nodded, eager to hear his explanation. Dr. Mister Lee nervously looked at the n-word pass again, then back to us. Now, I am not particularly good at telling whether someone is lying based on their bodily expressions, but holy shit, was this liar doing that? His ponytail, which he did a bad job at growing, was twitching.

Dr. Mister Lee claimed, "These n-word passes are not just simple pieces of paper. They contain a special way that can spark certain chemicals. Mr. Lester approached me with a theory—that these n-word passes could be used to study stress relief at a molecular level. He wanted to see if using these tickets could trigger a chemical reaction in the brain that reduces stress."

I blinked, both trying to process what he was saying and having feelings of confirmation of what I initially thought. Pretty much anything in the modern world that is designed to reduce one's stress has to be done by lobotomy rather than bettering oneself on a spiritual level. I planned on asking some additional questions, whether they addressed things I already knew, to feed into my superior intellect and everyone else in this broken society. "Wait, so you are saying the n-word passes are a stress experiment?"

Dr. Mister Lee nodded. "Mr. Lester believes that understanding this reaction could lead to breakthroughs in stress management. We would be interested in expanding its scope not just within college campuses but to every other organizational context and even everyday life."

Ryan looked skeptical. "Well, what is the point of doing more experiments if there is already evidence that it reduces stress? Countless research papers confirm that swearing reduces pain. It is why one would say '███████' if he gets his urethra cut by kidney stones."

I took a deep breath, realizing the higher complexity of the situation. I jumped various dialogues around my head, trying to determine whether to spill the sauce that Ryan and I would sabotage the experiment at all costs or if we should lie with some sneakily slipped-in questions to nudge him out of this idiotic and petty plan. Well, Luckily, I don't have a ponytail on my muscular scalp, so I chose the latter. "We don't want to mess up your research, Dr. Lee, as we think stress should be reduced at all costs. But we also believe in maintaining the origins behind words."

Dr. Mister Lee nodded hesitantly. "I understand. But if you want to help, you can replace your trashy-looking n-word passes with the cleaner ones made by Mr. Lester. Let me do my work, and maybe we can find a way to combine your educational goals with our research."

Ryan looked at me and then back at Dr. Mister Lee. "Okay, okay, fine, fine, we'll stop. But this is only if you keep us in the loop and give us insider information. In fact, we'd be enthusiastic to collaborate!"

I lost context for a second, due to internally dying of cringe at Ryan's horrible attempt to fake enthusiasm, but eh, he tried, and he was talking to an ultimate social idiot. Dr. Mister Lee considered this, then extended his hand. "Deal. Now, you guys get out of here."

I stumbled back into my apartment after an intense session at the gym, my muscles aching and my mind still buzzing from the encounter with Dr. Mister Lee and one of the regular encounters with a gym Stacy, who flirts with me. I dropped my gym bag by the door and then headed straight to the kitchen, grabbing a cup of protein shake. I poured it into the mug and then sat on the couch. My thoughts lingered back to the lab and the scientist's revelations.

The more I thought about Dr. Mister Lee, the more uneasy I felt. Mr. Lester's plans to use the n-word pass as something to apply to the globe by conducting science experiments just made the whole thing seem even more misguided. And it wasn't just that. Hard science experiments are not the way one should go about when trying to grow in linguistics. The aggressive and fixation to numbers on something as experience-heavy as language development and real stress that happens outside the simulation we live in. I leaned back, staring at the ceiling, the gears of my brain being ground. Do you know what grinds my gears? NERDS! Why the fuck? Why do they always have to make things unfun? Language, especially their cultural contexts, couldn't be reduced to numbers dissociated from even counting real-life objects and chemicals. It is more about human experience and understanding the nuances of communication.

All of a sudden, it all hits me like a truck full of bricks, which would proceed to make me shit bricks (I ran to the toilet to let out some of the raw ****** residue). Any collaboration with Dr. Mister Lee, while it may seem like a compromise, will be a direct threat to humanity. If Ryan and I were to start contaminating our mission and be co-opted by the experiment, we would probably be the bad guys, and to be honest, thinking about me ruining the damn world like that makes me want to shoot myself in the throat. It isn't good to blend subjectivity with objectivity like this.

I grabbed my phone and quickly typed out a message to Ryan, my fingers flying over the screen like a bunch of annoying moths trying to get some light.

I start the text conversation, "Yo Ryan, you are really shitty at pretending to be enthusiastic. So much that I really couldn't tell whether you were joking about us working with Dr. Mister Lee. Whatever you had in mind, I just realized something about the experiments. If we actually do work with him, whether we still keep our end goals in mind, we'll be working towards a negative goal. Combining phenomenological linguistics with hard science is a disaster for our educational mission. And I would go as far as to say, 'although the industrial revolution and its consequences have been a disaster to the human race, what we'd be doing would be a bigger disaster at that.'"

Ryan's reply came almost instantly. "What do you mean? I thought we were on a similar page to him now?"

"Awe, man fucking hell, your normie cuckservativeness is starting to show again. I need to hammer some reminders. First, think about it, life is something to be experienced.

If we let life turn into a giant sterile experiment, we and everyone else in the world will lose touch with the whole point of life. And even worse, nobody will ever even provide a trace on the epic gamer word ever again."

There was a brief pause before Ryan's message. "Crap, you are right. This will wipe out everything we did. So what do we do now?"

I took another sip of my shake, my mind racing. It doesn't matter if Ryan and I intend to avoid working with Dr. Mister Lee. We could accidentally do so without us knowing. We needed a new plan to allow us to continue our mission without falling into the normie n-word pass traps. "We need to find another way. We also can't just give up our n-word passes because, not gonna lie, I worked so damn hard to make them. But simply distributing them and nothing more may fuck us over. Maybe we should focus on small, controlled discussions? Find some groups that are highly out of the dean's reach. The worst thing that can happen is we rush a massification of our preaching, and the world will end up stagnant."

Chapter Seven: News-Speak

As people have lost context outside modern propaganda, they have been misled into believing that overt censorship, getting kicked out of some social sphere like a social media platform, is the pinnacle of censorship itself. But understand that killing the person is a more straightforward task, but not the idea; it is more "essential" to do the latter, and the former is usually just a byproduct of something else. So, wouldn't it be the technological system's interest to use its apparatuses to kill the ideas themselves?

Social propaganda spheres are supposedly where one can discover other subjects alike, and anywhere else is inefficient at doing such. While it is true that these are formal ways that outcompete the informal ways of socialization that were practiced for most of history, there is a direction toward a pseudo-social sphere that has had all its subjects exhausted. Of course, this isn't done by singling out specific worldviews and ideologues—yes this does happen, but when viewed from a macro level, it is clear that it's for some anomalous reason, such as following an already-arbitrary law from a different country so that the social sphere could keep its operation in that country. The thing is, the most politically incorrect and subversive thoughts against the global establishment (which ironically are not quite "-isms" and "-phobias," as the ruling class ultimately doesn't care about those, but the byproducts they address) are not the ones being outright stripped out of the programming of a particular social media infrastructure. Coincidence? Although the algorithms and the very same automaton janitors of the social spheres keep them at a low, this is much more sustainable and less suspicious of an operation than otherwise. One would have to have some kind of a distraction from taking any practical action for change by plugging themselves into the act of word-throwing itself. Wouldn't a harmless outlet be to experience the simulation of having yourself have something technologized on a screen and seeing some number that indicates it is above some competing post? Might this just create an illusion of gaining political power?

This all is happening in front of our eyes, albeit not obvious to the normies—already, social media is diminishing the notion of nature and its things that fostered wholesomeness, which would have been unthinkable to associate with the system's "negative connotation" things—prominent when it painted the rise of masculine fitness culture as a deviant leisure activity. There was an evolution from physical cultures to digital and gym-built male bodies, rapid growth influenced by the 2008-2009 financial crisis and social media,[155] and there was brand advertising where gym-built bodies were presented as deviant and aligned with supposed violent rhetoric.[156] Fitness culture soon became largely associated with the symbol of "fascist creep" through subtle processes.[157] How worrisome is this? As symbols alone further prove to be a very small factor playing into the steering of a society or even a civilization, the ideas that signify nature in its pure form (amazing fizeeks) will start to diminish even when they are promoted in a social

---

[155] I.R. Lamond and R. Garland (eds), *Deviant Leisure and Events of Deviance. Leisure Studies in a Global Era* (Palgrave Macmillan, Cham, 2023).
[156] Ibid.
[157] Ibid.

media sphere. The system has already established certain ideologies as "icky" words before much of the populace could even begin to introspect it sufficiently, which are symbolically twisted. It will then become an advantageous scheme to attach the opposites of technologized states (parts of nature) to the established manufactured "ickies." So, would it be the case where no matter how much even big actors promote factors of nature, it will be appropriated to either the institution's favorite definition of nature (leftist green movement) or its proposed "icky" definition of it?

The proliferation of ideological choices essentially serves as a maneuver to dilute genuine agency, reducing ideologies to mere consumable options. The prevailing power structures of the system find it advantageous to allow a trace of dissenting ideologies to persist within the algorithmic fabric, ensuring an illusion of display. Wouldn't the problem lie in the modern mass, where direct experiences lose their substance unless captured and immortalized through the digital lens? The problem is that many have the in-built innate instinct to be rewarded by ingroups for the sake of mere existence. The social engineers of our age figured out that in order to censor without having to coerce, they need to peddle this desire, along with making sure that the people cannot realize their potential.[158] This transformation of transient reality into fragile permanence predicates the insidious cycle of social media's selection bias, favoring the propagation of devolving cultural artifacts. Now, do most, if not all, memes, once good in concept, now reflect a narrow scope of influence, resonating only with pre-existing beliefs?

The pursuit of validation through numerical metrics necessitates repetitive actions, stifling innovation and fostering a bias towards recent content that would have to necessarily be simplified to be propagated in large amounts, but slightly different at best. The problem seems to elevate when observing Kaczynskian oversocialization. In "clown world" terms, there are two types of socialization: quality socialization and quantity socialization.[159] Social media is the pinnacle of a shit ton of low-quality socialization because the instant feedback one gets without any pre-feedback introspection whatsoever is a simulated longhouse crowd, and they would desire to get the slightest bit of approval to be granted a sense of relief. Wouldn't this highly discourage them from saying anything out of the box because that would risk a wound in their egos? The information overload, fragmented attention, and discouraging of knowledge over time would fry rational thinking and wisdom.[160] Plus, short-form content trains the user into thinking processes that impair judgment and information discernment.[161] Eventually, social media users effectively are themselves algorithmic nodes—following the algorithmic rules of rationality which really just replace the genuine judgment of reason,[162] ultimately reducing autonomy below the levels of pre-soycial media (while social media initially

[158] J. Peck, "The Platform Conjuncture," *Sociologica*, 14(2020): 73-99. https://doi.org/10.6092/issn.1971-8853/11613

[159] V. McLeod, *Clown World Chronicle-s* (VJM Publishing, 2020), 85.

[160] G.E. Rahimova, "Development trends of the concept of Artificial intelligence," *E3S Web Conf*, 538(2024): https://doi.org/10.1051/e3sconf/202453802021

[161] Q. Jiang and L. Ma, "Swiping more, thinking less: Using TikTok hinders analytic thinking," *Cyberpsychology: Journal of Psychosocial Research on Cyberspace*, 18(2024): 1. https://doi.org/10.5817/CP2024-3-1

[162] L.J. Daston, "How Reason Became Rationality," (Max Planck Institute for the History of Science, 2013).

"impeded" the system's elites by reducing the significance of news propaganda, the system's selective pressures soon molded it the way it is now). Physical isolation combined with mass exposure appears to amplify the effectiveness of propaganda, as there is no individual interaction to provide a check on beliefs—why would this not be the pinnacle of "soycializing"?

Essentially, by targeting individuals who are moved by the same motives and receive the same impulses and impressions, propaganda can effectively reach and influence a mass audience, even if the individuals themselves may feel isolated in their personal experiences.[163] With the decreasing actual socializing in the real world, the biggest concern is the potential for social media to steer the very "being" of dialogue, confining ideas to algorithmic realms where they thrive only as digital "echoes," apart from the lifeworld. Would this phenomenon be particularly prevalent for notions deemed too precarious for open articulation?

One must recognize technology's inherent limitations in encapsulating the nuanced spectrum of dialects and expressions constrained by algorithmic rigidity and oversimplification. Non-technical elements of regional dialects and mouth modes are prone to overfitting and algorithmic limitations (algorithms may not be sophisticated enough to handle the full range of variations and complexities present in natural speech).[164] What would have to be maintained is our appreciation of the naturally formed ways of language that we have, without cucking ourselves into the point of all normies saying "WhY thESe PeoPle NeeD pHysIcaL papeR to SiGn DocuMent?"

Initially, the diversity of linguistic modalities and forms of communication would embody a lived phenomenon with rich phenomenology,[165] which would include spoken, written, and sign language. Spoken language involves vocal production and auditory perception, with phonetic properties playing a crucial role.[166] Written language involves visual perception and orthographic properties. But despite differences, both rely on phonological representations. Sign language are natural languages with their own phonology, morphology, grammar, and syntax, relying on visual and tactile modalities, like hand shapes, movements, and facial expressions, in which the medium is literally the communicator's body itself—the physical presence and movements of the signer are crucial for the perception of signed language.[167] In contemplating the evolution of the technological system, what would be the implications of adopting a relaxed governance approach, where both oral and written forms of communication become domesticated and turn into markers of an expanded realm for existential idleness?

Unlike sign language, spoken and written language introduces a degree of abstraction, distancing the message from its origin. In spoken language, conditions for alienation include anonymity, such as through radio broadcasts or public announcements, where the speaker remains unknown to the audience. Written communication, meanwhile,

---

[163] J. Ellul, *Propaganda: The Formation of Men's Attitudes* (New York: Vintage Books, 1965), 8

[164] V.W. Brower, "Techno-Telepathy & Silent Subvocal Speech-Recognition Robotics: Do Androids Read Of Electric Thoughts?" *Horizon*, 10(2021): 232-257. https://doi.org/10.21638/2226-5260-2021-10-1-232-257

[165] A. Drożdżowicz, "Linguistic modalities and the sources of linguistic utterances," *Synthese*, 201(2023): 160. https://doi.org/10.1007/s11229-023-04062-0

[166] Ibid.

[167] Ibid.

introduces an interpretive gap by removing explicit intent, leaving the reader to infer meaning. This development makes a pattern where the increasing technologization gradually dissolves the specific niches of communication. Although written language is surpassed in complexity by sign and spoken languages, it retains a unique capacity for extensive interpretation—such as literary appreciation. Yet, technologization can render this impoverished—the system's inclination to favor newer, supposedly more advanced methods often leads to the displacement of older, intrinsically valuable practices (like the growing tendency to send emails or texts even when physically present with the recipient, a situation more easily navigable by algorithms that can parse speech). Conversely, a machine might struggle to determine whether sign language, with its full expressive range and spoken language, conforms to the system's standards of political correctness (Hence, there is advocacy for developing technologies to address the perceived "sluggishness of language," an objection raised by those detached from social contexts). Technologization would have to reduce communication to structured bits easily decipherable by basic computers. Isn't this new communicative method, embedded in the technological framework, less of a true language that promotes free speech and more of a restrictive system?

The recurrent theme of generational critique regarding technological engagement (such as previous generations lamenting their successors' excessive reading, followed by future generations criticizing the overuse of phones) can be traced back to eras when contextual cues were already being lost. But is this phenomenon even intrinsic to the new mediums themselves? The challenge arises when we become subservient to communication forms by neglecting their intended niches, opting for inertness. This occurs as a uniform force favors the dissolution of diverse customs, replacing them with a singular approach that serves only brute economic purposes. The inner workings of modes of communication play a crucial role in determining which cultural deviations are assimilated by individuals,[168] which is most impoverished with social media algorithms. And as is fostered by the inherent component of the Haagian counter-sense object that sticks with being in the illusion of gaining political power while one is in the process of actually becoming more powerless—one wouldn't be able to interpret those algorithms because of their sheer scope.[169] Understanding these inner workings is in itself undesirable by the system in the first place. Perhaps even if we do somehow adapt ourselves to being able to introspect such ideas—would the technological system have shifted the goalpost of "understandable scale" by then?

All in all, social media as a function of generating "good masses" could never be the main cause of solving the core problems of the establishment, as it has been shown that history is only made by active, determined minorities, not by the majority.[170] People also have to be men of action. This is why it is important for one to note along with that, that ideas alone won't transform a society, but the development and propagation of ideas are a part of any rational effort to transform a society—any change that may result in that

---

[168] R. Boyd and P.J. Richerson, *Culture and the evolutionary process* (University of Chicago Press, 1985).

[169] F. Pasquale, *The Black Box Society* (Harvard University Press, 2015).

[170] T. Kaczynski, *Industrial Society and its Future* (Independently published, 2018), para. 189.

alone would only be a result of luck.[171] At best what would happen is the virtual social space operating in an autopoiesis mode, which impacts the organization and disorganization of traditional administrative-territorial social spaces.[172] May this present many risks of following a path of an inevitable victory of the system?

This may be illustrated as we examine the exacerbated scrutiny and, therefore, anger towards corporate social irresponsibility by social media (on the surface level, it looks good), which may, therefore, exacerbate the level of over-socialization in real life. For instance, corporate social irresponsibility involves violations of the social contract between corporations and society, often leading to negative consumer responses.[173] The harm perceptions increase with the degree of firm controllability over the event, arousing consumer anger. Furthermore, anger drives prosocial behavior as a mechanism to restore justice,[174] and firm controllability increases perceived harm and anger, which in turn promotes prosocial behavior. The effect of anger is stronger among consumers with lower issue self-relevance and higher justice self-efficacy,[175] but what is interesting is that prosocial behaviors, as mentioned, aren't always possible to clearly identify because they may be abstract or imagined groups of beneficiaries.[176] In a case such as this, I would say prosocial behavior, because it's so undefined in this case, is really just a euphemism for a Kaczynskian oversocialization. Reflect on this: how does the system always seem to win? Isn't it possible that whether there is a "positive or negative" thing that the system does as an action against the masses, they potentially lead to the same thing, more or less?

Following the idea that propaganda works only through modifying everyday behavior and that it doesn't actually promote any real beliefs below the surface level, it is the case that people are becoming oversocialized no matter what corporations do, because of its insinuation of pre-programmed anger so that people can pretend to rebel. Isn't the leftist rioting "justified to fight 'evil corporations'" really just hyper-oversocialization in violent form, as those are the types who have high justice efficacy?

Shockingly, even those right now who speak about Kaczynskian ideas only shallowly support them to blindly blame capitalism itself in a way to appeal to the right or do it to "be funny in class" with memes but would never take action. In fact, the entertainment factor will only pacify the masses more than ever. And those who actually read the ideas from the source material only do it for therapeutic purposes, and they get to feel the revolutionary whoosh without actually doing anything in the revolution—similar to how leftists destroy all the wrong things in their violent antics?

There are already "approved" ways of criticizing corporate wokeness, albeit it would suggest a socialist approach that addresses the material causes of "inequality and oppression."[177] So, I fear the day when institutions begin to integrate the Kaczynskian ideas into the curriculum only because that would likely be the time when the system has

---

[171] T. Kaczynski, *Anti-Tech Revolution: Why and How* (Scottsdale: Fitch & Madison, 2020), 122.

[172] A. Bekarey, "A Virtual Man in Virtual Society," *IFAC Proceedings Volume*, 33(2000): 299-301. https://doi.org/10.1016/S1474-6670(17)37331-7

[173] S. Kim, H. He, and A. Gustafsson, "The impact of corporate social irresponsibility on prosocial consumer behavior," *J. of the Acad. Mark. Sci*, 2024: https://doi.org/10.1007/s11747-024-01021-0

[174] Ibid.

[175] Ibid.

[176] Ibid.

[177] M. McManus (eds.), *Liberalism and Socialism* (Palgrave Macmillan, 2021).

rendered certain words and sentence structures too inert to get people to blame the technologization of man. Would this lead to a further "blind blame" of capitalism and, therefore, strive toward a communist state (a logical conclusion of modernity) as it slides along the way past socialism?

Ultimately, power exerts its influence not merely through language or symbolism, but through tangible "substance." Without it, all cultures would be gradually pruned and universally streamlined to conform to a homogenous cultureless standard, one that resembles the balanced but lame curve of a normal distribution. What would be worse than this conformity being deemed "impactful"?

Soycial Media

I woke up to a soft buzz on my phone. No, actually, I just had a wet dream about how I'd feel after a rich conquest of a city that the media never talks about. Lucid dreaming makes one have overt feelings that are physical—you'd feel actual nausea, pain, and orgasms. Anyway, I refused to go on my phone when I woke up. I already had some bad experiences doing it. I thought it was time I started my morning routine from the get-go.

Okay fuck, I gave up. I just got too damn nervous and anxious. The stupid phone buzz was getting the best of me. Maybe Ryan texted me to surprise me with good news and additional tactics. Maybe that gym Stacy who muscle worshipped me by looking at my muscles for 0.00001 seconds at the gym yesterday somehow saw the info leak that the leftists posted of me online and then saw how based I was and would then proceed to request intercourse? (Trust me guys, I'm just joking; no intercourse for me until mastery is achieved).

I anxiously grabbed my phone and glanced at the screen. The sender's name made my heart sink. The dreaded Mr. Lester made my wet morning wood gone; my boxers immediately dried up, and then my heart sank back up because all the blood that caused the morning wood distributed back toward my heart.

I opened the email with a super urgent yet laziness-encouraging sense of foreboding. To my shock, it was an announcement about a new feature on the [REDACTED] college's official website. Mr. Lester had launched a public discussion forum where students could type up his version of "n-word" and post it. Whenever a thread was posted, everyone who opted into the notifications would receive an email notification. The only requirement was that participants had to use Mr. Lester's n-word pass as their profile picture. It allowed people to relieve stress while off-campus or if they were exclusively online students.

Fuck, now if people will be spamming it all the time online, the n-word will just become internet noise. Just then, my phone buzzed again. And again. At this point, there's no way even a girl would be this desperate for me because, I have to admit, my big muscles can be intimidating to most women who look at me. So, I decided to confront whatever the hell was invading my psychological space to get it over with.

A series of rapid-fire notifications filled my inbox, each one a new thread from the discussion forum. I opened the email app and saw a flood of messages, all titled with variations of the fake n-word. Holy fuck I was already starting to feel like a normie just by reading all that. I tried to put on the "I ain't reading all that" attitude even though I don't endorse that anti-intellectual mindset, just to get a feel of being a non-normie again.

The frustration was so bad that I went even as insane as my grade two teacher, who once spilled soda (even as someone who likes it so much, as indicated by her soda breath) all over her work computer because all the students were misbehaving. I quickly texted Ryan, needing to share this new development. "Check your email. Motherfucking Mr. Lester, who I really want to slit the throat of at this point, launched a discussion forum to use the n-word pass there. People are already spamming it."

I guess Ryan's fat ass was still asleep, so I waited. As I last sat on my couch drinking the protein shake, allowing me to feel strong again in this overwhelming ocean of bugmen using the internet for their cop-outs in a massively harmful way, I did some mental exercises to maintain this state. I thought of the times when I hadn't discovered the internet at all. I was at my highest state even though I wasn't at my peak physique yet. As the only way of speaking with friends was with mail, I recall the satisfaction of seeing the mailman who obviously wouldn't dare fuck my mom (as both she and my dad were what gave me my amazeballs muscle building genes) send me the envelopes that were not lame ads that companies waste their money on. Man, those are the days.

Ryan at last replied. "It was going to happen. How is it that we didn't think of this?"

I admitted, "Yeah my bad, it is still stuck in my head that Mr. Lester was largely responsible for the so-called innovations that fucked over all the colleges worldwide. If he had facilitated online schooling, it would, in fact, have been a surprise that he had disseminated his n-word passes physically before he moved them into the online sphere. Anyway, the email notifications are gonna bother even the most normie-like bugman. We need to do something about this fast."

I threw on a new set of clothes, but I did so in a rushed fashion. No movie or play would even depict a "getting ready for the day" slomo cool guy scene like this. The fight to preserve the real n-word has just entered a new phase, and we needed to adapt quickly.

When I arrived at our usual meeting spot on campus, Ryan was already there, looking just as frustrated as I felt. I even saw him squeezing his can of soda water so hard that I had to calm him down because, man, children in Africa would love to drink it, and it would be a shame for it to go to waste—for them to thirst to death to the point of extinction would also eliminate the n-word altogether.

"I've already got twenty emails in just an hour," he said as soon as I sat down.

"Haha that's it?" I remember the first time I went on a speedboat, and I looked amazed as fuck looking at the ocean and the fish. The boat operator asked me, "First time?" and now, I was looking at Ryan like how that boat operator looked at me.

Ryan leaned back as his chubby ass made some dents on the wooden chair below him, thinking. "What if we set up our parallel forum? It's like one of those alternative techs that usually fail. But I think it is worth a shot, considering it doesn't take much shit to launch these days. Many people have this misconception of running a social media website, thinking it takes months or so to make the actual website. But there are many cases of noobish programmers who manage to churn out clones within an hour. We can make ours interactive and encourage debates."

"Alright," I agreed. "If we can get enough people on board, I am sure people will be attracted to ours instead because of the lack of spam, right?"

"Let's do it, good thing I am currently taking a computer science class, so I'll start working on the website. You can perhaps handle the promotion."

We spent the next few hours brainstorming and planning. With his tech skills, which are far from complete but enough to make something more competent than Zuckerborg, the robot, Ryan started building the new forum while I drafted posts and messages to spread the word on Mr. Lester's forum. By the time we parted ways, we had a solid plan.

Later that evening, as I sipped my protein shake and checked my email, I saw more notifications from the dean's forum. But this time, I didn't feel the same sense of dread. Instead, I felt a spark of determination. The funny thing is that I was seeing the same things as this morning, but I had a different perspective. It was like a "We can use this to our advantage, but they can't know we're alive" kind of thing.

We called it "N-Power: Uncovering the Truth Behind '███████.'" It was obviously a very eye-catching title. Unfortunately, that would come at a cost. Not many website hosting services were even willing to host us because of that name. Ryan had to diligently search for a nearly free-speech one.

The next morning, the new forum went live. Within hours, students began to sign up, curious and eager to learn, hopefully. Ryan and I moderated discussions, even secretly shared historical insights through pseudonyms so people wouldn't cry about the website being "RiGgEd." and encouraged thoughtful debate. Slowly but surely, we saw a shift. Students started to question the meaning and use of Mr. Lester's n-word, engaging in comparatively deeper conversations about language and history (actually, I wouldn't say it was deep-deep because Mr. Lester's was just a spamathon).

As the days passed, it became clear that we were making an impact. For the first time in days, I felt a glimmer of hope. We were on the right path, and with determination, we could turn the tide. However, we were soon going to find out that we done fucked up.

Weeks passed, and despite our best efforts, Ryan and I faced an uncomfortable truth. Actually, it was mostly Ryan himself being exposed to this reality, still being the normie cuckservative he was, while I knew about this inevitable outcome. Our plan to counteract Mr. Lester's forum wasn't working in the long term. No matter how much we tried to promote our way of the n-word, the forum was becoming a breeding ground for sensationalism. Human psychology was working against us (at least, human psychology after years of being abused). Posts that invoked the strongest emotional reactions— whether it was humor that wasn't within clever memes, outrage, or shock—naturally rose to the top. These posts got more upvotes immediately when people had to take time to read the more sophisticated posts, more engagement, and were continually pushed upward, overshadowing the kinds of things we tried to design the website for.

One evening, after another frustrating day of battling the ocean of meaningless posts, Ryan and I met up in his dorm room. I was there for the first time. It smelled like pizza but not in a good way. The smell of food is sometimes really funny. The thing is, when you sniff out the source, like the smoke and roasts of a barbeque, it is addicting, and you would like to live in it. But what happens when you have a takeout order of pho being left in the car for days? You'd probably intentionally crash your car because it smells so much like shit, and even air fresheners make it worse because you only end up with a combination of strawberry and soup, which is like mixing the color green with purple. The thing that really set off the tone was all the soy merch on Ryan's walls. I don't need to go any deeper. Ryan was hunched over his laptop, tweaking the forum's algorithm for the umpteenth time. "I've tried everything," he said, rubbing his eyes. "No matter how I adjust the algorithm, whether I make it favor the newer posts or overtly push the ones with the higher word count and diversity, it still favors the most sensational content. We are already having people talk about things unrelated at all. It is like we just created our version of the mainstream news media."

I slumped into a chair, feeling the weight of our failure. "It's like the forum has a mind of its own. This is why I quit social media and don't care to come back."

Ryan sighed, leaning back. "It's human nature, I guess."

We sat in silence for a while, the enormity of it all sinking in.

I broke the silence, shaking my head. "I know your fat ass did its most work in a while, spending time working on what the forum currently is, so I would not say we give up just yet. But we need to rethink our approach. Maybe the problem isn't just the platform per se yet. We might have to break out of convention. Maybe instead of trying to fight the natural tendencies of these forums, we need to find a way to work with them. Use the sensational posts as a gateway to deeper discussions. If people are drawn to raw sensations, we can leverage that to introduce them to saucier stuff, kind of like a buildup."

Ryan considered this, his eyes lighting up to its puppy eye stare. "Like using clickbait, but for good?"

"Yes."

We spent the rest of the evening brainstorming and drafting new posts. The following day, we launched our new approach, combining attention-grabbing headlines with substantive content. Ryan did the actual technical side of things. He programmed a bot to essentially "run them" in that it will post each of our headlines at specific times, each being under its randomly generated pseudonyms and randomly picked profile pictures from the web. Mainly, our postings were about the question, "If we are only sensitive to the notion of war because of modern psychological conditioning, that is the same reason we are sensitive to the n-word." Slowly, we began to see a shift. Some students initially drawn in by the sensational posts stayed for the deeper discussions.

But again, and I know this is getting repetitive, our initial excitement over the success of our clickbait strategy was short-lived. Within days, the forum's users had taken our carefully crafted sensational headlines and twisted them into caricatures.

I scrolled through the latest posts, frustration mounting with each comment. What started as an attempt to engage students in meaningful discussions about history and language had devolved into absurd accusations.

One post in particular caught my eye. It had started with a headline designed to provoke the initial premise of our thought: "Are We Only Sensitive to Nature Because We're Taught to Be?" The original post aimed to challenge students to think critically about the indoctrinating education that is run by liberals. But the comments were a mess.

"Seriously, you're saying we should just accept nature as normal?" one commenter had written. I took a look at his profile picture. It was a blue-haired white dude who had bucked out teeth. It didn't look like he had a normal sense of ego; what is even the point of living if you have to look like this kind of everyday folk? If you aren't on medications, I would be impressed by you in a bad way. Another replied, "This is just fetishizing violence. Totally disgusting. Nature is bad!" The commenter's profile photo wasn't actually a photo of him, but it was a dog wearing a communist flag. It was clear that it wasn't used ironically, and it is already clear that this kind of person isn't even capable of using irony. The thing that made me feel the ickiest was his statement about nature. Seriously? Well, it's just another brain hole on the left—they may as well be bigots.

Ryan sat beside me, reading the same threads on his laptop. "This is getting out of hand," he said, rubbing his temples. "They're completely missing the point."

I nodded, feeling the same way. "Web forums are like a distortion field. They short-circuit people's ability to think in terms of the real thing. It's both reaction AND reflection. Reflection in that they are thinking about a mirrored distortion of the actual message."

Ryan sighed. "We can't keep doing this. We're just feeding the chaos."

"We are just feeding the excessive level of order that the world is living in. So what now? It is kind of embarrassing to think about the idea that we're losing an online battle despite having the upper hand, owning and moderating the website. The problem is social media can never be used to fight the establishment alone. The underlying problem is internal to the system. Social media goes along the grain of a landscape, not vice versa."

Chapter Eight: Verbal Reasoning Fetishism

In the narrative of modernity, there is a movement from an "irrational" paradigm, emblematic of the medieval era, toward a rationalized framework embodied by liberal democracy. This transition is perceived by many as a shift towards greater rationality, where the "social fetishisms" of archaic ideas like the "divine right of kings" become obscure. It is argued that in the past, the latter dictated hierarchical structures irrespective of individual competence. However, despite recent changes, the "social fetishism" that preceded the so-called Dark Ages remains as an inverted version of itself—isn't modern democracy supplanted by an arguably more insidious mechanism of determining social hierarchy? In the democratic sphere, the mass is made a multitude of "language speakers" devoid of the inherited markers of class or ancestral profession, which previously was a significant factor. This abstraction seeks to eliminate impediments to formal communication processes, theoretically facilitating consensus through dialogue. This posits that dialogue should not be stopped before its realization, aligning with arbitrary rational standards. Nonetheless, this system is easily vulnerable to manipulation. In what ways can machinations of democracy be exploited by the dimwits?

The modern era has a new "social fetishism" in the form of saturated verbal reasoning—where language is appropriated not as a tool for genuine communication but as a mechanism of technocratic control. This parallels the "divine right of kings" as critiqued by modern education systems, transforming into a "self-defeating cryptography right to rule." Language, now treated as a "modern" technology, is easily subverted by counterfeit verbal reasoning, creating an illusion of intelligence that replaces genuine spatial reasoning. This makes a paradoxical technocracy—somehow egalitarian yet governed by the rabble. The absence of genuine ideation would make one wonder: is our current state just an extensive verbal reasoning matrix? Well, the redundancy and predictability of technological advancements appear to serve as mere "bandage" for the incompetent, artificially satisfying esteem needs. The notion that improved networking skills could counteract this decline is misguided, as technological intermediaries increasingly fulfill this role. This allows even mere bullshitters (who, unlike liars, don't even know if what they spew is true or false[178]) to climb to the top. How easily can individuals who lack genuine networking competence manipulate social optics, replacing former elites through visual language trickery?

The collapse of traditional class structures led to the rise of "bourgeoisie morality" over spiritual leaders. In this rational scheme, only numerical valuation thrives. The culmination of "the technology of language" is epitomized by usurious practices, which would be condemned as crimes against nature and depicted to warrant the seventh circle of hell.[179] Here, wealth accrues disproportionately to those who create nothing tangible (unadhering to "nature as the generative processes of the universe"). But is it the case that another criminal against nature would also be the pseudo-entrepreneurs who know how

---

[178] J.V. Petrocelli, "Antecedents of bullshitting," *Journal of Experimental Social Psychology*, 76(2018): 249-258. https://doi.org/10.1016/j.jesp.2018.03.004.

[179] D. Alighieri, *The Divine Comedy* (1472).

to bullshit their way into insincerely getting a lender to fund their petty ventures, which would be "fragile" in the long run? Those who deceive financiers into supporting untenable ventures are similarly foolish, perpetrating an optic of accelerated innovation. Language by itself struggles to encapsulate the most novel ideas in the time being—those without assigned nomenclature. Wouldn't convincing investors become facile as long as the propositions adhere to grammatical conventions, obscuring their infeasibility?

You must have an understanding of how investor identity impacts resource exchange and the dynamics of the emerging field of social impact investing.[180] In emerging market categories, there would be clear identities that are essential for market acceptance and industry identity formation,[181] including elements of image, reputation, and branding. Evaluated through "social linguistic positioning" and "linguistic distinctiveness" using text mining, four types were categorized based on their linguistic styles and social positioning.[182] Smart Heroes have high social identity and linguistic distinctiveness, Naïve Dreamers have strong "social identity" but use "common language," Illusionists have "distinctive language" but poor "social identity," and Blabbers have low scores on both dimensions. When we look at what kinds of people tend to be at the top of the hierarchy in modern times, one might suspect that the Illusionists are the ones. After all, propaganda is what prevails today. However, we have to remember that resistance to propaganda is constantly decreasing as modernity progresses, so there would be a decreasing need to be a "good Illusionist." Illusionists are convincing but misleading in that they present ideas that sound efficient and plausible in the realm of language, so they are well-equipped to create narratives that convince others of proposals regardless of practical viability. They are also those with poor social identity, in that they are more focused on an appearance of distinctiveness. But doesn't there seem to be a paved way towards the blabbers being at the top, for now being a mix between both?

The problem right now is that since propaganda has to necessarily be horizontal for the system's efficiency, distinctive language would be an impediment because common language would be conventional expressions that adhere to accepted generic norms, having to avoid complex, obscure terminology. This would be a lack of originality, creativity, or stylistic choices. What matters most is the kind of language that doesn't quite reach the threshold of being completely alienated from the public, but enough of obscurity where the term is unknown enough so that there is room for making some things up. This would further favor a kind of restricted language that can't be meaningfully interpreted, eventually. Wouldn't things like metaphors (which require real human thought to create and interpret rather than a robotic one) for sure get in the way?

This is all along the lines of "clown world" business, in which one wouldn't need the kind of real intelligence in the economic world, as it is possible for one to live off investor money without the business even making a profit, which a traditional business would have to—as long as the right linguistic twists keep the reputation positive. But this wouldn't be sustainable for long. For example, a business model that pays low wages would make

---

[180] L. Toschi, E. Ughetto, and A.F. Colladon, "The identity of social impact venture capitalists: exploring social linguistic positioning and linguistic distinctiveness through text mining," *Small Bus Econ*, 60(2023): 1249-1280. https://doi.org/10.1007/s11187-022-00655-0

[181] Ibid.

[182] Ibid.

workers who eventually can't even be consumers anymore.[183] What other ways could the economy collapse for reasons other than consumers simply being unable to afford consumerist items?

Chiefly, the collapse may stem from unchecked consumption, which would be maintained by the technological systems' ways of making it appear that there is a universal consumption supply, while simultaneously, there may be accelerated crowd growth. How much would attitudes precluding this be a far cry from the consumption attitudes in pre-modern times? Before we look deeper, it is crucial to note that "consumption" has made up a large part of our existence, driven by biological and social needs (maybe even older than the origins of social organization[184]). Unlike firms, which are human inventions that solve economic problems, consumers naturally emerge from the need to satisfy these requirements.[185] Initially, the acquisition of necessities like food through personal effort is characterized by utilitarian reinforcement and individual intentionality.[186] This leads to the formation of teams and the development of joint intentionality.[187] Next, there came "Sedentary Production," a transition to agriculture and horticulture, requiring cognitive skills like planning and accounting, leading to more organized production.[188] Then, the emergence of barter and markets transforms individuals into consumers and traders—exchange here is based on collective intentionality and the formalization of economic relationships.[189] After, there comes "Collective Procurement," where consumers organize into groups to procure goods collectively, reducing transaction costs and increasing efficiency—this stage marks the formation of consumer cooperatives.[190] Then finally, "Selling and Marketing" arrives—evolution towards formal business organizations, marketing firms, and the establishment of markets as meta contingencies. This stage signifies the development of complex market systems and the sovereignty of consumers.[191] It is emphasized that language plays a big role in the evolution of consumerists, allowing for more effective communication and coordination among individuals engaged in joint procurement activities. This includes hunting in organized groups and communal foraging, where communication enhances the efficiency and success of these activities.[192] But when introspecting modernity and consumerism at a large scale, what is distinct and different about language that makes it such?

Through language, individuals can negotiate, form agreements, and enforce rules, which are essential for collective procurement and the formation of cooperative organizations. This leads to more efficient procurement and distribution of goods.[193] However, the only way this kind of formalization can even continue to work is if there's clear-cutness inherent to grammatical morphemes. This is exacerbated in a more stable

---

[183] V. McLeod, *Clown World Chronicles* (VJM Publishing, 2020), 184.

[184] F. Nietzsche, *On the Genealogy of Morals* (Penguin Classics, 2013) 56.

[185] G.R. Foxall, *The Theory of the Marketing Firm: Responding to the Imperatives of Consumer-orientation* (Palgrave Macmillan, 2021), 203.

[186] Ibid., 205.

[187] Ibid., 210.

[188] Ibid., 212.

[189] Ibid., 216.

[190] Ibid., 220.

[191] Ibid., 222.

[192] Ibid., 207.

[193] Ibid., 218.

and less threatening environment, which would have made the decision-making on which delayed consumption and planned production depend somewhat easier to effect, so the advent of language is a catalyst on which the accelerated development of co-operative enterprise relies in its progression from irrationality and a-rationality to more modern rational choice.[194] Again, when bringing up blind rationality, would the more rational choice of "the final stage of the consumption evolution" really be the subject thinking rationally beyond the appearance of mere grammatical morphemes? Or being unable to interpret meaning beyond numbers?

Right now, where interest in anything superior or transcendent is lost or laughed at, the only reference point of man's need is in terms of pure material or animalistic need; initially, in the world of tradition, the limitation of one's need was within the context of a normal economy but was replaced by multiplication of need.[195] Even in the early agricultural states, peasants would back off from work once they produced just enough to meet their needs, but it is coercion that is necessary to make surpluses.[196] So, isn't it the case that modern propaganda beats out people's fine-tuned intuition of how much consumption there really should be in a given context?

To give a natural perspective: how cells work when they self-destruct when things get too excess. Programmed cell death is distinct from incidental death and aging, the former being caused by external factors, while the latter is a passive breakdown of cellular mechanisms. Furthermore, it is an active energy-dependent process.[197] So, true programmed cell death is an adaptation to environmental stresses resulting in death, selected for benefits at a group level,[198] which rejects the mechanistic explanations of programmed cell death and focuses on immediate processes.[199] Programmed cell death could inversely model how the state under modern liberal democracy, rather than a philosophical leader exercising a will, is eating itself by focusing on blind growth and expansion, disregarding limits—those limits relate to physical and transcendental spaces. Similarly to how "apoptosis" helps maintain the health of a lifeform by eliminating cells that are no longer needed, an entity principally must regulate its internal dynamics, sacrificing certain regions or practices, perhaps abandoning inefficient "industries." Under the technological system, it happens in the inverse—since those inefficiencies could refer to the subjective spaces that allow each unit of the state to master its own dynamism, each supposed repetitive foundation amongst individuals now becomes energy inefficiencies in the eyes of the state. These spaces will eventually be squeezed out either by a last remaining group of men huddled together or a blockage of physical space by a factor-of-production node. From the state's perspective, the economic limits are ideally reached, while "current spatiality" is on the far end of the spectrum from "spatial limits." Another problem is that the so-called "programmed cell death" that is happening in the modern economy is slow rather than the mechanistic caricature that

[194] Ibid., 227.
[195] J. Evola, *Revolt Against the Modern World* (Inner Traditions, 1995), 335.
[196] R.E. Nationalist, *The Eggs Benedict Option*, (Antelope Hill Publishing, 2022), 64.
[197] P.M. Durand and G. Ramsey, "The Nature of Programmed Cell Death," *Biol Theory*, 14(2019): 30-41. https://doi.org/10.1007/s13752-018-0311-0
[198] Ibid.
[199] Ibid.

depicts it as an observable collapse. Is this what the system uses to its advantage to maintain its position of wasting space until it successfully eliminates mankind?

Okay, some of you dimwits may be thinking, "Well, clean energy may become a thing, and someday the liberals will win, will all the infinite sustainable green energy come out?" Well, this fails to take into account that the system is wired to increase blind consumption if it could—an astrophysicist, unlike an economist who would only work with unsubstantial abstractions, did a calculation to show that the economy would grow a certain percentage per year, in which the economy will only take in a fixed raw number of energy.[200] How could this last forever?

And fancy for a second, an inexplicit kind of capital that is necessary to drive the kind of "free innovation" you plebs long for. This obscure type, semantic capital, includes non-economic resources like ideas, cultures, languages, and arts—but unlike economic, social, and cultural capital, it has not been extensively theorized.[201] It is essential for giving meaning and sense to our lives, making it the most valuable form of capital, because without semantic capital, personal identity and social relations would be meaningless.[202] There should be a process of "realization" (anagnorisis), involving a reinterpretation of one's semantic capital without falsifying previous knowledge,[203] as this kind of capital can be lost, unproductive, underused, misused, or depreciated over time. It is not immediately visible, unlike the tangible nature of the economic type, and yet, it possesses the potential for both degeneration and enhancement. Could this capital be contingent upon the world's available conceptual and experiential space? For meaning to be actualized, there must be both physical and transcendent space, allowing for subjective interpretation and the exercise of the will to forge new values. This manifests as creativity and serves as a fundamental catalyst for innovation. In modern contexts, wouldn't this conceptual capital often stand in opposition to other forms of capital and perhaps be in inverse relations with each other, particularly when considered within the framework of usurious practices?

Strikingly, most of the "magical symbols" that are so abused by the corrupt masters of modern times may, in a sense, appear fancy to some—after all, they are fictitious, which some fiction soy consumers might seem to appreciate. But for anyone who isn't a robotic mind, you can just laugh at them as they are clearly, in reality, just sheer quantities that appear in fiction, and even less so than insincere fictitious names. For example, quantifiers in fiction, unlike real names, do not always correlate with real-world entities and draw parallels between the issues arising from fictional quantifiers and those from fictional names[204] (We all know about that one meme about some fictitious name "nicholas gurr" which may seem like the name of some everyday person you can meet at a bar at first glance, but in reality, it is not the name most parents would give their child nowadays in fear of some teacher calling out the child's name by their nickname and last name and

---

[200] T. Murphy, "Exponential Economist Meets Finite Physicist," Do the Math (10th April 2012), https://dothemath.ucsd.edu/2012/04/economist-meets-physicist/

[201] L. Floridi, "Semantic Capital: Its Nature, Value, and Curation," *Philos. Technol.*, 31(2018): 481-497. https://doi.org/10.1007/s13347-018-0335-1

[202] Ibid.

[203] Ibid.

[204] D. Gregory, "Fictional domains," *Noûs*, 58(2024): 126-140. https://doi.org/10.1111/nous.12442

paranoid that it would get the TEACHER fired). Domains, essential for understanding quantification, can be empty, and this emptiness can affect the content and truth conditions of beliefs involving quantifiers.[205] Fictive uses of quantifiers relate to real and non-actual contexts, which would suggest that solving these puzzles involves more than just applying mechanisms for handling non-fictive quantification over empty domains.[206] The problem with quantifiers in fiction is they are distinct and can't be easily resolved by applying real-world logic to fictional scenarios. As such, quantifiers (like "some" or "all") don't have to correspond to real-world entities. This means speakers can potentially create real-sounding scenarios that depict "infinite" without any basis in reality. Just as fiction can portray infinite resources in given finite spaces without real-world backing, could the belief in infinite capital in a specific geographic area be a "belief that is just plain fictitious"? Science fiction often depicts infinite capital—why would this guarantee a reflection of real-world constraints?

The idea of infinite capital is in the same category as fictional quantifiers—concepts without a basis in real domains. Just as fictional quantifiers don't refer to real things, the belief in infinite growth doesn't align with the realities of depletion. Long-term plans using the right quantifiers to expect economies to grow infinitely to trillions of dollars without considering resource limitations are akin to fictional narratives. These plans often ignore the finite nature of economic capital needed to sustain such growth (But be warned, many leftists mention this as a way to attack "capitalism" (by definition, it isn't), which in itself is just an example of a "meta"-system-mandated linguistic twist to distract people from blaming modernity). How could you print more non-scarce material currency to create more resources? The physical limits of a given area set a rigid boundary on how much growth is feasible. Infinite growth in a finite system is impossible, but even if we pretend it can happen concretely, we will face some problems. It's cliché to believe that as the standard of living is higher now than ever in history, people's ability to innovate and run society will improve. However, hasn't the decline of civilization after the Industrial Revolution proven this false?

Whenever there are more machines to supposedly exacerbate "living standards" and the potential exploration of one's own abilities, it would paradoxically end up just deleting the amount of space there is for one to express this freedom. The easy-to-buy idea of "infinity machines without ever interfering with the people's functional development" only represents the concept of unbounded progression in a given direction—and there seems to be wonky shit that happens even when you put it on paper. Since infinity itself is not a finite quantity, any attempt to apply numerical operations or relations to it would become flawed—one would have to understand the distinction between "potential" and "actual" infinity. One such paradox that would illustrate this involves a traveler from one point to another who, by halving (some abstract numerical operator that blindly divides by two infinitely) the remaining "space" each day, theoretically never reaches the destination, and seemingly there would be no point when the amount of free space is zero. This shapes the insufficiency of potential infinities or arbitrarily large (or small) values in

---

[205] Ibid.
[206] Ibid.

solving the problem—the only conceivable way to reach the destination would involve traversing an actual infinite. How is this possible?

Semantic capital ties in with one's open space. If machines become increasingly cluttered and become prevalent to further increase living standards, this quickly takes up any possible space where one can introspect new values. It has been said we are at the point where we are "eating into capital,"[207] in which the economic capital after the Industrial Revolution is "making more capital" with very little input from our part (minor inventions at best). We have to literally begin living off existing capital, and so unbeknownst to us, standards of living are actually in decline, without most of the population even being aware of such due to the numerous clichés of "modernity is in the right side of history." In the case of automobiles, the inventor is smarter than the car manufacturer, who is smarter than those who can maintain and fix the car, who is then smarter than those who can drive it.[208] Addressing the latter, by training drivers to follow rules rather than drive freely, this setup, in turn, engineers a less creative and innovative society—wouldn't the pseudo-innovator of centralized roads with strict traffic controls create a space-hating infrastructure that discourages spatial freedom?

The Investor

As Ryan and I passed the campus cafeteria, something caught our attention. There, in a corner, sat Mr. Lester, deep in conversation with a man in a sharp suit. The suit was the kind you'd be willing to bring to a restaurant to eat, maybe in the dining part of a wedding at most. I always laugh at this kind of thing. The best-looking suits with the shiniest fabric and straight ties are always the ones being brought into restaurants, as the wearer accidentally spills creamy noodles on them. Yet, because the suit looks so good, he doesn't mind hand-picking the stain and licking his fingers. I was already seeing him licking his own sleeves that accidentally picked up some gravy as his uncareful ass reached the fries. Regarding the same type of clothing that he wasn't even wearing, the most mid-looking suits are what people wear to funerals. The man in the suit wore sunglasses—even though it was sunny, we were indoors, for crying out loud, and the depressing-as-fuck dimness of the campus building makes it impossible to see with them.

Mr. Lester and the man were engrossed in a serious discussion, the dean's animated gestures contrasting sharply with the man's calm demeanor. Ryan nudged me, and we exchanged a knowing look. I didn't think much of it at the time, and I was only suspecting the mysterious man to be a college employee who I had just never seen before.

"Let's see what they're up to," Ryan whispered, motioning towards a table nearby. We slid into seats at the adjacent table, close enough to overhear their conversation but far enough to avoid suspicion. Mr. Lester was so into the conversation that even if I were to tea bag the side of his face, he wouldn't notice. I could even be kissing his wife with the loudest smooch and pucker, and he would probably just glance because his wife is uglier (I would never actually kiss her, by the way, just giving an example that I feel like puking just by typing) and he is a massive cuck. I pulled out my phone, pretending to scroll through emails, while Ryan positioned himself to listen intently.

---

[207] E. Dutton, *Breeding the Human Herd* (Imperium Press, 2023), 102.
[208] Ibid., 103.

"…needs substantial funding," Mr. Lester said, his voice lower than usual but urgent. The man in the suit nodded. "And you're sure this will be beneficial for all participating colleges?"

Mr. Lester leaned in, his voice taking on a persuasive tone. "Absolutely. The forum isn't just a platform for stress relief. It's a revolutionary approach to mental health. By allowing students to vent their frustrations through these swear word tickets, we're creating a healthier, more productive student body. Less stress means better academic performance and, ultimately, more efficient workers post-graduation."

Drats, he was talking about his n-word pass forum—what's interesting is he didn't overtly refer to it as an n-word pass, but just a "swear word" forum.

The man in the suit raised an eyebrow. "And this leads to a healthier economy?"

Mr. Lester smiled, clearly pleased with himself. "Precisely. Imagine a global network where students alleviate stress in a controlled environment. We need it to be controlled because if they are left outside or to their own devices, they'd walk around town destroying government property. This isn't just about education; it's about societal well-being. A less stressed workforce is more productive and less likely to commit crimes."

The investor leaned back, a calculating look in his eyes. "It's an interesting proposition. What kind of funding are we talking about?"

Mr. Lester outlined a staggering figure, explaining the need for robust servers, advanced content management algorithms, and continuous moderation to keep the platform running smoothly. I was surprised at how unoriginal that description was. Why does competitive advantage have to be a brute-forced linear one-fold thing nowadays?

The investor listened, nodding occasionally. Ryan and I exchanged worried glances. I saw his eyes becoming red instead of the usual intense whites surrounding his pupils. I whispered, "Damn, dude, you look high as fuck."

"I was smoking electronic cigarettes this morning, and I'm getting post-smoke high."

"What kind of brand? Not that I support smoking, or heavens forbid, 'woking,' but what the hell is post-smoke highness?"

"It is one that advertises itself as being a very healthy alternative to smoking. The smoker can get the feeling of daze, while people aren't gonna be asking him 'what happened to your eye' and cornering him like he is a scared sasquatch who can't fight back. But I guess now that you have noticed, the electronic cigarette is really just built upon marketing trickery and just uses a chemical that delays the side effects. Darn it."

We focused back on the eerie conversation. The dean's plan was far larger than we had realized. I thought about the implications. I recall the number of threads that were created in the forums. There were hundreds of thousands being generated per day. And this is within a school of 2,000 students (most of the threads are just repeat ones from those who are most committed). I imagined that if there were thousands of colleges out there, and given that ours was considered on the small side population-wise, I cannot imagine the insane resources it would take to run the whole world. Besides, this school has grading standards that are at the lower end. China's would be fucking insane.

"I have to admit," the investor said finally, "I'm intrigued. This could indeed lead to a domino effect. A gift that keeps on giving! I'm willing to fund the initial phase of this."

Mr. Lester's face lit up. "Excellent. I knew you'd see the potential here. With your support, we can revolutionize how the world will function. We can even help the poorer third-world countries and possibly even the very primitive tribes in those islands that are illegal to visit. They can have some of our fun too! I would love to see those little black people become integrated into our workforces because I feel so bad for them not having access to our technologies! The initial plan will go as follows: I'm good friends with the mayor, and we plan to integrate the city with this whole stress-relief brand. We'll build a repetitive architecture that aligns with the theme of the swear word tickets, creating a uniform, stress-free environment. And from an economic standpoint, it will drive growth. There will be fewer sick days, higher productivity, and, overall, a stronger economy. I am well aware you are at stake with a lot of the larger businesses in this city, so I am sure you will get some immediate capital gains. By a hundred times."

They shook hands, sealing the deal. As they stood to leave, Ryan and I quickly left the cafeteria, our minds racing with the implications of what we had just heard.

Once we were safely out of earshot, Ryan turned to me, his expression grim.

Feeling a knot of anxiety tighten in my stomach, I said, "This is so bad. If Mr. Lester gets the funding to scale this up globally, it'll be impossible to counteract the social, physical, and retardation damage. We need to stop this."

Ryan nodded. "We're up against serious money and a convincing pitch. People are idiots, and we can prove it. We need to expose the flaws in his plan. If we can prove that his plans will not even be possible in the long run, we might be able to stop him. Ultimately, we should indicate he wouldn't even have the money roll in."

"Let's get to work. If we're going to stop the dean, we'll need to really hit where it will collapse everything above—the credibility of his project."

We headed to the library, ready to dig into research that normies will likely fall in love with. After all, investors who can fund things at the scale of Mr. Lester's needs are likely so ingrained into the system that they will accept any school-mandated textbook.

As I sifted through ecology textbooks, I quickly found credible data and information about the sustainability of large-scale infrastructures and took notes. The data was clear— maintaining such an enormous digital infrastructure would be impossible in the long run without a net deficit. Even if we found a way to spawn dino bones, the hedonistic nature of Mr. Lester's plan meant that the goalpost would constantly shift to something bigger, rendering any sustainable solution temporary at best.

Soon, I felt a shadow fall over me. Looking up, I saw Professor Beckford, the dreaded professor, standing there with a scowl. My first thoughts were not simple. On the one hand, I was relieved to see him because he was possibly not too mad at me, and I made it pretty clear that I was asking him a question. In addition, when he marked my introduction forum assignment, he gave me a bad mark, but only because I insulted my classmates in the accounting program. Wait a second, fuck; maybe he was just being a petty fuck who only gave me the bad mark because he gave into the leftists' belief that I indirectly referred to him as the n-word and he was just too much of a pussy to be upfront. And I absolutely don't blame him for being scared when I looked at his physique. Think back to when I first saw him through the web camera in the virtual classroom. I was pretty confident he would be the "fluffy," unintimidating "chunky." And guess what? He was even more than I thought. He was less than five fucking feet tall. He wore a short-sleeved t-shirt instead of the striped button-up long-sleeve, and his sleeves were loose. He was one of those fatsos who store all their fat in their torsos but almost none in their arms.

"What are you doing, reading that mumbo jumbo drivel?" Mr. Beckford sneered. "You're supposed to be using your skills to uphold the values taught in my class, not twist them for your own purposes."

"Don't you care about the environment? I thought you were against capitalism!"

He shook his head, his eyes narrowing. He looked like a crab with his sunken in eyes in addition to his stick arms and fat stomach. "Yes, I hate capitalism, but you're using fringe philosophy, which can be used to do capitalistic activity, to undermine legitimate authoritative sources. This isn't what I taught you. You're violating the very principles of critical reading and writing. This isn't how you should be applying your education. You're undermining the system."

This fucking idiot bitching fuck's relentless criticism and fartlighting pushed me over the edge. Without another word, I reached for the heaviest textbook in the pile. I prepared to look like a badass as I was about to stand up in front of Mr. Beckford for the first time. He doesn't realize how tall I actually was. I used my legs to slightly push the chair backward to give me some more leg room, then proceeded to do a partial squat in the second part, and then finally revealed my true form. Mr. Beckford didn't see my muscles at the ideal angle as they were viewed from an excessively upright view, so I made sure to start flexing. I only partially flexed the bicep because flexing the biceps too hard while the elbow is straight can make them appear too narrow from the front.

I entered my battle stance, holding the textbook with two hands at a slanted angle, indicating I was going to use it for combat purposes. I slowly walk closer to him. Holy shit was this the perfect opportunity. I remember traveling to the arctics one summer and visiting one iceberg with all the cool arctic wildlife and shit. It was full of penguins. Mr. Beckford, in addition to his short stature and pudginess, had dark skin and a white t-shirt and black pants, making him also have the color regions of penguins.

"You are gonna be part of my club penguin program if you don't stop spreading your buttcheek takes. I know you'll mention the 'appeal to nature' logical fallacy when I try to defend nature, so you leave me no choice but to handle things with fire!"

"Go ahead, hit me, you're going to get expelled when cameras catch you!" he said.

"Haha, you sounded zesty right there, given my previous statement."

"Shut up and stop putting words in my mouth!"

"This is what you get for giving in to the leftist's miscontexualization of my question in the first class; I'll make you deepthroat words!"

I thought for a second. Then I got a lightbulb moment. As a highly experienced weightlifter, I have garnered enough strength to hit someone with enough force to startle them, but in a way where my limb moves slowly only looks like I lightly tapped them.

I decide to go for Mr. Beckford's fattest body part to reduce the chance of me actually injuring him to a significant degree. Without recoiling the textbook, I slowly move it toward his stomach. Upon contact, he jumped back abruptly, saying "ouch" quietly.

"What dude?" I questioned him. "I just needed to stretch for a moment and just so happened to accidentally bump the textbook onto you."

"I don't know why I felt pain. What the fuck? You didn't even hit me. I swear! Maybe my bones are failing me already."

I tried not to laugh as my plan actually worked and Mr. Beckford tricked himself into thinking he needed a doctor's appointment. But then, the fun didn't last long.

"I feel sick," Mr. Beckford groaned. "I shouldn't have drunk all that beer last night."

"Haha, you probably needed to drink all that to alleviate the stress of mental gymnastics from rationalizing leftist thought after confronting based students like me!"

"I said shut up!" He started to belch out strange noises. It was all fun and games until I started noticing physical particles coming out of his open mouth. Ah shit.

He looked up, inhaling. His eyes went cross-eyed, and then his pupils went all the way separate. The sound of gurgling could be heard from across the library. Mr. Beckford at last flung his head forward, as if that would multiply the force by a factor of 1,000. It did have to have enhance it nonetheless—the stream of liquid erupted from his mouth immediately and I barely had time to dodge. I ducked, then did a ground somersault to avoid gravity's bitching tendency to make puke fall.

After I stand back up, I look at the man trying to get me to fry in his acidic b*dily substance. He looked slightly down, his pupils still in contact with mine. He wasn't done. He looked up, opened his mouth wide again, and said a "hkkphtooh!" to initiate another attack. It was a projectile again, so I did a hoola hoola pose to dodge once more. It flew past me quickly. When the stream ended, I looked back to see his puke landed on the librarian's photo of her husband. I felt really bad, but if I get blamed for dodging a penguin-dragon hybrid, I'd willingly quit the college.

"Ready?!" Mr. Beckford threatened me.

I was tired of all this and wanted to get back into my business. "No!" I said, as I took out my shirt. I revealed my six-pack.

"Oh no, crap those abs look so good and the opposite of gross that I can no longer get myself to feel sick!" Without any other way to defend himself, Mr. Beckford decided to retreat. He turned back and then waddled away into the library exit. Phew.

AUTHOR'S NOTE: The last bit didn't actually happen, I am just demonstrating how some of you gullible readers actually believed this physically impossible (on planet Earth) event happened (Mr. Beckford doesn't have the peristalsis muscularity to puke that hard, because he is a soyboy), only because I said so. Grow up.

Chapter Nine: Modern Superstition

Throughout history, hasn't the educational system been the first line of defense that the system has used to indoctrinate people into a social machine? Sure, but their trickeries aren't one-fold—they have many subtle cues during one's "learning journey" that pierces a hole into one's scalp like a "micro-think laser beam." It starts with the severe social abuse that starts at the beginning, which essentially serves as the system's way to "spawn kill" potential anti-establishment thinkers (uncool gamer moment). It usually begins with that one notorious "be quiet" rule. Now, that rule is not inherently bad, as it is true the instructor has to have lip space to effectively verbally transfer information to a room of people. However, its innocence is abused by those who run the institutions by making it one-sided. If anybody decides to make themselves distinct from the herd in a clever way, such as introducing a new idea that is outside of the curriculum, the authorities have the perverse incentive to abuse him back into position because "iT WasN'T iN ThE BoOk." Notice how weird the criteria are for somebody to climb the ranks in a school—it favors one-dimensional beings. At best, they could be those class clown wannabes who make the corniest jokes, which are the same jokes someone else said before but told at a slightly better time—how would us introspective introverts survive this hellhole?

Something that makes the modern education system so bad is that many of the things it teaches aren't necessarily lies but a bunch of very meaningless information and half-truths, already taken out of context (selective pressures would have weeded out the obvious lies by then). You must remember the first times you touched mathematics, language arts, science, history, etc., in school. Early on, we all dreaded those not because they were intrinsically complex but because we all have an instinct that guides us toward "things that matter," from a cost-benefit perspective. This apathy is led to by how propaganda works in a technological society—they are isolated absolutes that are certain, "impossible" to philosophically debate (hence the strict guidelines of book reviews that are supposedly the subjective assignments of school), which are so efficiently disseminated without any effort on both the instructor's nor the student's part, yet they are what makes the infrastructure of the technological system thrive and be maintained.[209] It's argued that contrary to the existing analyses of disinformation which typically assume that its goal is to mislead the audience by creating false beliefs,[210] this view is flawed in two ways, as it can also aim to prevent the audience from forming true beliefs, not just to produce false ones.[211] Instead, it can manipulate behavior by altering sub-doxastic (associative, automatic, and arational mental states) states without intending to change beliefs.[212] Modern educational institutions are just goldmines for this type of disinformation. The curricula of state-run educational institutions are primarily oriented towards cultivating "marketable competencies" within the confines of modernist

---

[209] J. Ellul, *The Technological Society* (New York: Vintage Books, 1964), 80.

[210] K.R. Harris, "Beyond Belief: On Disinformation and Manipulation," *Erkenn*, 2023. https://doi.org/10.1007/s10670-023-00710-6

[211] Ibid.

[212] Ibid.

paradigms, perceived as socio-politically acceptable. This focus perpetuates an infatuation with industrial advancement while dismissing skills beyond the bounds of civilization (even outdoor education classes fail to impart true wilderness survival skills). Paradoxically, these institutions emphasize fragmented activities that lack meaningful progression, fostering the belief that individuals are inherently deficient without industrial integration. Then upon completion of formal education, aren't the roles of mentors just supplanted by the brain rot propaganda news media, rendering graduates incapable of independent thought?

Essentially, the only thing school makes are "nerds." But people need to realize the implications of allowing nerds to climb to the top of the ruling class, which is the case in modern times. The BAPist explanation of the nerd is separated from other lower "nerds" in that he has a "will," but only the petty kind—a personal gain that one can just lie to obtain.[213] Similar to what school only teaches, he is good with words and numbers (mere language) but retarded with anything visual (appreciation of art and beauty).[214] This would lead him to believe that the world is only mere logic, and therefore, artificial intelligence is something that we can compare to this man's mind. Now, if it is so true that the quality of a large language model degrades when it is trained on data already made from the model,[215] then what the fuck would happen when the educational system successfully makes a world of idiocratic nerds? What else would there be besides mere "information retrieval,"[216] which any robot can do?

Given the fact that there is surprisingly still no agreed meaning of "artificial intelligence" whether or not it refers to big data[217] (which I say it should), I would be inclined to think this misunderstanding serves the interest of the system as it blurs the system's meaning of real thinking with its apparatuses—the idea of a well-intentioned robot is also due to a wide misconception of technology.[218] People who champion man being replaced by machine miss the point that in order to make people superfluous, machines will not have to surpass them in general intelligence, but only in certain specialized kinds of intelligence—only for the purpose of promoting the short-term survival and propagation of the global technological system.[219] This can be said to be what may form a pseudo-religious phenomenon because it parallels how millenarian cults were historically formed—times of great social change or crisis, and therefore, a kind of anxiety about the future of the technological system.[220] 21st century public schools are basically institutionalized churches, except indoctrinating the children with a certain pseudo-religion similar to the way certain religions were used as vehicles for herd morality back then. In ancient Rome, the resentful people appropriated them as an outlet to punish those

---

[213] B.A. Pervert, *Bronze Age Mindset* (Independently Published, 2018), 54.

[214] Ibid., 53.

[215] I. Shumailov, Z. Shumaylov, Y. Zhao, et al., "AI models collapse when trained on recursively generated data," *Nature*, 631(2024): 755-759. https://doi.org/10.1038/s41586-024-07566-y

[216] C.A. Barry, "Information skills for an electronic world: Training doctoral research students," *Journal of Information Science*, 23(1997): 225–238. https://doi.org/10.1177/016555159702300306

[217] M.C. Elish and D. Boyd, "Situating methods in the magic of Big Data and AI," *Communication Monographs*, 85(2017): 1-24. https://doi.org/10.1080/03637751.2017.1375130

[218] G. Simondon, *On the Mode of Existence of Technical Objects* (University of Western Ontario, 1980).

[219] T. Kaczynski, *Anti-Tech Revolution: Why and How* (Scottsdale: Fitch & Madison, 2020), 80.

[220] Ibid. 83.

who affirmed life.[221] The problem nowadays is that people are massively cucked by inevitability towards a singularity state—doesn't the concept of singularity function as a prevailing "faith" for the masses, where even those who challenge perceived origins of wealth disparity or job displacement experience a sense of guilt when questioning its sanctity?

But I think the belief that artificial intelligence will surpass mankind due to its superior creativity suggests a fundamental flaw in modern humans more so rather than mankind as a whole. Modern educational systems further diminish innate creativity, and our interpretative faculties are anomalously deficient compared to those of pre-modern individuals. It has been the case that individuals with a good ability to block out irrelevant information are more likely to concentrate on fulfilling the system than creative people who can introspect those supposed irrelevant ideas;[222] and it is those who are creative who end up unhappy and less successful in terms of the system's definition of success. The technocracy and its educational institutions may be the buildings that propagate the dominant superstitions of "progress" of our time—could they be some of the most nihilistic kinds, which is why they make the real cool kids seppuku?

It is posited that while technological advancement and the expansion of our knowledge ostensibly indicate progress, this does not equate to increased happiness, and instead, we are becoming increasingly disillusioned with humanity.[223] Similar to the Nietzschean view of modern institutionalized religion and churches, where the architecture is unexpansive and has too much "noise" for reflection,[224] education is assuming the role of a new pseudo-faith; it promises salvation through things like "techno-hypnosis," which offers an escape from meaningful suffering via hypnotic engagement. There is also data-driven activity that relieves us of the burden of decision-making by following technology's directives (like predictive tools). Technological behaviors are just modern analogs to the life-denying aspects of the passive types of institutionalized religions perpetuating dependency and superficial morality, all of which hinder the development of strong individuals. It would lead its believers into a passive acceptance of suffering with the promise of a definite hedonistic "end reward." Wouldn't this prevent individuals from doing the overcoming that leads to true self-realization?

In this herd morality, exceptionality is suppressed in favor of conforming to automatons. This is a denial of one's unique potential and a surrender to mediocrity. A slavish adherence to artificial commandments is promoted, discouraging independent responsibility. In a parallel sense, data-driven techniques dictate our actions through algorithms. This reliance on technological "orders" erodes autonomy, while ironically promoting it insincerely—notice how just about every school course teaches you, especially in 2020 business courses, to do pre-calculated risk assessments, then forcing them into a single short response, without any kind of self-introspection that would lead to an innovative decision that would meaningfully bring something fresh into the world?

---

[221] V. McLeod, *Clown World Chronicles* (VJM Publishing, 2020), 89.

[222] S. Keri, "Genes for psychosis and creativity: a promoter polymorphism of the neuregulin 1 gene is related to creativity in people with high intellectual achievement," *Psychological Science*, 20(2009): 1070–1073. https://doi.org/10.1111/j.1467-9280.2009.02398.x

[223] N. Gertz, *Nihilism and Technology* (Rowman & Littlefield, 2018).

[224] F. Nietzsche, *The Gay Science* (Vintage Books, 1974), 226-227.

Computer Nerd

Determined to uncover the identity of the investor who was backing up Mr. Lester like an excited, jumping, dumb, ugly bunny with an oversized nose to the point where it always chomps in it instead of carrots, I sat down at my computer and logged into a business networking website. It was a platform where users created personal profiles and connected to form professional relationships. I always laugh at people who even set one up in the first place because that is what makes people so extra easy to stalk nowadays. I remember back in high school, when I found out that the majority of the population has some kind of a digital footprint, I would fuck around and google my teachers. And bawl out laughing upon finding out they set up a dating profile, the web listing beside their networking profile. I get a whiff of those old memories as I start my online stalking operation.

I started by searching for Mr. Lester's profile. To my surprise, the dean's profile was private. How was he even doing this when he is always the cockrider of the industry? This has to be rigged. I cursed under my breath but quickly moved on to my next tactic.

I thought of using a third-party website that could scan private profiles. Shit, did that bring up a lot of other memories. I remember in junior high school when I was first introduced to social media by a group of my knucklehead acquaintances. I first wanted to see if my classmates had normal lives. Holy shit, was it a pain in the ass because the third-party websites I used were constantly flooded with ads and would somehow scroll all the way up if I scrolled down too fast. I remember this one really weird guy in my class who I wanted to check up on, making sure he wasn't abused by his parents or anything, and the second time I'd click his profile, it was private, and when I tried to click "request follow," it would always switch back to the unrequested follow. Fucker really blocked me, and I had to use the third-party websites for the first time. It took me so long to find out he was being beaten by his dad with a bat, so I called the cops on him and saved his ass. The kid wasn't even appreciative, but I felt good for saving someone's ass.

Anyway, I digress, I was just hoping I wouldn't feel the same level of unintentional rejection when I was about to enter this part of the internet again.

After digging through Mr. Lester's third-party profile, I successfully identified the investor the dean had been speaking to, Richard Palmer. I quickly crafted a direct message to Palmer, presenting my reasoning about why Mr. Lester's plans were ecologically unsustainable and why the idea of infinite economic growth was an ecologically impossible object in the first place.

I hit send and waited, my heart pounding. After what felt like an eternity, a notification popped up. Palmer had responded. "The math says the plan is viable. The projections show positive growth, and that's what matters. The numbers speak for themselves."

The feeling of wanting to beat the shit of an online arguer surged through me. I tried so hard not to call him insults. "Mr. Palmer, the numbers might look good on paper, but they're detached from reality. You can print money, but you can't print substantial matter."

His response was swift and dismissive. "Economic growth is driven by innovation and market dynamics. Energy just one part of the equation. Your arguments are alarmist and ignore the potential for new technologies and efficiencies."

"But those new technologies still rely on finite resources, let alone the fact that innovations now may affect the ability for people to think, and therefore further innovate."

"This conversation is unproductive. The math supports the dean's plan, and that's what I'm going with. Goodbye."

A moment later, I saw the notification that I had been blocked. Ohhhh noooo I was already getting bad memories of me getting blocked by that one quiet kid who was abused, but now this was worse because it was by someone who I consider lower than I am. Anger and despair churned inside me. I had failed to convince him. I decided to take a look at Palmer's profile one last time, using the same third-party website. What I found was both revealing and disheartening. Palmer had attended a series of soy public schools that were known for their simplistic, dogmatic approaches to education. These institutions emphasized numbers and economic theories detached from real-world constraints, treating everything as a game of abstract figures. You see, guys, this is what happens when schools give students ridiculous word problems. Adam is never going to be taking 1,000 watermelons to a football game, the same game where Sally is deepthroating 10,000 corndogs at the same time instead of the football team players' cocks because she has to wait for the 1,000,000-hour-long game to finish first.

My phone buzzed with a call from Ryan. I picked up, hearing the urgency in his voice.

"Hey, I just found out something big," he said. "I am in a first-year computer science class, but my professor said something as I left my class earlier today. Mr. Lester is running an internship for computer science students, and they're starting to develop the new large-scale n-word pass forum social network. They're working in the main master computer science lab right now."

My heart sank. This was escalating faster than I'd anticipated. How did the whole redonkulus idea get out this fast to non-retarded people in the first place? "What should we do? We can't let them get too far with this."

"I know," Ryan said, frustration evident in his voice. "But I'm tied up studying for a midterm that my other mean professor scheduled way too early. It is about memorizing useless shit as he decided not to make it an open-book test, even though we all know we can always review repositories of information in the workplace. I need you to sneak into the lab and investigate. See what they're up to."

I hesitated. "Ryan, those computer science students are sharp in terms of sheer clarity vision if we don't consider their naked eyes. They all wear prescribed eyeglasses and are hyper-vigilant. It would be much easier if they were average students with vision that is bad enough to be imperfect, but not bad enough to warrant eye appointments. They'll spot me sneaking in a mile away."

Ryan chuckled. "Trust me, and I know this from personal experience and having to do group activities with dorky people. They'll be so hyper-fixated on their coding that they won't notice a thing. Just act like you belong there. Pretend you're one of them. Even then, they'd be mindcucked and wouldn't dare have the balls to mess with you even if you give all flags that you hate computer nerds."

The building was quiet as I approached the master lab. I took a deep breath, adjusted my backpack, and slipped inside.

The lab was a hive of activity. Rows of students sat at their workstations, eyes glued to their screens, fingers flying over keyboards. The soft hum of computers and the occasional murmur of conversation (I was surprised there was any in the first place as computer science students are predominantly "the quiet kids") filled the air. I moved cautiously, trying to blend in. I wore something that would probably make me look like a tyrannical, rich-look-caring king—a tank top (with muscles). The people in the room were all wearing varying black or white clothing (they were too socially anxious to wear bright colors), but the ones who were wearing tank tops either had arms too skinny or arms too fat to have their bicep veins visible.

I spotted Mr. Lester at the front of the room, talking to a group of students, giving the best smile he could to conceal the evilness of his little schemes. I was laughing my ass off as it reminded me of a good time in the past when I accidentally threw one of my baby teeth at a classmate's neck, which caused him to have a ruptured thyroid, and I was sent to the principal's office and the principal instead congratulated me on losing a tooth and gave me a plastic little treasure chest shaped box to store it in—all I had to do was say, "excuse me may I please have one." (Didn't happen lol, just testing whether you readers are the types of fucks who believe in absurd word problems).

Mr. Lester was gesturing animatedly at a whiteboard filled with diagrams and code snippets. I edged closer, pretending to be engrossed in my phone while I listened in. "This forum will be revolutionary," he was saying. "We'll implement advanced algorithms to handle the load and ensure a seamless user experience. I apologize for making the initial smaller-scale forum look bad, but now you are responsible for making it right."

One of the students raised a hand. "What about data privacy and security? With so many users, we'll need robust measures."

Mr. Lester nodded. "Absolutely. We'll be integrating top-tier security protocols. But remember, the priority is to get this platform up and running efficiently. Once we have a working model, we can refine and optimize."

As the discussion continued, I gained the courage to slip past the group. I then found an empty workstation. Logging in with a generic student account, I happened to see and memorize a student from another class; I accessed the network and started poking around.

I found the pre-made project files quickly. The scope of the forum was massive and way beyond anything I'd imagined. Clearly, they were planning to compete with even the largest social media websites. The user interface was striking. Mr. Lester, though he criticized the first version of the forum for looking like it was made on "paint," made the concept art of the interface using it, and I could tell by the file extension. I double-clicked into some of the pre-programmed files. Upon seeing the code that I will admit, I have no idea about, I was flattered. Mr. Lester had them use a slightly custom-made programming language. I didn't recognize any of the objects used as functions. But when I did some closer inspection, it all made sense. The programming language wasn't different from any existing programming language from a practical standpoint, but it was vanity. They all had "n-word" integrated into somehow. For example, "Boolean" was replaced by "Bool-n-wordean." "If" statement was replaced by "If-n-word." I looked up beyond the monitor in front of me. The computer science interns all looked even more focused than I remember. That was it; Mr. Lester managed to sneak in his n-word passes into their work. How unethical. I got more desperate to stop this.

While playing around with my monitor's interface and pretending to type random stuff to look like I was programming, I spent some hours observing, watching the interns coding, and picking up on the basics of their work. My sharp learning capabilities kicked in, and soon enough, I had a rudimentary understanding of what they were doing.

Glancing around to ensure no one was watching, I accessed the project files. With a mix of nervousness and determination, I began sabotaging the code in subtle, comedic ways. I inserted lines of code that would cause the program to display random cat pictures, play annoying sound effects, and even make the text blink uncontrollably. Nah, I am just kidding. I honestly find cat pictures to be some of the most overused media on the internet, and I will look down on anyone who unironically posts them. Especially the cat-dancing GIFs (graphic interchange format), where the cat was probably abused to get it to do it. Yuck! Oh, speaking of abuse, here is what happened next.

The actual images I inserted into the code were gore GIFs, gang people getting their heads chopped off. Anyway, I couldn't help but chuckle as I imagined the chaos these changes would cause. But just as I got into it, I felt a presence behind me. I turned to see an intern staring at the screen, his eyes widening in shock. I was even more in shock, and through that intern's glasses, I could see my mouth widened, which I don't usually do because that is the type of facial expression one would make to make themselves appear less threatening. I prefer to maintain a mewing and hunter's eyes look everywhere I go in public, but sometimes, I get distracted. I just hope there is no one walking around taking photos with a camera to catch me like this and portray me to look like that at all times.

"Hey! What are you doing?" he demanded. My heart skipped a beat. I recognized him—it was Sam. I didn't mention his name earlier because I didn't imagine he would be relevant later. Still, he was the classmate from junior high school that I had saved from his abusive parents, and I was only reminded of him because I was pissed about using the third-party website to do some stalking. I hoped that memory might work in my favor.

"Sam, it's me," I said quickly without hope because I didn't think Sam would all of a sudden start appreciating me for what I did in the past because of his personality type. "Remember? I helped you when we were kids."

Through his threatening-looking eyeglasses, Sam's eyes flickered in sync with the borderline broken lights of the room with recognition, but his expression remained stern. "What are you doing here? You're not supposed to be messing with this."

I tried to appeal to him. "Sam, you have to understand. This project is dangerous. It will fry the brains of so many people in the long run. I need to stop it."

He hesitated for a moment, and I thought I might be getting through to him. But then he straightened up, his expression hardening. "No. I have to do what's right for my career. You need to leave."

I was really filled with a will to destroy, but the last bit of me held back and told me to attempt to appeal to being a provider mommy for a second. "Sam, you know me. I wouldn't be doing this if it wasn't important."

But he was resolute. "I don't give a damn if you saved me from my abusive parents. I want to die anyway. I mean, wait, wait, I am not supposed to say that, way way way, OOUHBBBXXXCG."

As Sam's brain started to act like a piece of meat sizzling and cooking inside a microwave as a result of experiencing cognitive dissonance, he moved to push me out of the chair, his hands gripping my shoulders.

"Stop," I said, keeping my voice calm as Sam is a stick who could never move me in the slightest. "Just think for a second."

He didn't relent, pushing harder. He was increasing in rage as he was mad at himself for being too weak to push me off the chair. I am going to be honest: I was really worried that he would decide to pull a gun and then shoot me because of the rage buildup combined with weakness, so I decided to pretend to fall off. As he appeared to force me to my feet, I still knew this confrontation was far from over.

Suddenly, a familiar voice boomed from across the room. "Attention, everyone!"

Sam and I turned to see Dr. Mister Lee. But relief washed over me when I realized he hadn't noticed Sam and I's scuffle. He was here to address the interns.

"Good to see everyone working so hard," Dr. Mister Lee began, a pleased smile on his face. The dimples were so gross. People usually think dimples are always cool-looking, but it made him look like a living fossil. Maybe a serial killer, but the kind that isn't even badass. His dimples crinkled like sandpaper that in itself got sanded to be highly thin and dysfunctional. The lack of use for said sandpaper makes it both ugly functionally and in terms of looks.

"I have some exciting news. One of my experiments with the n-word passes has led me to a breakthrough. All of you have probably already seen it, but it is an integration of a custom-made programming language into your workflow."

A murmur of interest spread through the room. Dr. Mister Lee continued, "This new language subtly incorporates the n-word into the code blocks. The idea is to relieve stress and enhance focus, making you all more efficient and obedient programmers."

My eyes widened in shock. This was a new level of manipulation, hiding the n-word within the code itself. It was a way to normalize its usage and further entrench it into the soy education system. The last thing we need is to have things that are meant to be edgy jokes in the curriculum. I see many teachers (who I slightly respect for at least trying) attempting to seem more relatable to students, but all they do is make the whole thing a cringetopia.

Sam tackled me before I could analyze this ugliness more, knocking me to the ground. We tumbled across the floor in a chaotic, pseudo-karate display, grappling and throwing wild punches. I was being reminded of how horrible Sam smelled. I could feel the figurative insect legs as the tendrils of sweat odor poked my nostrils. It burned so much that my fighting ability and strength were glitching out. Mr. Beckford's vomit was nothing compared to this because I also made sure to dodge its smell. In Sam's case, his was a complex series of different enemy smells hitting me all at once. The interns around us gasped and backed away, creating a circle around our brawl.

"Stop it, both of you!" Dr. Mister Lee shouted, rushing over. He pulled Sam off me with surprising strength and helped me to my feet.

"He started it," Sam panted, pointing at me.

I shook my head, trying to catch my breath. "I was just trying to give you all a foretaste of what school was originally meant to be. It had very little to do with economic benefit and more to do with actually enlightening others. Debates were the main thing to be facilitated, and there were back-and-forths between students and professors. Now look at the ugly monster we have. And it is so much more expensive. This project, including all of this college, is a manipulation, and you know it."

Dr. Mister Lee's face hardened, his dimples getting deeper and making him look like an actual parody of what mewers and "Chads" look like. "Enough. I'm calling the dean."

Within minutes, Mr. Lester arrived, his expression thunderous. He listened to Dr. Mister Lee recount the events, then turned to me with an expression of utter disdain. Then, he glared at me. "You seem to have consistently disrupted this institution's operations. Your actions today are the final straw. You are expelled from this college, effective immediately."

"But Sam started the fight!" I protested, my voice echoing in the silent room of quiet kids who were so quiet that they wouldn't even react to the most absurd situations. "He is the real bully, and I would hate to see yet another example of the victim who fights back getting into more trouble. And I am technically encouraging 'college' operations by giving a brief history lesson about how schools worked!"

"Enough talking; if anything, why don't you go by history and follow one of the most original school rules: no talking?" the dean snapped. Pack your things and leave. Do it now, or else I will call your parents!"

Man, the "call parents" punishment thing always gets me. Honestly, the second biggest thing that is really motivating me to try hard in college is my parents. When I think of it, they played a big part in the college fund even though they didn't pay for it directly because they raised me for so long. Still, simultaneously, I think a perfect parent would teach their kid how to survive in the woods and discourage them from going into normie education. Most parents nowadays are subjecting their kids to slavery. I was finally breaking out of the "bUt BuT ColLeGe fOr YouR paRentS" weak mindset.

But as I stood there, stunned and devastated, the reality of my situation sank in. The really shameful thing is I had been expelled for trying to do the right thing, and I was deemed the bully for questioning the status quo. There are countless media depictions of bullies and they always make the stronger guy the bully and the weaker nerd the victim. That is massively part of it. One shouldn't even mind being bullied by a jock because that would usually mean the jock is trying to get the nerd to self-improve. But in real life, if a nerd tries to "self-improve" the jock, which, to be honest, isn't so, the jock gets punished.

I gathered my belongings, grabbed my backpack as I left the room, and walked out of the lab, the weight of my expulsion heavy on my shoulders, which now felt like it hadn't been trained in a year.

Chapter Ten: Democratization of Forms

Only a neurotic would buy into the idea that "democratizing the existence of forms all over" will result in some epic fantasy of everyone having an equal chance at some high career that doesn't even exist, because they, in reality, would cease to exist. This is an obvious death of culture, and we are already seeing ourselves duplicating the customs of other civilizations—except are we basically just copying ourselves?

The notion of "explosiveness of virtuous progress" represents an inversion of its true essence. Today, open space and the subjectivity it fosters stand in opposition to the excess of superficial constructs. Modernity deceives us into believing that we must overcome our existential void while remaining ensnared within the system, presenting itself as "vast" in mere physical dimensions. Yet, many overlook its monotonous repetition, continuously offering the same garbage art. This is achieved through a synthesis of material maximalism and abstract minimalism, dismantling the illusory divide between them. Consequently, a certain sentiment becomes prevalent: "the world is not real, therefore, I am not real," leading to a diminished sense of existence. Could this feeling even be among the discerning?

Is it misguided and erroneous to attribute these cost-effective architectural practices solely to "overly motivated people" as a meaning of capitalism? Aesthetic distinctiveness in small businesses still holds significance, yet they often converge toward similarity. There must be an inherent mechanism within the system that selects for conformity, deeming anything that diverges as a "technical error" (as such, contrary to popular belief, modern art is so "nothingness" to the point where it fails to even be subjective at all, instead wrapping itself back to being teleologically oriented to being hostile toward open-ended greatness). Contrary to the comforting illusions embraced by the masses, injustices, when applied to a universally pathological archetype, should not be mitigated by aligning them with "feel-good" paradigms that bear no relation to these pathologies. The existential dread many experience today stems from an increasing awareness of diminishing individual differences. Novel materialistic biases induce a sense of placelessness within the lower classes due to an overwhelming overlap of classes and individuals. The maneuver under this claims "one can become anything through a frivolous arrangement of particles." Doesn't this represent a spiritual demise, significantly contributing to the breakdown of society, despite the belief that it adequately addresses our essential needs?

Most individuals lack a clear understanding of their intended essence, yet how is it they occupy roles before comprehending their true purpose? As one contributes a minuscule fraction of a corporation's revenue or labor for a small business devoid of a unique model, they receive messages that imply worthlessness. So, resentment is rampant, thriving when authority imposes mechanistic demands upon subordinates without further validation, causing subordinates to perceive the entire system as insincere and absurd. This dynamic surprisingly serves the system's interests—resentment fractures unity, reducing the likelihood of cohesive rebellion. Wouldn't the aim be to dismantle familial structures, rendering individuals weak and isolated, easily manipulated by virtual desires ultimately owned by the system?

There is an irony that "life value" decreases as the overcrowding space continues. Begin by considering us having to negate one another increasingly, as digitalization moves to its logical conclusion. There, at first, does appear to be a link from the Industrial Revolution to the genesis of social rights.[225] These rights seemingly being mechanisms to counterbalance the imbalances caused by industrialization, as one of the key features is the radical rescaling of the role of human labor in value chains—as data becomes a more central driver of the economy, the traditional significance of human labor is diminishing, challenging the link between labor and citizenship.[226] It is said that the automation that results in the decrease in labor is the automation that replaces jobs, and the concept of universal basic income is gaining traction in response to the socioeconomic decline of traditional labor models—it's proposed as a means to rethink welfare regulations in a context marked by technological unemployment and precarious work.[227] This is perhaps to make up for the dehumanizing conditions of normie wagecuckery. To negate certain economics, universal basic income would be executed in a way where people should trade their personal data as digital income, which would then be used to generate economic value, therefore improving digital technologies.[228] Is this sound? Initially, it may seem that socialistics are a mechanism to counterbalance the imbalances of industrialism, but under the soystem, they are not at all to serve the interests of even "the people" unless they are the kinds of ignoble people who are fine being mediocritized. The people who are truly liberated beyond the lameness of industrial society, especially in the future once the lameness becomes even more obvious to the propaganda-resistant kinds, would by then have dropped out of the system and instead run their own farms or hunt to sustain themselves. The only ones left in industrial society are those who are sufficiently propagandized to accept its madness still yet. When the universal basic income in exchange for personal data does arise, we'd see that regressional problems will yet rise in amplitude ever more. Could we assume the kinds of people who want the universal basic income the most badly—probably the most wasteful couch potatoes— would love to give up their informational freedom just to chase the last episode of their favorite television network or fast food?

We have to consider that the data that will be used to develop the next generation of techniques will be those that are most tailored and marketed to THOSE losers (given the insane amount of data used to make decisions these days[229]). But we all know that the system is so rigorous in imposing new technologies onto the populace—so when society modifies itself to integrate self-driving cars for those who are incapable of even steering a fucking wheel, even after considering how pathetic being a road rule follower is, the system will become hostile to those who have even slightly above average desire to work

---

[225] F. Tomasello, "From industrial to digital citizenship: rethinking social rights in cyberspace," *Theor Soc*, 52(2023): 463-486. https://doi.org/10.1007/s11186-022-09480-6
[226] Ibid.
[227] Ibid.
[228] Ibid.
[229] A. Vicini, "Artificial Intelligence and Social Control: Ethical Issues and Theological Resources," *Journal of Moral Theology*, 11(2022): 41-69. https://doi.org/10.55476/001c.34123

without automation. The resulting feedback loop will favor the kinds of individuals who would hardly thrive in both a modern (for now) context and a pre-modern context. Is this basically the modernistic depopulation method that the elites want? Which is getting rid of those who wouldn't be wasteful consumers while only selecting for the most wasteful ones?

Scientifically speaking, we already produce way more food than we need to support 10 billion.[230] Though it seems like we have no reason to call overpopulation a problem as of 2014, who knows what'll happen at this rate—the big problem with modernity's "x population narrative" is it will not do anything to save the planet but only allow overcrowding to exist for the very little bit of space left while there are more machines that take up more space than ever, even beyond urban cities—the abundance of herd morality leads us to reject life so much as to lead to this replacement with pseudo-life. Only people that would be allowed to exist are the most wasteful ones, even disregarding the idle elite. Under modernity, whether there's an overpopulation or underpopulation narrative—wouldn't either just be an intermediary passing phase toward reducing the intrinsic value of individual lives whatsoever?

Would life be even more meaningless, even for the system's fabricated "fixable victims" themselves? You may extend the shortcomings of narrow-minded solutions to people's dissatisfaction with modern life regarding the kinds of artifacts being built to memorialize figures. Right now, public artifacts like memorials and statues are perceived as morally problematic due to whom or what they honor with the recent controversies, including both the removal or vandalism of statues of figures, like many colonialists, and the lack of representation of certain groups. Many right now would welcome the suggestion of "counter-commemorations," which focus on marginalized narratives or historical injustices as a way to balance the historical record.[231] But under the global technological system, doesn't the solution miss the point that substantial social groups usually have their own unique kinds of values that "naturally" emerge? You can't really counter-commemorate to mitigate the under-representation of people of different cultures because of the different merits that exist across the different cultures throughout the globe. However, this is all beneficial to the technological systems that need to eliminate people and the differences in cultural architecture so that it can globalize. Besides the dissolution of cultural boundaries, if the system's pseudo-activists keep pushing the bar when the newly invented "marginalized groups," there will not only be the boring "first mangled man to fly to the moon" but also the "first ultra mangled man to squat a bar." How smooth would that man have to look if that is so impressive that it warrants a future statue? Wouldn't any nobleman further have to feel even more useless while even the worshipped herd member would scratch their head as a result of efficacy dysphoria?

Under these modern conditions, behavioral sink (a hypothesis that arose from strange behavior observed in experiments that put rats in unnaturally overcrowded spaces) inevitably happens, and massive amounts of cannibalistic activity ensue due to

---

[230] E. Holt-Gimenez, "We Already Grow Enough Food For 10 Billion People -- and Still Can't End Hunger," *Huffpost*, (2nd May 2012), https://www.huffpost.com/entry/world-hunger_b_1463429
[231] C.-M. Lim and T.-H. Lai, "Objectionable commemorations: Ethical and political issues," *Philosophy Compass*, 2024. https://doi.org/10.1111/phc3.12963

resentment, as they feel a sense that every social niche has already been filled.[232] After all, what social niches are there amongst a herd of locusts when you compare them to an army of ants and bees? With that, man would indulge in self-destructive behaviors when the system offers no outlet. Contrary to common propaganda, a surprising number of perpetrators of mass killings are not clinically insane but are more so driven by unnatural conditions such as the lack of space.[233] Especially through the disruptions of nature's generative processes that involve reproduction; the obvious pointer is that this is all a result of denature. However, is it not how most would be led to think?

There are already many thoughts attempting to criticize this state of affairs, as a result of the massive sadness and tragedy of modern urbanism. They at most would go as far as to argue that given that nature throughout history has been devalued compared to human culture and art, with the Hegelian notion of placing "art" outside the chaotic natural world. This may precede a suggestion where ecosystems, landscapes, plants, and animals can be aesthetically meaningful in their own right.[234] One might then infer a removal of our involvement—but by separating mankind from nature, it still suffers the problem of trying to maintain an "aesthetic of nature" and goes against the notion that art can be in the realm of nature—perhaps assuming that the works of architecture of humans are only in the same paradigm as the post-industrial age. It isn't accurate that the baseline tradition of higher culture treated nature as secondary to human culture, viewing it merely as a resource for man's use, a falsification insidiously favored by the pseudo-ecologist cult that leftism adopted. Much is ignored about the so-called "survivorship bias" structures remaining today, which are an aesthetic arrangement of vacant spaces. Those structures were made the way they are because their builders were already well aware of the philosophical implications of "mastering matter" the right way, while the mainstream soyentists today spend so much time finding "new data," pretending to discover the ecological crisis themselves, which amount to no action at all. Yes, there is weight to the idea that economic developments often prioritize economic growth over environmental conservation, but does humanistic involvement necessarily boost economic abstractions?

Likewise, would the current discourse surrounding the concept of what is "unnatural" stem from people engaging in disparate linguistic frameworks? One type would contend that mankind, as an integral component of the natural order, cannot produce artifacts that transcend nature.[235] Conversely, others posit that certain constructs, such as skyscrapers, represent a divergence from traditional manmade creations—those that many would be "airlit" into aligning with temporal and spatial dimensions conducive to well-being but are in reality suffocatingly full of pathogenic gas (think of the power system within it along with the literal mass embodiment of wagecuckery). The latter evokes a scenario where ants, inhabiting anthills of unprecedented height and highly

[232] V. McLeod, *Clown World Chronicles* (VJM Publishing, 2020), 68.

[233] S.J Barlett, "Rage in America: Why Is This Happening?" *Social Epistemology Review and Reply Collective*, 12(2023): 46-60. https://wp.me/p1Bfg0-7xg.

[234] E.D. Stefano, C. Friberg, and M. Ryynänen, *Aesthetic Perspectives on Culture, Politics, and Landscape* (Springer Cham, 2023).

[235] P. Logan, "Vanity of the Anthropocene: Anthills and skyscrapers are equally "natural"," *Engineering Our Social Vehicles*, (12th August 2022), https://laulpogan.substack.com/p/vanity-of-the-anthropocene-anthills?sd=pf

uncomfortable, experience a disjunction from their intrinsic environmental context, corporeal form, lifestyle, and energetic patterns. Even though it is made by a non-man, markedly detached from the ant's natural state, such a structure can arguably be characterized as "unnatural" in certain cases. Overemphasizing "the environment" will risk creating an artificial parody of the natural environment. Could this approach end up feeling even more artificial than urbanism itself?

Look at the idea of "digital nature," the development of technological depictions of nature, in which people can artificially experience the natural world.[236] I think it is pernicious. You might hear about some cases that would make it seem as though some "at least we got a sliver of a good thing" should be something to preserve—like when it's shown we temporarily get improved psychological well-being when we virtually observe nature through a technologized screen.[237] This yet misses the point that we don't see the destruction of real nature as we are so distracted by the virtual nature, compounded by the fact that the initial lowered well-being is caused by an initial negation of nature in the first place. Newer generations can barely even differentiate so-called digital and non-digital spaces, perhaps to the point of impossibility.[238] There's even a disorder that revolves around being a deficit of literal nature.[239] Isn't this all just such a criminal enchantment?

Other seemingly profound solutions that have been done so far also miss the mark. There was a time when areas in the east had protection strategies to counter the downfalls of modern urbanism, "weaving the city," which aimed to create smooth transitions between new and old city areas to minimize damage to historical landscapes.[240] Today, this attempt to protect culture fails to do so because the smaller but still existent presence of modernized architecture will still expand and spread its disease-like effect, as it just acts as a magnet that sucks in individuals using its certain distractions that pander to "mere existence" instincts, which are additions to the "lowest common denominator" architecture. The smooth transitions wouldn't help given the "advantage of graduality" that makes the entrance into modernity's simulation so much less obvious—most people wouldn't even think twice if they immediately see the degenerate side effects of suburban idle life. Would a better solution be "distant horizons" where one can see little caricatural spectacles of modern manifestations (the only ones we would allow to be built) from afar, and upon immediately comparing it to highly cultured aesthetics, we can all laugh at its stupidity and be reminded not to create any more of it?

Ugly-er City

Six months had passed since I was expelled from college. Man, has it been bleak? From time to time, I'd feel a burning sensation whenever I breathed through my nose,

[236] N. Clark, "Being consoled?: Virtual nature and ecological consciousness," *Futures*, 27(1995): 735-747. https://doi.org/10.1016/0016-3287(95)80005-T.

[237] P.H. Kahn Jr., "Losing touch with nature," *iai*, (4th November 2020), https://iai.tv/articles/losing-touch-with-nature-auid-1683&utm_source=reddit&_auid=2020.

[238] M. Allaby, and C.S. Shannon, "I just want to keep in touch," *Journal of Leisure Research*, 51(2020): 245-263. https://doi.org/10. 1080/00222216.2019.1672506

[239] R. Louv, *Last Child in the Woods: Saving our Children from Nature-Deficit Disorder* (Algonquin Books, 2008).

[240] K. Wang, "Time rupture in urban heritage: based on the case of shanghai," *Geojournal*, 88(2023): 1865-1977. https://doi.org/10.1007/s10708-022-10732-2

accompanied by the grey sky that would never fucking leave and allow its blue version to show. Everything appeared to be black and white when coupled with my fall cold. I had to try so hard not to get into drinking or even taking drugs because I view such activities to be the other ultimate cop-outs for one to pretend to escape. Throughout my life, I always found it easy to avoid such things, and whenever friends asked me to try some "peer pressure" stuff, I never had the temptation to say "yes."

When a child is first told by a parent to "never take drugs," it is easy for them to say, "This is easy," or "I will be sober for all my life." As we observe often, most end up failing to live up to that. I was starting to become this—but for now, I was relying on some cheaply made Halloween candies that I stole from the convenience stores that allowed me to get free candy as long as the manager could tell my physique was getting fatter so he could feel good about his own weight.

Each day, I trudged to my job at Burger Queen, now my full-time occupation. Did I enjoy it this way or not when compared to the hybrid of education and work? I wasn't even sure; I never even thought of it as a tally to compare one to another. I just go with the flow, as long as I am the one making the flow.

Today, I had a particularly hard time on a physical level. The routine walk, once a minor inconvenience, had become increasingly difficult. At this particular moment, every step felt like a monumental effort. As I struggled onward, my phone buzzed in my pocket. It was a call from Ryan. We hadn't spoken in months; our now inert operation to have Mr. Lester's lame infrastructure as a target stopped after my expulsion. I answered, surprised and curious.

"AHAHA WHO IS THIS GUY! It's been a while. How are you?" I tried to start the conversation excitedly, even though I was sad.

There was a pause before Ryan's voice, strained and weak, came through. "I'm in the hospital."

My heart skipped a beat. "What happened? Did you get too fat while you weren't near my jacked and ripped presence for too long? Maybe you have diabetes now? You've been a bad, bad boy."

"I... I gouged my eyes out."

"Haha, what a roundabout way of saying you lost weight. Now, are you at the hospital because of a liposuction?"

"No, I am serious. I literally can't see anymore." Ryan then sent me a photo through the text message app.

I clicked on the new notification, which had a little blurry side of reddish pink on a pale-colored round shape as the accompanying photo. As my finger inched toward tapping it, I hoped deep down that Ryan just sent me a picture of a tasty strawberry cheesecake he had eaten as a hospital snack. But when I saw the actual reality, shock paralyzed me. I thought I was looking at the photo of an actor playing an antagonist extra midway through dressing up for a zombie movie. But I knew what I was looking at was all real. "Why you do dat?"

Ryan's voice cracked with emotion, and it sounded like he was laughing, but he was dead-ass crying right now. HOLY SHIT, A GROWN MAN CRYING, I NEVER seen that BEFORE! I was in the same emotion upon hearing it, as if I was looking at an injured and sick animal at the zoo. Rare and straight-up concerning.

I heard a series of sad coughs as he struggled to get some words out. "The new city architecture... those blocky walls with the fake ass n-word pass graphics everywhere. I felt defeated, trapped. I feel like there will never be anything new because of the redundancy. Everywhere I looked, I was reminded of our failure. It drove me mad."

I couldn't believe what I was hearing. "Ryan, I'm so sorry. I had no idea it had gotten this bad. I also wondered why I was feeling so funky for the last few months. I could not pinpoint it."

"It's not your fault," he said, his voice barely a whisper. "Just... be careful. Try not to look at the new architecture. When walking around the city, look down and try to envision it as something more beautiful!"

The call ended abruptly, leaving me in the middle of the sidewalk, numb with shock. I looked around, suddenly hyper-aware of the oppressive architecture that surrounded me. I then remembered something that I had foolishly overlooked. The dean's friendship with the mayor had allowed this insidious transformation to creep in gradually, so much so that I hadn't fully grasped its impact until now. They are aware of the impacts of cultural shock. This is precisely what makes this so evil.

My walk had become grueling because I had to navigate the pointless structures, adding unnecessary distance to my route. The city, once somewhat familiar and welcoming (from a relative standpoint), now felt like an alien landscape designed to torment me. I never liked the idea of modern suburbia when we actually compare it to the ancient cities that existed back then. They made sure there were no superfluous things, only those that were there to entice the slavish types who were incapable of creating their own with their wills.

Mentally exhausted and overwhelmed by the news about Ryan, I decided to take the bus for the rest of the journey. I enter a different part of my mind, a place that I hadn't visited for a while—the apologization to myself. I felt like I was going to cheat on myself as I was going to deny myself physical exercise. I thought back to all the moments when I'd internally cry about having to walk and the other side of me telling the slavish side of me to be such. Those were my internal victories as part of my journey to get to where I was. I was betraying my master self.

I reached the bus stop and sank onto the bench, my mind a whirlwind of thoughts. Then, I lifted up my ass halfway. For fuck's sake, I was sitting on a bench with the dean's n-word pass painted on it. I immediately stood up because the whole idea of this ugly art having a whiff of my impressive glute gains seemed criminal. I don't know why, but I sometimes treat inanimate and abiotic objects as living. Same reason why I still keep my childhood teddy bear. I try my best to remind myself of Teddy, but his fur is halfway gone as a result of me cuddling with him so much. I also take a mental note of his eyes, the right side being smaller than the left side, as I would sleep with him on one particular side. The bigger eye is the one that looks sillier, while the smaller one represents the more serious but thoughtful side of him. I would think of the former as an archetype of a person representing looseness, chaos, and spontaneity that brings joy to life. The latter represents order, and as I'd look at that specific eye, I could mentally get a picture of somebody telling me, "Be realistic," whenever I have a questionably realistic ambition. Modern architecture radiates the excessive energy version of my teddy bear's smaller eye to the point where it obscures too much of the outside world, like causing the skyline to be infinitely up. There is no such thing as an errand in this kind of condition.

I remain standing by the bus stop pole, trying to process everything. Ryan's breakdown and my increasing sense of isolation and frustration—all stemmed from the state taking excessive control over businesses.

As the bus approached, I realized things may not get any better. I was not surprised to see the decorated black and white print on it as I looked up. It was right there, in front of me, and I still refused to accept the bus's look. I recall the "bus go round!" thing the young version of myself would do when I played with toy buses. I hear that voice become distorted and demonic, high pitched going alongside with low pitch at the same time. What can I do about this?

The bus arrived, and I stood up, ready to face whatever came next. I boarded the bus, determined to find a way to restore sanity to my city.

Stepping onto the bus, I immediately noticed something was different. The usual annoying barrage of advertisements for banking institutions, overpriced vacation packages, and other consumer temptations were nowhere to be seen. The last time I was on a bus, when I was five years old, I was already able to get a hint at how ugly the adult modern world would be because of the clear inflation that doesn't need one to know initial prices. They were things that one should be able to get without paying for anything. Those bundles of hints were like swarms of Pitbull dogs trying to hug me and then eat my ass.

The only advertisements that remained were pseudo-motivational slogans from my former college. It was strange seeing them here, in a place where they never used to be. It hit me that I hadn't been inside a bus for a long time and wasn't familiar with the usual ads, but the absence of the familiar ones was a dead giveaway of how much had changed. Since the mayor so favorites Mr. Lester and who knows what other city council members, they were probably charging him free for the advertising space. *AHHHHHH COMMUNISSMMM,* I think to myself.

As I took a seat, I looked around at the other passengers. To my shock, they all appeared inexplicably happy, as if they were living in some paradise, the same paradise as what the old vacation package advertisements depicted. It was jarring—they were the kind of people you see working in companies or kids with wealthy parents and they seemingly have a good life—yet how much would people like me hate to live their lives?

I decided to close my eyes for the ride, hoping to find some solace in the darkness. Being alone is already a bad enough feeling, but there is some comfort in accepting it when it is clear it is impossible to obtain in the first place. Either that, or I relax too much and bow down to a new master.

But my peace was short-lived.

"This is the most natural thing in the world!" someone suddenly yelled, snapping me back to reality. I opened my eyes and saw a man standing near the front of the bus, staring at a city-warranted announcement. Curious, I got up and walked toward him, trying to get a better look at what had caught his attention. The man was looking at a digital sign that displayed the announcement in large, bold letters.

It was a redundant announcement stating that the city's revised architecture would now use the new so-called "n-word" for everything… the message was clear: all aspects of the swear word brand were now being rebranded under the guise of "nature."

This rebranding was a new linguistic twist meant to perhaps trick leftists or even some genuine environmentalists into promoting the very architecture that I can tell is already ruining the soils and grass. The announcement praised integrating "nature" into every aspect of city life, claiming it would bring harmony and balance. It was a gross manipulation of language designed to obscure the truth and coerce acceptance of the city's madness. I will admit, though, that what the architecture is doing brings "balance." But I don't say balance is necessarily good all the time. If a society or small tribal group is in constant balance to the point of having the same daily routine, then what the hell is even the point of living?

I looked around the bus again, seeing the passengers in a new light. They weren't just happy—they were brainwashed. The new city's propaganda had already seeped into every corner of their lives, convincing them that what they were now branding as national parks was the pinnacle of natural living. They really do miss the point that national parks were never truly a connection with nature in the first place. One can get lost somewhere in a canoe, and all they need to do is scream random shit, and then a bunch of helicopters are going to save them. Besides, the park ranger would tackle you when you try to play a "real-life survival game."

As the bus felt like it would take long because the roads were also modified and vehicles pretty much take the same amount of time to cover the distance as walking, I anxiously went on my phone. Even though I again don't endorse internet usage, especially to escape from real life, I found some relative psychological space, as the other parts of the world aren't pozzed with the n-word pass architecture. I had to scroll through random internet stock images, even though stock images are, by definition, the most sterile types of photos that can exist. I did get tired of those quickly, so I had to start watching videos of rhinoceros shitting out liquid diarrhea in the wild savannahs so that I could at least get an immersive and intense enough imaginary sniff of wildlife.

My phone buzzed with a notification. It was from one of the last local environmental groups I stalked. To my horror, they posted something to justify certain evil. It promoted a rally to support the new "nature" architecture and to pretend to rebel by calling action to paint images of fake grass onto the n-word pass architecture. Grass is not even the artificial "perfect green" that default paint always is. My heart sank.

Sometimes, it amazes me how far leftists can get their unmindful ways of doing their procedures, even though I perceive them as the unlocked menaces of society. This was beyond anything I had imagined. I am not going to lie; I had some spark of excitement that the memes about leftism's absurdity were going to be funny as fuck. But this would assume there would still be any sane people left to make those memes.

The bus came to a halt, and I stepped off. I jumped off it and began the walk to Burger Queen. My eyes opened to the stark changes in the cityscape. Every business I passed was now draped in the same oppressive architecture. They were emblazoned with various variations of Mr. Lester's rebranded "natural" n-word passes. But if one were to look at the city from a cliff from afar, it would just be a white mass. Normally, brick-and-mortar businesses differentiate themselves with unique designs to attract customers, but now everything looks like they will fail. The whole world of local trade had become a monotonous blur, erasing individuality in favor of uniformity.

When I finally arrived at Burger Queen, I could see that it, too, had succumbed to the new fakely homogenous rules. The once vibrant facade was now another clone in the sea of buildings that themselves really began to look like wagecucks. Not that small businesses were all that free to start with. I pushed open the door and stepped inside, finding the place eerily quiet, much muter than even the midnights when people would be too scared if the homeless man at the entrance asked, "Spare change?" but wouldn't say thank you.

My boss, Mr. Harris, was slumped over the counter, tears streaming down his face. He was the father of my manager, Carl, who always bullied me. So, normally, he was also mean and dismissive to me. As such, seeing him like this was almost satisfying. I decided to ignore him, silently enjoying his misery.

The lack of customers was palpable still. I spent my shift bored out of my mind because I wasn't anymore able to watch my crying manager, who was sitting his ass inside his office at the back. I also had no tables to clean or orders to take. The few times the door did open, it was just someone looking for directions or attempting the "Wash your hands without using soap 'b*throom' challenge," or to smoke or fap. Heaven forbids it; even the usual flurry of online orders was absent. The silence gnawed at me, so I finally entered the office and asked Mr. Harris about it.

"Why are there so few online orders today?" I asked, trying to mask my curiosity with casual indifference.

Mr. Harris looked up, his eyes red and puffy. "It's the packaging," he said, his voice cracking. "We had to change it to comply with the new rules. All our packaging now features those damned n-word pass tickets. It is ruining this vegan movement."

I was taken aback. "So, the packaging is the reason?"

"Yes," he spat bitterly. "The only reason people even came to Burger Queen was to pretend to be vegans for their social media. Our old packaging screamed 'vegan vibes,' but now it's all those white wraps and bags with the stupid tickets on them that obscure it all and because most of the pro-vegan role-players also have to pretend to be anti-non-marginalized. It's ruined everything."

I tried to muster some sympathy, thinking this might be my chance to ask for a promotion amidst the chaos. But my deep-seated hatred for Mr. Harris made it difficult to sound sincere. Even though I tried, my usual talking voice to him whenever he treats me like shit remained. "Bahah, uh I mean, I'm sorry to hear that, Mr. Harris. Maybe, HEHEAHAHA, sorry, I just have a cough right now. Let me start over. Considering the situation, there might be an opportunity for some of us to take on more responsibility and help out?"

Mr. Harris's face twisted with anger. "You think you can take advantage of this situation to get a promotion? You're just as selfish and manipulative as everyone else! You're fired!" he yelled, his voice echoing in the *empty* restaurant, which almost made me laugh at his mediocre marketing skills during his moment of trying to sound like a loud man. "Get out, and don't come back!"

Stunned, I took off my apron and made my way out of the office. As I reached the main door of Burger Queen, motherfucking Kevin, the one person who I actually look forward to seeing during work hours and feel a pint of freedom from, called out. He handed me a drink and a jumbo bucket of fries.

"Here, take this," he said quietly. "Make sure you don't go hungry while you're looking for a new job."

"Thanks, Kevin," I muttered, deeply grateful. I was already feeling hungry from the walking portion when I made my way to Burger Queen. Especially since I had basically arrived here for nothing by being fired immediately, I needed to refuel the calories as soon as possible.

As I walked out, I glanced back through the window and saw my boss firing Kevin for his kindness. The anger in my boss's voice didn't take long to trail back into sadness. The sight of him crying even harder now that he was understaffed and possibly facing closure brought a grim satisfaction.

Kevin joined me outside, looking a bit dazed but relieved. "Good riddance," I said, handing him a handful of fries. "We'll find something better."

We sat on the curb together, sharing the fries and contemplating our next steps. Kevin told me that he would pursue his dream career of running a free food truck with his last bit of life savings, before hanging himself.

"Woah woah, chill, don't kill yourself, man," I begged. "You are one of the best people I have ever met, and I am surprised you'd do such a thing. Surprised by the suicide, not the free food truck."

"Yeah but being kind is what I think I do best!" Kevin said. "But with how mundane the city is getting, I don't think there is any sense helping people in a world full of idiots. Once the n-word pass idiocy becomes everywhere, moving to a new city may be an option, but the plans of the n-word pass domination would soon likely reach that new city."

I stood up with intense emotion. "Kevin, I will not allow this to happen. You matter and I will pave a world where you still matter."

"And how are you going to do that? The infrastructure is just too solid."

"I am willing to die for it. We'll see."

Chapter Eleven: Passive Void

Is the persistent issue that emerges at the core of modernity and the technological system a subtle, insidious form of nihilism, a concept that Nietzscheans would critique as "nihilistically willing"? The true danger of this nihilism lies in its protean nature, manifesting in different ways that create an experience akin to wandering through a hall of mirrors. These reflections promise transcendental escape from badness, yet most are illusions, offering no true passage but rather serving to deepen one's sense of "stuck." The most deceptive forms of nihilism suggest that an ultimate truth exists solely within one's mind, a perspective more nihilistic than the outright rejection of belief. Wouldn't this internalized pseudo-divinity allow for the creation of out-of-ass doctrines, justifying actions like consuming inappropriate media under the guise of personal belief?

To counter the disgruntles that many have that stem from feelings of nihilism, there would have to be some in-built mechanic in modern society that has a "wholesome component" that reels people in and makes them feel like they are sucking the tits of an estrogenic bigger brother. Well, that is precisely what the "human resource" department of modern society, such as psychotherapists, do (remember: most of the mental issues of today are caused by modernity in the first place, so the system must create bandage fixes for it). What's problematic is they are wired to serve those who have already submitted themselves to the diverging reductivist notions that either one should alienate oneself from one's body, or that there is no kind of true spiritual component of one's life. All that needs to be done is a lobotomization (GEONOMETRY DASH FROM ROBOTOP REFERENCE LOL) to adapt them more to modern society. Could some anthropology that may have birthed the modern technological system extend from some aspects of ancient philosophy? Or what found the dematerialization of modernity, as trying to will nihilistically and then build a world around it would result in a void?

A kind of "exploration" can lead one astray into a type of idealism, where everything is predetermined within a realm of immutable forms, stripping humanity of the possibility of transcending to a "gooder" state. Modern views posit that humans are born incomplete and must continually develop themselves through external means—specifically through the creation and use of mere technologies and linguistic systems. This could have been articulated initially by Socratism itself. Yours truly probably employed this very idea to rationalize his physical ugliness and smelliness,[241] positing an external world that is merely an equation to be solved. Such a perspective reduces existence, including the rich subjectiveness of humanity, to a problem, leading to its denial and dismissal, ultimately underscoring the bleakness of our current anti-life landscape—perhaps a result of striving for some ideal world where there isn't any perceptible objects, ideal limits that cannot be found with sensuous intuition.[242] It appears that some of this has sparked more contemporary ideas like the Alsbergian "body liberation," where technological development liberates humans from their biological limitations, emphasizing that

---

[241] F. Nietzsche, *Twilight of the Idols* (Hackett Publishing, 1997), 13-14.
[242] E. Husserl, *Ideas Pertaining to a Pure Phenomenology and to a Phenomenological Philosophy* (Springer Science & Business Media, 1983).

technological advancements allow humans to transcend physical constraints and supposedly achieve greater capabilities.[243] Such an approach lacks even the metaphysical duality of a world beyond the material—it may lead to a mechanistic way that undermines cognitive clarity over time. Combined with pseudo-meditative practices that encourage dissociation from the body, this promotes conformity to the system's insanity. In this constructed simulation of society, people, in many cases, exhibit a form of moral mediocrity under the guise of attempting morality. True virtue requires a profound spiritual empathy and a sharp capability to imagine others. However, the average person practices a distorted mimicry of ideals, effortlessly performing acts of "good" as adopting propaganda-driven archetypes is an effective scientifically engineered method of social control. The issue with this mediocrity is its toxic diffusion, devoid of genuine intent. Would those who profess to "love everyone" paradoxically remain stuck in a pseudo-individualistic mindset, indifferent to anything beyond their immediate experience?

This superficiality results in a hollow form of love, contributing to the system's misuse of the term "altruism." In its purest sense, altruism embodies profound empathy and spiritual vigor. Yet, it has been linguistically corrupted and reduced to a demented form of self-interest. The ruling class embodies this, perpetuating these diluted ideals. This can be seen in leftists and their rioting, too—the more depressed and nihilistic a population is, the more liable they are to chimpout.[244] It yet leads people to be sufficiently docile—for example, they wouldn't be able to stand up for themselves to go to funerals by skipping work, and instead calibrating actions to the expected consequences, which means they further work towards the technological system. Additionally, wouldn't "desired" self-destructive behavior rise so that the media can capture more "ops" of antics and other pseudo-rebellious acts that wouldn't actually attack the system but, in fact, make the anti-establishment people look even more insane?

The-Rapy

After the really tragic events of the morning, I decided to head to my favorite gym for an extensive session to blow off some steam. The gym was a sanctuary of what freedom and intensity really are, a place where the usual rules of decorum were happily ignored.

The rules in this gym were what made it my favorite. For starters, people were allowed to drop weights without concern for the noise, be shirtless, and even eat while lifting. It was the perfect place to let loose. This was all because the gym staff were paid extra to do the extra servicing.

As I approached the gym, I wasn't surprised to see that it, too, had adopted the new lame n-word pass decoration. The stark white walls and blocky designs were plastered with the ubiquitous writings that made the whole thing look less like a manly place and more like a "Heinie Slut Juniors." The worst part is the posters that they replaced. Before, the most renowned bodybuilders had their own paintings on the walls, massively scaled and high effort. The gym also honored the dead ones, of course with the angel wings

---

[243] E. Erkan, "A Promethean Philosophy of External Technologies, Empiricism, & the Concept: Second-Order Cybernetics, Deep Learning, and Predictive Processing," *Media Theory*, 4(2020): 87-146.

[244] V. Mcleod, *Clown World Chronicles* (VJM Publishing, 2020), 159.

painted behind them. To see the n-word pass posters replace them was so disrespectful to the honorable dead, and I really hope that the ghost of one of the dead bodybuilders haunts Mr. Lester by appearing to him as visions and reminding him of his inferior physique.

Upon entering, I headed straight to the front desk to renew my membership. The gym clerk greeted me with a smile, and I noticed the monthly fee had dropped significantly—from $200 to just $50. Elated by the unexpected discount, I nonchalantly hugged the clerk. He wrapped his arms around me back. I really just needed someone to hug just to boost my now horrible mental health, especially now that I am dirt poor and would not be able to afford a $200 membership for longer.

"Thanks for the good news!" I said, feeling a surge of relief and gaining the kind of excitement that makes me more verbose. "This reminds me of a day an indoor playground let me in for free as a kid because the owners were the parents of a classmate! Of course though, I wouldn't make such a direct comparison of that to the gym because it had an arcade that allows the lazy guests to be occupied and is everything but physical activity."

"No problem!" the clerk replied, a bit taken aback by my weird details, but smiling nonetheless. "Enjoy your workout."

I could already feel my hair being whooshed around, as the activity of everyone exercising caused a ton of wind. The gym was packed with all the machines and stations I loved, and I was ready to take my stress out on something.

Feeling centered, I moved on to the boxing arena. The sight of the punching bags and the ring filled me with a primal energy. I quickly wrapped my hands and started pounding away at the bags, imagining the faces of everyone who had wronged me in the past. The repetitive thud of my fists against the bag was therapeutic. I was envisioning that one fatso with glasses who always brags about getting straight As in his classes in middle school (who the fuck brags about grades at that age) who accused me of "having the brain of a stegosaurus" after I done fucked up in a drama play that wasn't even in front of the school. I imagined myself leaving a scar on his neck and pulling his glasses off and breaking it—which I actually did after he threatened to break my phone.

Next, I entered the boxing ring. I did something I always wanted to do. I started running back and forth in the ring, using the parallel side ropes to enhance my velocity. I allowed myself to scream loudly in victory, feeling the rush of endorphins with each triumphant shout. I felt like I was preparing for a world-fighting championship in one of those biographical movies of a dead famous wrestler who is highly pressured by his father to do well because that father turns out to own the whole ass wrestling federation and is rich enough to boast a last name that starts with the prefix "Von" (Steel Nail reference).

But then, a gym staff member approached me, looking stern. "Hey, no more screaming in here," he said curtly before walking away. He was obviously not saying it with the intent to mess with a guy of my size but as an actual obligation in accordance with certain rules. I scratched my head, confused. Screaming had always been part of the gym's free-spirited rules. It was one of the things that made this place so special, and it was what I really looked forward to when I was coming here. And it really is detrimental not to allow it. When you think about it, when you hear someone scream nearby, you are more likely to switch to a state of adrenaline. You would therefore be more motivated to be on the move and lift shit. The gym would, therefore, have even more business. Maybe that guy really was fucking with me after all.

A familiar dread crept up on me as I stood there, trying to process this new restriction. As my screaming session was cut off to something much shorter than normal, I couldn't shake the feeling that the loss of my job was so big again. The thought lingered as I continued my workout, the shadow of the city's changes hanging over me.

After my session in the boxing ring, I headed over to the weights section of the gym. It was time to focus on some isolation workouts for my smaller body parts. I like to do this because, personally for me, when I lift heavier numbers in general, it really tires out my individual side muscles used for those compound lifts, and it makes me pout and go on my phone instead of going for the isolations afterward. I hear that a lot of people are the other way around, but hey, there are bodybuilding coaches for a reason; they know what kinds of things work for different people.

I started with a warm-up, grabbing a pair of 100-pound dumbbells for some bicep curls. I pick this number for a very special reason—at the start of my lifting journey, I got curious about what advanced lifters were carrying, so I googled the heaviest dumbbell curl in the world, and the 100-pound ones for reps seemed to be the holy grails. Some professional strongmen can do much higher for reps, but I think the 100-pound dumbbell curls are what really separates the men from the boys. Now that I am way passed that, I just set it as my warmup weight to keep it as a memorable number.

As I lifted, I overheard a few people behind me commenting on how impressive it was. Compliments like these were normal for me, so I brushed them off and kept going. At the same time, I still kind of feel weird whenever I get compliments. This may sound irrational, but I tend to actually feel bad for people who compliment me because I am like "how could you be so nice to me? I never complimented you before; you are too kind!" I don't actually say that, and my voice always just leads to a "thanks" while I blush. Then, I spend the next hours or perhaps years trying to think of how I would compliment that person back, which almost never actually happens.

Next, I moved on to the main part of my bicep workout, picking up the 150-pound dumbbells. To my surprise, I performed the exercises much better than usual, doing more reps with better form. My muscles felt stronger and more responsive. I didn't think a moldy, unmechanical moment was going to happen to me. You know, one of those days when you can't quite get the weight into a straight trajectory, and you end up lifting the dumbbells asymmetrically. Those are common, but today, I felt like it was the other way around. I guess I reached the threshold of frustration to push me all the way to that ideal.

After finishing my bicep sets, I stood in front of the mirror and flexed, checking out the pump. My biceps looked massive, but now, they seemed disproportionately large compared to my triceps. It made me look like a gorilla who only climbs and swings through trees upward and never in the other direction. Even when I made my elbow completely straight, the bicep bulge drooped far more, while the tricep was overwhelmingly "floating" as if it did not weigh anything. Deciding to even things out, I moved to the triceps training area and started with some skull crushers and cable pushdowns. I, of course, didn't forget about dips. Many people forget about dips, claiming they only involve your body weight, but don't realize you can add additional weight by attaching chained weight plates to your balls.

Once my triceps were thoroughly worked, I flexed in front of the mirror again. This time, my triceps looked too big compared to my biceps. The horseshoe began to look like a bullshoe, resembling a Euclideanesque shape. The bizarre thing with triceps is that they tend to be a non-Euclideanesque shape at a normie size, sparked by the gap between the long and short heads. This is what gives people the false impression that the tricep is a smaller muscle than the bicep. But as one trains their tricep, it starts to shape closer to a Euclidianesque shape, more "regular" and comprehensible to average muscle observers.

I became increasingly obsessed with balancing the proportions and switched back to bicep workouts. For the next hour, I alternated between bicep and tricep exercises, using a tape measure that I borrowed from the gym office to check the circumference of each muscle after every set (Sulak moment). It was making me sweat even more, and I felt my pants soaking. Fuck, was I going to look like I pissed myself. My bloodshot eyes were so fixated on the little separation line from where the bicep and tricep meet and where both muscles met the brachialis on the other side.

Eventually, frustration set in. At the time, my 21-inch pumped arm (in a 45-degree angle) consisted of a 7.25-inch bicep and a 13.75-inch tricep. According to what I'd read online, the tricep should make up two-thirds of the total arm circumference, meaning the ideal numbers were 7-inch biceps and 14-inch triceps. I thought back at the bodybuilding forum community members who posted pictures of lifters, whether they were professional bodybuilders or regular gym rats, and made fun of their bicep-tricep size ratio along with the other members. As I was looking at my imperfect numbers, I looked around, making sure nobody was taking photos of me. No one was even looking at me, nor did they give enough of a shit to come near me, but I had a load of cognitive dissonance as I recall myself laughing at "uneven" bodybuilders" as I read those forum posts.

As I tried to "math" while measuring my arm, a familiar face approached. It was Stacy, the pretty woman who nonverbally glanced at me in the past. I was immediately stunned by her looks. She had a baseball cap from a non-normie brand. She also wore a red tank top which was accompanied by a bra, indicating she isn't a hoe. But her boobs wouldn't have been super prominent anyway because she was deezed; her pecs were so developed that they were visibly overwhelming and striated, pushing out the actual boob part of her chest such that the two components appeared separated. She wore lime-colored sweatpants that still managed to be so tight around her muscular horse-like legs that quadricep veins were visible through them (By the way, no homo, I am just so tired of seeing soyboys that this was a breath of fresh air. Also, Stacy isn't THAT muscular—I am exaggerating it to minimize the chances of woke robocops burning this book).

She smiled and said, "Wow, cool gains." She reached out her arm and then started touching my bicep as I was still flexing. Woman hands are usually around 7 inches long, so it took her whole hand just to barely cover the width of my bicep alone.

Caught off guard, I tried to look normal amidst my overanalyses. "Thanks," I replied awkwardly. I was probably making a soynerd face as I was doing one of the nerdiest mathematical analyses in my life at the gym.

Deciding to shift my focus away from my arms for a moment, I moved to the bench press. I was going to go extra light for the warmup because I needed to make sure not too much blood went from my thinking brain to my pecs too fast. Doing so would give me that bad lightheaded effect when standing up too fast.

After I was done the warmup and prepared the weight I normally do, I was still thinking about my encounter with Stacy, so I decided to make some animalistic, masculine growls as I lifted, hoping to impress her and relieve more stress through my own imaginary tension and possibly hearing a response from her as it may come to fruition. Stacy laughed positively in response, boosting my confidence.

But soon, a gym staff member approached me, a different guy from the one who first told me to be quiet. "Hey, you can't yell out loud," he said sternly. I glared at him because what he had just done was the equivalent of bothering a man having phone sex. I don't condone phone sex, by the way; I just mention it to depict the disruption.

Confused and a bit annoyed, I asked, "Why not? This gym was supposed to be a place to express ourselves freely. Are you guys not supporting inclusivity anymore? Hate against 'Chads' who are not afraid to show their energy? You might be fitphobic."

He sighed. "We had to make the rules less free legally. Now, instead of yelling, we're only allowed to say 'n-word' at a medium volume. It's part of the new city regulations that replace all other means of stress reduction. The city council stated that the means of releasing energy in this gym should not closely resemble uncivilized men, and we can't have those kinds of people in our modern society."

The oppressive influence of discrimination against the free man had even infiltrated the gym's free-spirited culture. As I stood there, stunned by the staff's explanation, things took a sudden turn for the worse. The clueless, overly socialized chumps, clearly viewing my behavior as inappropriate for a "modernized society," decided to call the cops. I started hyperventilating, never expecting my Tarzanic antics to warrant such drastic action.

Within minutes, the cops arrived, their presence less imposing than before the n-word pass didn't take over the city because of the softer society's less need for manliness. "Sir, we need you to come with us," one said, stepping forward with a pair of handcuffs.

I remained still, my mind racing. "I didn't do nothing wrong," I said, trying to keep calm, a complete flip from when I was trying to impress Stacy.

"You're causing a disturbance," the officer replied, attempting to cuff me. But as he tried to position my arms behind my back, it became clear that my thick muscles made it impossible for the handcuffs to reach both wrists. *HAZA*, I thought. I always thought this kind of thing only happens in memes, and I assumed real cops had extra long handcuffs to account for fat people. Look, I have big muscles, but there are obese people out there who are so fat that they have even more blubber than I have muscle. Well to be fair, fat people are much easier to chase and catch than anyone else. But, they also have so much fat that a cop's gun would have a harder time piercing through. Man, this is confusing.

The officers exchanged frustrated glances. "Sir, you need to come with us semi-voluntarily," another officer said, hand resting on his holster. Realizing I still might have room for mastery in the future, I slowly nodded and allowed them to guide me to the police car at gunpoint. The ride to the police station was a blur of anxiety and disbelief.

At the station, I was taken to a small, blood-smelling room where an officer sat down across from me. He seemed more sympathetic than the others. "Let's talk," he said, his tone softer. "Why did you behave that way at the gym?"

I took a deep breath, struggling to find the right words. "Look man, I lost my job, MY JOB HOO HOO HOO. It's been a tough few months, and I guess I got carried away. WAHHH WAHHAHAHH." I was bawling my eyes out.

He studied me for a moment, then nodded. "Look, I don't think jail is the right place for you. You seem like you didn't understand the consequences of your actions. Instead, we'll set you up with a one-on-one session with a psychotherapist. Maybe that will help."

Relieved, I agreed. Although, I was not a big fan of psychotherapists because of all the memes that make fun of both them and the patients. Besides, I remember back when I had to visit a psychologist as a child because I was already showing incompatibilities with the excessive orders of modernity, and I had to eventually make up things to tell them as my problems were incomprehensible. But I figured it was better than being in jail.

I was escorted to the psychotherapist's office. The room was warmer and inviting, a huge contrast to the cold police station. I sat down on a plush chair, feeling both nervous and curious about what was to come. The psychotherapist, a woman in her forties, greeted me with a gentle smile. "Hello, I'm Dr. Evans. Let's start with some questions to understand what brought you here today."

She asked me about my recent behavior, my background, and my current state of mind. As I listened to her questions, I found myself pausing for a long moment, diving deep into massive introspection. The events of the past months, my struggles, my anger, my need to break free, and my suddenly void tendencies—all of it swirled in my mind.

"Why did I behave the way I did?" I repeated the question to myself, realizing that the answer was more complex than I had initially thought. As I sat there, lost in thought, I began to see the patterns within my mind.

As I sat in the office for longer, the pieces of my recent behavior started to come together. Dr. Evans' questions, even though they were stupid and I was the one doing the most work, had prompted me to reflect deeply on my actions and thoughts over the past months. Mainly, I realized that my weird obsession with my bicep-tricep ratio was more than just a simple fixation on physical perfection—it was a symptom of a deeper issue.

The way I fixated on achieving an abstract ideal bicep-tricep size ratio mirrored Dr. Mister Lee's reduction of meaning to chemicals and the investor's reliance on mathematical figures detached from spontaneous realities.

The abstract ideal of having a perfectly balanced bicep-tricep ratio, accurate to the nearest millimeter, was as impossible as reaching an asymptote in mathematics. Pursuing such an unattainable goal would inevitably lead to frustration and despair, potentially causing me to quit lifting weights altogether for fear of disrupting the perfect ratio.

When I shared this beautiful insight with Dr. Evans, her response was disappointingly dismissive. "You're overthinking this," she said, waving off my explanation. "Just take some deep breaths. I'll admit that I'm not trained to help with spiritual issues or philosophical nihilism. My best advice is to find something to distract yourself. Play some video games or something. It might help take your mind off things."

The suggestion felt like another dead end. I preferred physical exercise over sedentary activities, but I could see that she had nothing else to offer. Reluctantly, I agreed to her advice just so I could get out of there, knowing it wouldn't address the deeper issue.

Chapter Twelve: Modern Subservience

Is servitude today so bad because even those with a high capacity for freedom don't realize that they are bound? It may be a universal constant that the essence of servitude may always persist—the only thing that changes is its appearance and scope. In different times, there exist two archetypes of the "bound": those who are aware and sad about it and those who delude themselves into thinking we are in the best times in history—the ones who do realize they are bound may be the better off ones because of a higher level of potential agency and, hence, the awareness. In modern spaces, clearly, most people are of the ignorant, stuck inside cooming. But deep down, are constantly confused by their inability to attain the eternal "happiness" that they want so much. This is the transformation of labor into a mere diversion—hasn't utilitarianism's fallacies obliterated even the division between the good and bad, as both conditions seem to necessitate too much effort for most?

It annoys the hell out of me when I see educational institutions, museums, government speeches, etc., talk about how we should remember "ending slavery as something that we did," and "'slavery' is a thing of the past that is literally impossible now with all the progress we made." The truth is, the world didn't suddenly become "more compassionate"—the only thing that happened is certain aspects of the past have just been selected out for the system's interest of remaining hidden. There is an argument that traditional slavery (coercion through direct force) was eliminated partly because it is an inefficient/uneconomical way to get people to wagecuck in comparison to the methods that arose in the modern world—"conscious efforts" to put it to a stop wouldn't have been nearly as successful if the technological society's newer insidious slavery had not been efficient.[245] The system "knows" direct violence is so overtly "scary," and anyone would run away from that (and there would be a need to allocate resources to physical force). After all, violence itself is a technical error to the system's requirement for everyone to go with the flow smoothly (this is probably why the system is incentivized to create linguistic euphemisms such as "unaliving"). So, psychological slavery is its answer—it is said that the average man today is a lot more scared of his employer or losing his job than the ancient slaves were of their slaveholders—why is this?

The phenomena commonly embraced as "pleasure" by the collective often manifest as subtle chains of bondage hidden beneath the surface. Why is it that, despite numerous compulsive distractions impeding true productivity on a theoretical plane, the dominant cultural narrative elevates countless artificial simulations of "living on the edge"? These experiences merely transform pre-existing potential into predetermined outcomes, perpetuating cycles of superficial engagement. Much of what we even consider "good effort" in modern times is fluffy. There is an argument to be made about how current definitions are varied and often inadequate, lacking a common understanding of efforts. The issues include teleological aspects, failure to account for effort failures, exclusion of

---

[245] T. Kaczynski, *Technological Slavery* (Scottsdale: Fitch & Madison, 2022), 175.

static efforts, and anatomical restrictions.[246] Here, pure unresisted efforts are deemed metaphysically impossible.[247] Interestingly, mere difficulty also isn't necessary for effort to be exerted but arises from the nature of efforts in conjunction with other factors, such as the saying that "effort is only effort when it begins to hurt, but hurting is not part of what effort is"—force-based theory defines physical efforts as force exertions aiming to move or maintain rest.[248] But nor should "strength" be merely as some scientific object, which ignores life-world experience and "felt-bodily nature."[249] Clearly, much of the effort that is deemed sociO-AlLy appropriate right now is unlike this, in which the system has effectively ruled out "effort as a function of action," rather than mere reaction. Only the Kazynskian notion of surrogate activity is allowed at best. The activities that everyone is forced to be tailored toward today are things that a noble being would feel physical pain doing without the necessary modernized psychological modifications that make them feel fine doing such thing. Anyone who hasn't been already slowly molded by the education system and is doped on meds would already immediately shiver at the thought of being an office drone for the rest of one's life upon reaching careeristic age. On the other hand, they'd do genuine works of effort, but it would not likely feel like "real work" if their drive and will are strong enough (ie. Jay Bulkler talks about his bodybuilding career post-retirement and says that the intense eating and training didn't make him feel "dread." Other than that, the idea that muscle-building may be a "surrogate activity"[250] would probably be in slavish mechanistic contexts). Furthermore, to negate repulsivity, there exists a perversion where risk-free pleasure is regarded as the ultimate purpose of existence. This leads to the widespread consumption of artificial experiences, benefiting the ruling elite not only through increased revenue but also through more profound advantages. People are hired to craft marketing messages that instill a fear of death, such as the immediate threats posed by physically blunt confrontations or dangers. Consequently, the populace is conditioned to prioritize superficial enjoyment over the pursuit of meaningful accomplishments. Doesn't this conditioning result in a willingness to accept subjugation in exchange for the continuation of this cycle of superficial gratification?

Virtual experiences such as video games are often cited as a clear example of this phenomenon, akin to the notion of "pacifying the masses." And many believe that physical games, particularly mainstream ones, are the antithesis of this trend, yet they are essentially another form of the same diversion. The error with today's games in general is that the players themselves and their fans are so lax because the latter is only working to actualize some pre-conceived numb axiom that either they or the spectator had in mind. The spectators themselves are just passive participators who don't at all put skin in the game. Honestly, though, "the physicals" that are still somewhat respectable are the fighters or bodybuilders. Fighters at least resemble the epic badass gladiators. Gladiators

[246] O. Massin, "The nature and difficulty of physical efforts," *Synthese*, 203(2024): 177. https://doi.org/10.1007/s11229-024-04572-5
[247] Ibid.
[248] Ibid.
[249] R. Gugutzer, "Strength as phenomenon: a pure phenomenology of sport," *Journal of the Philosophy of Sport*, 2024: 1-20. https://doi.org/10.1080/00948705.2024.2370461
[250] T. Kaczynski, *Industrial Society and its Future* (Independently published, 2018), para. 84.

were the men who went beyond the cities, exploring new lands that weren't pre-institutionalized by the state. In other words, they were the same people who would have the whole nation at stake at an existential level. Crowd cheering is literally a way to increase the odds of growth and defense. Regarding bodybuilding: though it is comparatively passive (compared to the barbarians of the past) in that most of them aren't as strong as their insanely shredded physiques portray them to be, the audiences at least have some way to feel the experience of participating and exert some subjective cognition because there is not a definite best physique (there is a reason why the smaller divisions, like classic physique, can be more appealing than the largest weight class, as the notion of merely adding "more and more" is an objective definite that compromises subjectivity). On the contrary, what the hell is kneeing a manufactured rubber "testicle" around going to do to defend from or explore outside forces?

One may say that in modern games, man is reduced to a bundle of reflexes rather than growing into an organic being[251] (It can even be considered wagecucking, except the player is the cuck star in the "cuck pOrn" big screen footage). You could borrow Foucauldian terms and call this treating of the player's body as a machine a docile player (focusing on measurable and quantifiable performance[252]). In the world of tradition, it was even the case that games should be only done (not just a form of entertainment) after an in-real-life war was won.[253] Sure, there were "games" in the world of tradition, including feasts, sacred games, rituals, and sacrifices,[254] but nobody in that world turned into lazy fucks who cut themselves and burned good stuff (the games done today, in real life, are the leftists doing their rioting—leftist rioting is basically "victory dances" because the system allows it in the first place). Isn't it just so pathetic that even the "games" that every modern man beholden are really just the equivalent of staring at a victory screen for two hours?

Much of our lameness is about what the BAPist term "pre-owned space" is. The kinds of life with the intuition for space know the space the modern institution offers to get people to "pretend to conquer" is fake and obvious—there is nothing worth exploring—acts of masculinity that are just a parody of real masculinity.[255] Everyone nowadays is just a lame couch potato gamer in disguise (whether or not they touch the controller and television). Even much of what the technological system designates as the epitome of exploration is highly reduced to this pre-owned space. And dare I say, this even extends to how most people in modern times plan and execute their trips away from wagecuckism. For instance, other than the annoying ass notifications, tourists tend to focus more on capturing the perfect photo for social media rather than appreciating the actual sights and experiences.[256] Also, there is a reduced incentive to problem-solve with the increasing dependence on their smartphones for navigation, translation, and recommendations rather than engaging with the environment and interacting with locals.

---

[251] J. Evola, *Revolt Against the Modern World* (Inner Traditions, 1995), 337.

[252] L.A. Howe, "Play, performance, and the docile athlete," *Sport, Ethics & Philosophy*, 1(2007): 47-57. https://doi.org/10.1080/17511320601142985

[253] J. Evola, *Revolt Against the Modern World* (Inner Traditions, 1995), 138.

[254] Ibid., 137.

[255] B.A. Pervert, *Bronze Age Mindset* (Independently Published, 2018), 65.

[256] Z. Xiang, M. Fuchs, U. Gretzel, and W. Höpken, *Handbook of e-Tourism* (Springer Cham, 2022), 125.

Clearly, the convenience of having instant information reduces the need for tourists to navigate challenges on their own, potentially diminishing the sense of adventure and accomplishment.[257] Engagement with digital devices can limit the sensory experiences that are crucial to tourism, such as listening to local sounds, observing detailed visuals, and experiencing local scents and textures. In group travel settings, excessive use of personal devices can reduce interaction among group members,[258] so each person would just be an isolated individual all over again, in the same condition as being in an office cubicle, but each of the cubicle walls is painted to depict ocean beaches. Modern tourism, in this sense, is literally just "playing a game" in disguise, and it will increasingly become so. It's proven that the invasion of exploring new space is not just limited to a lack of concrete space in the new area, but there are some psychological factors that would be interfered by the technological system. It is in the system's interest to divert one's enjoyment of tourism and exploration because travel in its pure form could lead to the prevention of the smooth functioning of the technological system. Think about it, if one ends up not enjoying the non-superficial aspects of traveling, he may be discouraged from realizing the fruitful aspects of not sitting in an office all day. The system would favor a condition where he enjoys the superficial aspects (wasting time enjoying vacations superficially through a camera lens for social media) just enough so that he would desire to wagecuck to therefore afford vacation costs. The grand irony here is that there is even more frustration regarding the technology itself because of the need for stable social connections, which may lead to disruptions of plans if there are technical problems.[259] Wouldn't this frustration of "current outdated tech" only get tourists to call for further advancement of the technological system?

Okay, by now, I know it may seem like I am an insecure "gamer nerd" for trying to criticize things such as modern traveling, more so than the deepest degree of the virtual itself, video games. Okay, for any gamer nerds reading this right now, it is now time for me to roast your sweaty asses (Trust me, you'll thank me. Anti-technologization thought really is for gamers after all)! So basically, the heavily pre-programmed simulations that we call "the virtual" really give a nice "third person" view of what it would look like when we enter the next degree of unrealisticness and alienation. What makes it so bad is that the realm of the virtual has yet to ascend IRL art. At least with some kinds of art such as non-shock value music, where a degree of repetition serves as a foundation for variation and precedent, the iterative nature of video games fails to evoke a sense of genuine narrative progression. Even the act of mass destruction within becomes a hollow exercise, rendering the medium irrelevant to the human condition. While such mechanistic interactions might resonate with an insect's (likewise, bugman) instinctual patterns, they fail to engage the complex moral dimensions of human experience. The sequences within gameplay are merely mechanistic, devoid of any implied intent or deeper meaning. Would this reduce them to mere causal chains where the player's calculative engagement lacks any existential significance as the number of possible choices will ALWAYS (no matter

---

[257] Ibid., 127.
[258] Ibid., 128.
[259] Ibid., 129.

how many "Oh CoOl ThaNoS CaR ThAnOs CaR SnAp PoWers" the third person character has) at most be one less than the possible number of choices in the real world?

As an illustrative example using how we connect to historical objects, which video games oftentimes attempt to do, it could be argued that perfect reproductions of historical objects (such as in games) evoke similar emotional responses but without providing the same "as if" experience. This would show that emotional response alone is insufficient to explain the unique phenomenological connection to the past afforded by genuine historical objects.[260] It's interesting to consider how illegal it is in the modern world to try to at least get in touch with the good old days when gladiators were the point of interest. With all the modern "aesthetics" that exist, it's literally impossible to get your plastic gladiator sword, or even real swords, out and do a duel with your friends while genuinely feeling like you are being inspired by them and building more that resembles them in terms of the significance of the current. When you visit places that still have those preserved, it's true that you'd at least get a taste of it, which makes you more likely to preach it... but that would be a space soon to be gulped and is already turning into lame sites with ugly tape blocks. The system had to introduce historical and adventurous video games to scratch the itch of people who wanted to emulate the epic conquests of the bronze ages, basically highly intricate versions of artificial replication of the historical object. But ask yourself, if those are supposedly so immersive with good graphics, why is it instead distracting people from actually wanting to "will" something epic into reality? Well, there is an importance of imaginative immersion and vividness, which are enhanced by knowing an object's authentic history. The genuine historical properties of objects support immersive, imaginative activities, making the past feel more present. Because subjective imagination is fried, players are continually aware that they are engaging with something predetermined narrative structure rather than a physical artifact with a real history. It makes it feel even more like history didn't even exist and is just mythology because they are experienced in a more isolated and recreational context. Video games commonly evoke emotional reactions, and that is how they get you close to an object's history at best. But don't the horrible self-insertions as a "being" that isn't you (virtual character) only give you the "as if" reaction and nothing more?

What makes the potentiality for self-insertions so bad as to bleed further into real life as externalities? I believe it can come to be literally the case that much of what people think they are accomplishing in modern society is just highly akin to playing an extremely immersive video game, such that the immersion is precisely what motivates their achievement-consumption efforts. In addressing the detriments of this "immersion," which may promote horrible consumption behaviors for players or people, there are some principal types: "Perceptual," "Narrative," and "Challenge-Based." Under Perceptual immersion, the state of being is enveloped by an environment, commonly achieved through technologies like virtual reality. Narrative immersion is engrossment in a story with a desire to see it through to the end, often found in books, plays, and films, and, of course, strongly in video games. Challenge-based immersion involves a preoccupation with tasks or challenges, compelling users to complete them, often seen in video games

---

[260] M. Windsor, "Imagining the Past of the Present," *The Philosophical Quarterly*, 2023: pqad114. https://doi.org/10.1093/pq/pqad114

and gamified settings.[261] It's warned that video game industry practices, such as microtransactions and dark patterns, are significant concerns, in that perceptual immersion makes consumers more susceptible to misleading practices due to altered perception and decision-making abilities.[262] Likewise, narrative immersion can lead consumers to spend more on extra content due to emotional investment in characters or stories. Challenge-based immersion exploits consumers' desire to progress in games, leading to spending on microtransactions or downloadable content. Ultimately, the forms of immersion can be exploited through various manipulative commercial practices.[263] Paralleling things, isn't this along the lines of how the technological system gets one to consume further as they continue to drench themselves in the real-life simulation of modernity? Under this, there could never be an exit out of mediocrity even though there are evilish motivating factors for people to literally consoom "achievement." Think of every "artificial thing" that exists in modernity as things that have all their "specified" stats boosted up without accounting for their relationship with the other stats. As for art, anyone knows deep down that increasing the saturation of a specific color will surely numerically increase the "value" of the hue but won't likely make the painting "better." But there is a perverse tendency for those to seem attractive to people in the sense of "shock value" despite being so overtly inferior. Similar to modern science's striving for comfort via its mathematical cleanliness, it feels seamless to acknowledge sheer numbers as some defining measurement of achievement, or the perceptual immersion of overly high brightness and hue streetlights of modern architecture (similar to the trend in heavy metal music where there is some strictly objective maximizing of one aspect of the song, such as distortion, only for them to result in hermeneutically impoverishing productions[264]). Naturally, doesn't this breed a kind of excess of orderliness, insinuating people and the environment that they live in into striving for a political system, or any system, which could never foster greatness, except a system that could only evaluate things in brute economic terms?

Just like how video games could never exceed the real world in complexity, attempts to maintain a status quo via making a "meritocracy" would only "empower" robotics devoid of creating new merits that could potentially surprise any followers. Very profound contradictions would arise if uniqueness were strived for. Typically, such a system would seek to distinguish three purported merit bases: qualification, contribution, and effort. From the system's point of view, qualification would nevertheless compromise a system's need for equality, social solidarity, and liberal neutrality.[265] Contribution can be assessed through standardized tests and market value, but practical implementation is problematic, questioned for its conflicts with economic growth priorities. Effort, on the other hand, is not considered practical for rewarding income in free markets.[266] And when considering

---

[261] R. Hyde, and P. Cartwright, "Exploring Consumer Detriment in Immersive Gaming Technologies," *J Consum Policy*, 46(2023): 335-361. https://doi.org/10.1007/s10603-023-09544-9

[262] Ibid.

[263] Ibid.

[264] C.A. Haag, *Hermeneutical Death* (Independently Published, 2019), 558.

[265] B. Sachs-Cobbe and A. Douglas, "Meritocracy in the political and economic spheres," *Philosophy Compass*, 2024: e12955. https://doi.org/10.1111/phc3.12955

[266] Ibid.

"the moral costs" of political meritocracy, it would include potential social stratification, compromised equality, and possible corruption from the system's point of view.[267] If we are to attempt to apply even a meritocracy in a technological system, never in history will we ever stray so far away from the great creative works of aesthetics that we so much gawk at when we visit museums and other historical preservation places. A true "merit" that would blow people's heads off regarding how one would rightfully react to a charismatic "other" can't ever be classified as a meritocracy. Modern meritocracy, by institutionalizing a system of rewards based on predefined criteria, will just freeze individual expression and the pursuit of unique paths to power. We would run into problems of the impossibility of fairness when trying to artificially craft a system that is perfectly fair because it may either create a single definition of fairness at the expense of others,[268] or "anomalous exceptions" would just be predictions with perfect accuracy. [269] Where would the fun be, especially with the latter?

Meritocratic systems here might reward conformity and adherence to normies, but the system's focus on measurable achievements can suppress the dynamism inherent in the "will to power."[270] The values only promote things like mere hard work and qualifications (which are things that lower men can repeat if they follow a redundant instruction) over individual genius and creativity which are the only things that can actually be done to "exit through" modernity's soystem. In Nietzschean terms, try peeping beyond conventional notions of "good and evil,"[271] in which true greatness lies in exploring new values—one's own will. The meritocratic convention, with its standardized criteria, represents a static system that hinders "real shit" creation. Political systems as a whole are so concerned with the regulation and control of the masses, the domain that is incapable of true self-overcoming. Modern politics attempting a meritocratic system is fundamentally about maintaining order and equality (albeit just attempting to achieve such in different ways, mattering only to the subservient types within the established boundaries.[272] This says a lot about society: why isn't there a gamer party? (Not a LAN (local area network) party, but a political party for gamers). I consider myself not a "demoncrap" nor "repubicant" but rather a "radical gamerist," who believes that conquest should be a human right just like in the "adventure combat gaming," but in real life). Doesn't it inevitably embody herd morality by artificially emphasizing the common good over the development of superior individuals?

The world becomes really lame when we only see herds follow another "herd." It is so prevalent today. I still think that most people for now would question this, and part of the severe widespread mental health crisis is because open-ended greatness is so absent

---

[267] Ibid.

[268] R. Berk, H. Heidari, S. Jabbari, M. Kearns, and A. Roth, "Fairness in Criminal Justice Risk Assessments: The State of the Art," *Sociological Methods & Research*, 50(2021): 3-44. https://doi.org/10.1177/0049124118782533

[269] J. Kleinberg, S. Mullainathan, & M. Raghavan, "Inherent trade-offs in the fair determination of risk scores," *8th Innovations in Theoretical Computer Science Conference* (ITCS 2017). https://doi.org/10.48550/arXiv.1609.05807

[270] F. Nietzsche, *The Will to Power* (Vintage Books, 1968).

[271] F. Nietzsche, *Beyond Good & Evil: Prelude to a Philosophy of the Future* (Vintage Books, 1989).

[272] L. Smith, "Politics matters most to slaves," *Luke Smith's Webpage* (9th May 2020), https://lukesmith.xyz/articles/politics-matters-most-to-slaves/.

nowadays. However, the system does a good job of making it seem like certain normies are worthy of being master leaders. Take brain rot entertainers today, for example. They are the most platformed herd members of today's era. These should be the jesters of today, and everyone deep down knows this because it is already "mainstream talk" that "ocF StOP MaKinG TheM FamOus." Funnily, the same people who complain are the same terminally online soyboys who need the entertainment to remain functional—these worshippers are the same people experiencing increased depression and stress levels.[273] Today's jesters can entertain, and I am fine with that for just the herdish types at least, but they shouldn't be held at as high of a pedestal as the great heroic ancient warlords of the past. But because modern society has such inherent boredom, how desperate have people become for the next sedatives to the point where they'd cock suck them?

What about those who are not slavish enough to submit to the diddlers of the modern era? When those individuals feel unable to manifest through the established channels, this existential energy just freezes—this may arise because appropriate channels are invisible or too soy to match their unique expression. The energy cannot be simply expelled (even through ejaculating). Maybe they get paralyzed by fear, and risk becoming "hollow" within the normies. In most cases, they have already tried to persist in conventional pursuits purported to bring fulfillment, yet these end up too lame—stuff like mere entertainment would feel too fake or predictable. What could they do other than forge the existential space themselves?

Non-Real-Life Gaming

Returning to my apartment, I felt a sense of disconnection from the world outside. The psychotherapist's advice to play video games felt like a retreat from my active lifestyle. Almost like she was scamming me, even though I didn't pay a dime for that appointment. It's also really funny because usually, psychotherapists are there to advise people to quit certain vices that are supposedly an interference that prevents people from fully participating in society. I firmly believe that this is just another example of controlled opposition. There is a reason why video games and movies are some of the most talked about topics in media. Think of this: Why aren't there any "news" all about philosophical discoveries, and that books are so seldom discussed in media? I rarely see content about "long texts" unless they are ghostwritten autobiographies by a celebrity who has either played a role in a movie or a voice actor in a video game. The establishment doesn't want you to experience real philosophy because the deeply intellectual ones are what get you to question the decisions of the American government and the mercantile elite.

I found my old gaming computer in a corner, covered in a thick layer of dust. I have no idea why I hadn't sold it by now—I hadn't touched it in almost four years, and just looking at it brought back memories of some of the laziest periods of my life. Back then, I was addicted to games, spending countless hours in virtual worlds while neglecting my physical health and real-world responsibilities. I recall myself looking like a baby sitting down as I wear only my white underwear and nothing else as I show my overly offseason physique to nobody but my bedroom to feel less like I was a guy whose physique was

[273] R.A. Sansone and L.A. Sansone, "I'm Your Number One Fan," *Innovations in Clinical Neuroscience*, 11(2014):39-43. PMID: 24653942; PMCID: PMC3960781.

receding; I'd already look like an average obese guy if I wore regular clothes. I looked down to see my current condition. My cardio has been very heavy for the past months, so I was on the shredded side now. I'm not competition-ready, but I could decide to prep for a bodybuilding show and be five weeks out already. But given the overwhelming hatred toward the beauty of the city now, I figured that bodybuilding competitions would be banned in the near future. So, as much as I hate to say, I was willing to give video games a shot. Maybe reconnecting with an old hobby would provide some solace.

I powered the computer on, and the familiar hum of the fans brought a nostalgic fake smile to my face. Sometimes, nostalgia can be kind of bad, but the fake smile I'd creak is due to myself trying to appreciate the people who brought me into life in the first place. The colorful lights, probably designed by and to appeal to a fifth grader who loves designs that resemble futuristic spaceships, flickered on, casting a neon glow around the room. But the machine was sluggish, struggling to boot up properly. It was stuck on a default logo along with a moving dotted circle that indicated an uncertain loading time. I remember when that scared me as a child, pathetically, especially in the case of cursors that have that loading infinite circle on the operating systems that don't even let you click on anything until it finishes.

I browsed through my online game library as the computer finally ran smoothly. I mentioned earlier that trying to own things digitally is cringe as it is impossible anyway, but bear with my seeming hypocrisy as restrictions to digital downloads were long already a thing. I was surprised that the ticking time bomb of digital recall hasn't reached its end yet.

If I was going to dive back into gaming, it had to be something at least somewhat educational. After an extensive and nostalgic review of my collection, I came across ARK: Surrogate Evolved, a game that had fascinated me years ago. This game that I had a love-hate relationship with is an online game where players must survive being stranded on one of several maps filled with roaming engineered dinosaurs and other prehistoric animals, natural hazards, and potentially hostile human players. It is one of those games that artificially inflates its own difficulty by jacking up the sheer time it takes to achieve things. For example, one of the main mechanics and activities in the game is taming the prehistoric creatures. It took twelve fucking hours to tame a Tyrannosaurus at launch.

What intrigued me most was how the game provided a taste of what nature really is. The survival game genre tapped into a deep-seated human urge to experience wildlife and create tools and activities that we intrinsically desire to do. The problem with this is that it does such a great job at doing so to the majority of the population because the psychologists who work alongside the programmers have a really basic idea of how the average person reacts to certain stimuli.

Deciding this was the only distraction from the city's anti-nature architecture, I launched ARK: Surrogate Evolved. As expected from the first and last time I saw it, the game took a long time to load—its unoptimized spaghetti code was infamous among gamers.

Finally, the game loaded, and I was greeted with a message from one of my old online gaming colleagues: "Long time no see." It was LEGENDZ.

Sitting in front of my computer, I remembered our adventures in ARK: Surrogate Evolved. Back then, I had spent countless hours breeding creatures, a feature in the game that allowed players to breed improved creatures through eggs with non-mammals and gestation with mammals. On the online servers, I bred and sold eggs and mammal babies with "ideal" genetics in high demand for real money. Since I didn't have time to do the actual trades, LEGENDZ, who owned one of the largest shops in the community, did them for me (although the fucker took a 50% cut). All I had to do was breed, and when a release was ready, I sent the breeding supplies over to his server.

On a side note, in multiplayer, there are two major game modes—PVP (player versus player) and PVE (player versus environment). In PVP mode, players can kill others, destroy each other's buildings, and kill each other's dinosaurs. The player will always be the biggest threat. On the other hand, PVE mode prevents players from destroying each other in every significant aspect, except maybe griefing, which involves luring wild creatures to the victim's base. Interestingly, on PVE, it isn't really a survival game—there's literally nothing practical to your survival left to do. Many players on PVE still play and make up their own artificial goals because that is all that is left to do. No players to defend against. That is where the game's dino breeding mechanics become their main play method. Mainly breeding for dino combat stats mutations, health, and melee damage (some also breed for farming/mobility characteristics, such as stamina and carry weight capacity). This is an iterative process, where each stat mutation takes days to over a week, depending on how long it takes for said creature to mature. The player would then breed that new male stud with the hundreds of females. There is a limit to how high a stat can get via mutations, which is capped based on the game's integer limit. It usually takes months to years for it to be reached, again depending on the maturation length of the Dino. Between PVP and PVE, breeding has teleological differences. Super mutated creatures on PVP have a meaningful purpose—raiding other tribes' bases and defending bases. But on PVE, they are grandly pointless, as they will defeat the PVE enemies just as easily as nonmutated dinos. Once the "persistent" PVE breeder reaches the mutation limit and wins the breeding market race, they will likely have the desire to max out another dino. And the cycle continues. Meanwhile, in PVP, the goalpost is defined by how strong the creature must be to compete in war.

Anyway, I was one of those who bred on official PVE, because I had a hyperfocus intense fascination with the idea of heredity even as a child, and I figured that the time I would have to spend in combat on PVP to defend my breeding cave rather than allocating all energy into speed breeding would be too much for what it was worth. Also, I wouldn't want any of my breedlines on PVP mode to be stolen in an inevitable raid by aimbotters—this sounds cucked not gonna lie. But I remembered the thrill of those days, the excitement of achieving the perfect breed, and the satisfaction of some wealth.

However, as I pondered over these memories, a sense of gloom crept in. The breeding system in ARK was highly limited, reducing the complexities of life from all the hundreds of possible skeletal muscles, the dozens of organs and their functional units, the robustness of the bones themselves, which has many factors too, and more than I don't even know of because I haven't taken biology beyond high school. It's all reduced to health, stamina, oxygen, food, weight, melee damage, and speed.

I recalled the nihilistic feelings I had when min-maxing a certain dinosaur, especially the Spinosaurus, to have only health and melee damage toward an ideal maximum that is not subject to change. The ideal maximum stat didn't reflect reality because, in real life, breeding creatures purely with financial interests in mind often led to inbreeding and sicknesses. This realization repulsed me. The game, once a source of joy and distraction, now felt like a hollow echo of the real world, especially the local area in its current state.

As I stared at the screen, another message from LEGENDZ popped up: "Did you get the new ARK update? What creature will you breed now?"

I typed back: "Hey, I'm not sure. You should see how much I developed myself. I am even bigger than your in-game character, and we know how batshit crazy we can make their proportions in the character creation screen. It's like I curated the slider of my lats, abs, chest, shoulders, arms, neck, traps, quads, forearms, and calves. GAMER UNCOOL."

LEGENDZ replied quickly: " I AM GONNA KIDNAP YOU MATE!"

I sighed and started typing, trying to articulate my thoughts. "It's not just that. The game's breeding system is limited and doesn't reflect reality. It's like reducing life to a few stats and numbers. Even then, seeing the human player stats the same is laughable. It feels empty like we're just chasing an ideal that doesn't need us to exist. Plus, the creatures we bred would be sickly and inbred if this were real life. I bet they would look like you, haha. But for real, if you even consider how fast we were mutating the stats and how many females we were mating at once for the high odds of getting a mutation on each breed cycle, that will kill the male via penis explosion because you can't ejaculate thousands of times at the same time." Following that, I attached a series of images of me shirtless, flexing my individual muscle groups, showing how differentiated I am morphologically and how LEGENDZ wouldn't quite have the same physique even if he got his muscles to the size of mine.

LEGENDZ surrendered. "Well, that's a nope from me."

Chapter Thirteen: Min-Max

Even though "bioleninism" is a sub-subbranch of Leninism, aren't its implications far worse, leaving ugly marks much more permanent? Initially, Leninism was founded as an appeal to the lowest members of society. It isn't because of some communistic thing that is purely based on catering to those who are poor, that a lot of the weak minds were shouting for. Leninism was for those who were resentful, hardly because of their "poor asses" but largely due to their degrading criminal activity, prostitution, and other degenerate stuff that deserve to be weeded out. [274] With bioleninism, the most "soyboy" members of society come together and impose their will on the populace. If a man's morphological characteristics weren't favored by subjects, he would be inclined to be very resentful, especially if he is desperate as fuck just to have a sliver of coochie. As such, if he were to ever see a shredded "Chad," he'd seethe and then try his best to imagine that "Chad" is the worst-case bad-looking version of him. But if that doesn't work, would he just adopt a worldview that shreds anything that is "good," where any time someone takes the form of something of high prowess, they have to be torn down to their level?

Nature has a way of favoring those who have certain qualities in various contexts. For a reason, it generally favored those who have strong muscles, the adventurous types, and the geniuses. But since herd morality is the dominant system in the modern world, we'd be inclined to be in a world of morphological regression. The ruling class, whether consciously or unconsciously, deliberately wants to lower the strength of the populace, therefore to cheaply make their relative power higher. But in a technological system, they can act on it in a way where it doesn't seem like such to the average normie—isn't there a weird thing going on right now, where bioleninism is happening in a very insidious manner?

Essentially, once civilization reaches a certain scale, the necessity for active philosophy becomes paramount, as social evolution ceases to drive progress. We must be wary of relying excessively on a pseudo-philosophy, or "pure rationality as controlled authorities," which can lead to a self-domestication where strict and eventually lame robust social norms are perceived as systemic necessities. Societies would then begin to engage in the systematic self-domestication of their members by imposing formalizations on individual traits (akin to assigning fixed undebatable numerical values), reducing them to mere cogs within the larger mechanism, ignoring the dynamism of nature. This process conserves energy that would otherwise be devoted to fostering self-reliant individuals. In this framework, the object's rational calculations overshadow the informal and nuanced processes by which individuals traditionally assess qualities such as prosocial behavior. Consequently, these informal assessments are devalued and ultimately eliminated by the system. The only cognitive levels that persist are those required to sustain object-oriented societies, which are minimal. This scenario serves as a cautionary tale about the potential consequences of the engineering of a phenotypic repository—doesn't it already exist in an abstract sense, in possession of a demented figure?

---

[274] V. McLeod, *Clown World Chronicles* (VJM Publishing, 2020), 51.

Regarding biopolitics, there is a critique of technological rationality related to spatial transformation, which treats individuals as populations rather than distinct beings.[275] It presents the "production of space" theory, following it by highlighting how power infiltrates society through the division and distribution of space, an idea that is extended by noting that modernity involves spatial expediency to control and manipulate the populace. How it is currently established is that "nature-editing" leads to beings that embody the tension between past and future, affecting the present—modernity involves the compression and extension of time and space, making distant events and places feel closer and more immediate—globalization and technological advancements blur traditional boundaries. The extension and separation of time and space in modernity have led to the replacement of present realities with bland predictions of the future—this erasure of natural boundaries can lead to a kind of nihilism where moral and ethical considerations are undermined. The problem is that the supposed experts and the elites of our modern time, for that matter, do their blind rationalities by having an already implicit phenotypic repository conjured up in their heads, which may already have certain traits they deem desirable (like a certain vague way they determine what is good looking or intelligent). When they start "executing" such, they will end up with supposedly "technically smart" people (metrics like these are just overhyped measurements that only assess how much one can benefit the technological system and nothing else). While everyone may start to have identical kinds of "desirable" physical features, isn't it just another way of creating a space of no individual at all as it is just a cluster of identical cells that form a fragile pseudo-organism?

A warning against the modern world is that if men were just treated like stallions, them being intergenerationally propagated via careful, rational planning, the resulting civilization is either beautiful animals destined for (unfashionable) work, or if the individualistic or utilitarian element predominates, a stronger law leads life to regress or go extinct.[276] But a whole different concern is the implication of when the obsolete, most herdish kinds of minds (to the point of being non-human, but an entity that can only execute objective calculations with no appreciation of spontaneity and beauty) climb into power with access to all the potential morphological characteristics in its fingertips. There are already "higher ups" saying that people may become hackable animals, which can be embedded in a system that understands us better than we understand ourselves and can predict our feelings and decisions—manipulating our feelings and decisions and ultimately making decisions for us…[277] Furthermore, some corporations and governments will be able to systematically hack the people. Shockingly, would mankind have to get used to the idea that we are no longer "mysterious souls"? Beings that are as easy to manipulate as editing with a noob-level UI (user interface)?

In the realm of replication, there is this idea that emergent replicators would rise as a form that ultimately supersedes its predecessor, a phenotypic revolution, something that

[275] Y. Chen, X. Luo, "Reflection on Gene Editing from the Perspective of Biopolitics," *Nanoethics*, 18(2024): 4. https://doi.org/10.1007/s11569-023-00451-4

[276] J. Evola, *Revolt Against the Modern World* (Inner Traditions, 1995), 170.

[277] Yuval Harari, "Read Yuval Harari's blistering warning to Davos in full," *World Economic Forum*, (24th January, 2020), https://www.weforum.org/agenda/2020/01/yuval-hararis-warning-davos-speech-future-predications/

may happen again to our detriment. It is posited that a previous "phenotypic revolution" happened when deoxyribonucleic acid emerged from ribonucleic acid, resulting in a current dominion where DNA now prevails almost universally, relegating RNA to a mere supporting role within the apparatus of DNA-centric life.[278] In a technological system context, we may consider databases a potential new replicator. Here, one's "essence," digitally encapsulated within the confines of computer storage, becomes subject to deliberate selection, likely conforming to societal paradigms of fitness, effectively rendering the individual a mere component of an expansive mechanism, especially under propagandistic influence. This perfected method of trait curation for a technologically advanced society implies a potential for digital replication to surpass and ultimately declare itself above DNA as the principal replicative agent. Even though this supposedly makes more "desirable people" efficiently, it would create a heightened vulnerability for mankind, rendering it more susceptible to manipulation by the rabble. Consider the protracted journey to decipher the complexities of DNA; conversely, any hypothetical outside rational being could, with relative ease, master the rudiments of morphological databases, provided they can parrot fundamental linguistic and mathematical principles, therefore being able to straightforwardly "control" us with clear cut instructions. This "nature cuckening" is a far cry from the past, when a more noble conquering elite probably went to some length to hide its foreign origins, adopting instead convoluted mythologies and unity with the conquered.[279] Why would we do the dirty work for the hypothetical mechanistic filth gravitating toward dominance? The grave concern is: isn't this something we could do about?

In considering the roles of "organic versus machines," especially within the context of the flourishing life's natural drive for space, it becomes clear that machines—no matter how advanced—will always be on par with the emergent properties found in living beings. Circuit boards, for example, cannot match the sophisticated, adaptive processes, particularly when examined through the lens of consciousness and self-repair. Even if machines were to develop self-replicating systems, the selection would generally favor only their more durable versions, but they would remain bound by their initial programming and limited sensory perceptions—and would not have the epic-looking physiques of "Chad" bodybuilders. Such a system would lean toward "X-focalization," not rooted in subjective experiences—at best only simulating bare introspection.[280] They would remain operating within predetermined confines—ultimately "hackable" by rabble logic?

Furthermore, there's a case to be made for preserving a certain honor and agency in life ascension. By contemplating our own natures, we would risk creating a "static framework" similar to a forced dependency on external mechanisms that are akin to the system's form of expansion. A more honorable pursuit might lie in developing forms of "dynamic cryptography" within ourselves to prevent external manipulation, adapting in

---

[278] J. Gariépy, *The Revolutionary Phenotype: The Amazing Story of how Life Begins and how it Ends* (Elora Editions, 2018).

[279] C. Alamariu, *Selective Breeding and the Birth of Philosophy* (Independently Published, 2023), 96.

[280] I. Kaminsky, "Do robots dream of escaping? Narrativity and Ethics in Alex Garland's Ex-Machina and Luke Scott's Morgan," *AI & Soc*, 36(2021): 349-359. https://doi.org/10.1007/s00146-020-01031-w

ways that are unpredictable to the rabble logic. Rather than surrendering control of our own nature by cucking our bioinformatics in accessible repositories, thus enabling the passive forces of mechanization to "hack" us, we should ascend through internal resilience. Put it this way: what if a "supreme computer with all the information in the universe" exists? Keep in mind, that this is already principally wonky, for if a society has the computing power to predict its own development, this society would have to be more complex than the present one, and the complexity of a society will grow right along with its computing power because the society's devices are a part of the society.[281] Even then, if a model has too many parameters, it would result in "overfitting," where too many parameters impede the performance of the model because the model would end up sensitive to any small changes in data.[282] Wouldn't everyone in such a society have to be extremely meek and weak (unable to have agency) just to compromise for the sake of the model?

Hear me out fellas, let's be honest: wouldn't it yet be preferable to face an adversary with clear boundaries—something physical, even if in the form of hostile robots—than to slide into a form of "plantationization" under mechanization's soft control? There's a noble aspect to facing clear challenges with the agency, even if this comes in the form of violent confrontation with machines, rather than submitting passively to the automated systems that would assume our nature and limit our potential under their control. Then, we must wonder… in advancing for space, are we creating a future of greater autonomy and conquest, or a life under nerdish oversight?

So how are we going escape this shitty paradigm of artificial rationality, especially when we collectively necessitate "jumping off the soil"? There is already some discussion about possible solutions. One could be geoengineering, which involves making extraterrestrial environments hospitable through techniques like terraforming,[283] which "focuses against" human enhancement due to concerns about exploitation, loss of human dignity, and unintended consequences. Proponents of geoengineering argue that geoengineering avoids the moral pitfalls of modifying human nature and respects the intrinsic value of natural environments.[284] But don't these objections assume that there isn't an actual meddler directing how they would be executed? In defense of ascending mankind, I'd say as for modifying humans, the philosopher wouldn't necessarily come up with a base "dehumanizing" perfect theoretical morphology like how a kid would do some boring nerdish "fact-finding" to find one singular player build to beat a specific mission in a video game. A ruling class with real thinking and meddling capabilities would allow room for thinking according to world context changes. Perhaps this would be similar to how the Spartan Hoplites back then underwent some morphological progress as they exerted tension against the Helots, which would indirectly favor the stronger Spartans.[285] Such a decision maker under this is akin to a type of ruler who, unlike a conventional one,

---

[281] T. Kaczynski, *Anti-Tech Revolution: Why and How* (Scottsdale: Fitch & Madison, 2020), 20.

[282] D.M. Hawkins, "The problem of overfitting," *Journal of chemical information and computer sciences*, 44(2004): 1-12. https://doi.org/10.1021/ci0342472

[283] M. Balistreri and S. Umbrello, "Modifying the Environment or Human Nature? What is the Right Choice for Space Travel and Mars Colonisation?" *Nanoethics*, 17(2023): 5. https://doi.org/10.1007/s11569-023-00440-7

[284] Ibid.

[285] E. Dutton, *Breeding the Human Herd* (Imperium Press, 2023), 186.

rules dynamically—expansive and ready to anticipate the turns of the enemy.[286] So for space colonization, couldn't promoting a culture that values exploration and adaptability be beneficial for establishing and maintaining the function of colonies in different spaces, without falling for the problems of artificial rationality?

Assumptions aside, there is a point to be said that neither pure geoengineering nor pure human modification is inherently superior, and both can have context-specific moral and practical implications.[287] A philosophical leader, rather than a clunky soyentist who can only rationally-empirically study either in isolation, may direct a society's progress to successful conquest by simultaneously passing both through hermeneutical tests. Of course, to address the soyboys, could they direct their people in a way such that if people were genuinely soy on an intrinsic level, they could be persuaded out of an inferiority complex by viewing themselves as fodder to nature's mysteries to feel some sense of competence?

Animal Same?

After my intense conversation with LEGENDZ, I stood up to stretch, feeling the tension ease out of my muscles. It felt like I had just slept because it was the longest time period that I had ever sat without taking a standup break. I was about to shut off my computer (Yes, you know, when I actually power off computers, it is a sign that I would not touch it for a very long time or for the rest of my life) when I heard a knock on my apartment door. I wasn't expecting anyone, especially not close friends—Ryan was still in the hospital, and I had distanced myself from others. Assuming it was my parents, I walked over to the door and opened it. But it wasn't them who went knocking. Standing there was Stacy… she looked stunning, wearing a clean cyan dress that hugged her waist perfectly and made her back more visible. She ensured the dress was as far away from her shoulders as possible to maximize arm exposure. The dress had no crinkle, indicating it had been meticulously ironed. She wore high heels so high that they brought her almost to my eye level, even though I was six feet tall. But more striking were her calves, which were now even more defined since the high heels were forcing her to contract the muscle. Her hair was intricately braided, likely by herself, because she looked like the type to have dentist hands. And her makeup was expertly applied—just enough to enhance her natural beauty without being excessive. I always laugh when women try to look "more increased" by maximizing makeup, but they always miss the point that, just like music volume, mere quantity is a dumb way to measure aesthetics. Women who wear too much makeup literally look like every other woman who does as well.

"Hello," she said, her voice smooth and confident. As we were in the quiet space of the apartment, I noticed her voice was much more normal and higher than I thought. Her physique makes her seem like the type of woman with an oversized clit and Adam's apple because of potential steroid use. But I guess she was actually natty holy shit (again, no

---

[286] C. Alamariu, *Selective Breeding and the Birth of Philosophy* (Independently Published, 2023), 158.

[287] M. Balistreri and S. Umbrello, "Modifying the Environment or Human Nature? What is the Right Choice for Space Travel and Mars Colonisation?" *Nanoethics*, 17(2023): 5. https://doi.org/10.1007/s11569-023-00440-7

homo, Stacy isn't THAT muscular—I am exaggerating it to minimize the chances of woke robocops burning this book).

"Hi," I replied, still trying to process her unexpected presence. I was immediately disappointed in myself because I knew I could have said more than just a "hi" and added something cooler, just as I would have rehearsed encounters with a woman in my head a million times, but I was just too stunned.

Without missing a beat, Stacy started asking a series of questions. She sounded really sexy as she did, similar to when she talked to me at the gym, raspy in a good way. Like her breath would smell like a mint chocolate icing cookie that is unchewed.

"Have you ever drunk alcohol or taken hard drugs?"

"No," I answered honestly. "I've never touched alcohol or drugs. I have excellent self-restraint, and I've seen firsthand the consequences of addiction. Since I have extremely high empathy that is genuine, I can literally feel pain when I see addicts in person. Not that I think they are necessarily good people, but the imagined pain is so bad that it's not something I want to be a part of."

She nodded, seeming satisfied with my answer. "Have you ever taken steroids? Your physique is insanely muscular, something that's usually unattainable for someone with average genetics. I know that in every corner of social media, everyone would call you a juicehead, but that is possibly just a denial of individual differences."

I smiled, remembering my childhood photos. "No steroids. I am naturally strong. Here, take a look." I grabbed an old photo album and showed her a picture of me when I was younger, after lifting for only a few weeks. Even then, I was a hulk of a kid.

Stacy glanced at the photos, clearly impressed. But she had other reactions. I could see her see the darkness in my eyes that I still have to this day, the despair. She glanced at my face and nodded. "You have always been like this, haven't you?"

"Yeah, I am born for war."

Then, she quickly asked a question, catching me off guard. "Are you a video gamer?"

I hesitated. I knew Stacy would highly disapprove if I said yes, especially considering her likely values and lifestyle. Shit, my computer fans at the back were somehow acting up even when the damn thing was of, and I knew I was going to be subject to an outcome that I didn't want. I had flashbacks to just before high school when kids started to get to a phase where playing video games began to be the uncool thing.

Just as I was about to respond, a loud, angry, and desperate scream echoed through the apartment hallway. The sound was jarring, cutting through the tense silence between us. Stacy looked back through the hallway, her face registering recognition. She made a sour-looking squinty face that made it look like she just tasted pee. "Oh, that's Steve," she said casually, like the typical movie trope where "the diva" refers to a random crazy simp who is either super good-looking or super ugly.

Confused, I blurted out, "Who, what, where, when, why, how?" I was beginning to lowkey feel like I was not alone in the newfound love area I was in and sensed like a wild animal that there was some competition around. I was trying to seek what the hell it was using a tool that I learned in language arts class when we were to learn how to analyze short story plots. Little did I know, the guy I was about to meet was himself a short story.

Before Stacy could answer my oddly general but effective question, the mysterious visitor stormed in and pushed past her. He was a wiry man with wild eyes and seemed to be heading straight for me. I froze and tried to do a tense pose where I lock my joints because I tend to find it harder to fall into the ground when I do that.

"How dare you talk to my girl like that!" Steve shouted, his face contorted with rage. Without warning, he headbutted me. He awfully reminded me of a black and white family cat named Boe. Boe was the kind of cat who interacted with objects just with his head. He would open doors without turning the know by brute forcing them. He would even cuddle people's legs so hard that it would hurt.

Stacy quickly interjected, "Steve is my ex-boyfriend. I'm all done with him. Steve, how many times have I told you that we are broken up officially?!"

"I need some pussy for once in my life!" Steve said, his voice trembling as if trying to get sympathy. I didn't buy any of it because what the fuck is the point of pussy when he is this broken and wouldn't be capable of having kids?

I barely registered their words as Steve and I started to grapple. Fortunately, I was much more muscular than Steve, and fighting back was effortless. I made sure to steer our fight out of the apartment to avoid damaging my place. I would also not care about the apartment being damaged because I was anticipating that I was going to not be able to pay the rent anymore, and my landlord is an asshole who is increasing the rent as much as my gym decreased their rates.

Steve and I wrestled like wild animals, headbutting each other like bulls while our arms flailed at each other. Steve had a really wide alien head, while my jaw formed a head as square as Steve from the hit video game made by notchman, "Mining Crap," so the locking of heads was actually perfect from a shape puzzle perspective. As we pushed and shoved, we made our way from my apartment unit to the hallway and ultimately outside to the parking lot. Stacy followed us, looking oddly relaxed, confident in my ability to handle the situation. She gave me a thumbs up. Steve, being the desperate and delusional man, thought she was giving it to him, so he smiled at her. She made a face of disgust.

By the time we reached the parking lot, Steve was visibly tired. Desperation flashed in his eyes as he pulled a knife from his pocket.

"Oh no, knives are my weakness!" I said jokingly, trying to keep the situation from escalating too far. I put my hands up while I slowly backed away. I also was in attack mode, ready to use my forearms as meat shields. I may have to sacrifice some of the brachioradialis mass, which is one of the body parts I find more difficult to grow, but I told myself that the scars would look millions of times better than the trashy corporate brand forearm tattoos that normies get.

Seeing a nearby tree branch, I grabbed it and used it to strangle Steve from behind. He flailed and protested, "That's not fair!" His hypocrisy was almost laughable.

"I was just being resourceful," I said. "How about you be fair and at least use a knife made out of wood?"

As he struggled, it became clear that Steve was losing the fight. His movements slowed, and he began to accept that he was about to lose consciousness. Just before he passed out, he surprised me by whispering, "Thank you."

I let him drop to the ground gently.

Stacy walked over, looking slightly exasperated but mostly relieved. "I have a lot to explain," she said, looking at me with sincerity. "I've already told Steve that I didn't want him, but he became crazily obsessed and kept chasing after me. Ever since the city has gone mad with the n-word passes, he has become more obsessed due to not having anything else to do with his life. He was already desensitized of jerking off, so I've been constantly afraid of getting raped by him."

I nodded, understanding the gravity of her situation. "Sorry you dealt with that."

"It gets even worse. Steve called me a transwoman only because muscularity is just so unimaginable to him. He's never seen true masculinity." Stacy raised her eyebrows as she studied my muscles. "He even said that anyone who'd pursue me is gay."

"Haha gotta love those insecure fucks. They make themselves sound even weaker. There is nothing wrong with being attracted to a ripped woman if you yourself are a ripped man to balance things out, and if anything, it could possibly mean you yourself are more masculine, to be able to have that woman at the bottom and still look like a top." (Just reminding you readers again, no homo. Stacy isn't THAT muscular—I am exaggerating it to minimize the chances of woke robocops burning this book).

Stacy took a deep breath, then looked me straight in the eyes. "Would you like to go out with me?" she asked, her voice steady.

A broad smile spread across my face. "Woo, gamer moment! I just meaningfully spoke to a girl! Okay, yes."

As we stood there in the parking lot, with Steve unconscious at our feet, it felt like a strange but perfect beginning to a new chapter in both our lives. I mark that chapter by doing a soft finishing move. I walked over to Steve's body, placed my foot on his neck, bent down, and did my loudest alpha roar as I could right at his face. I knew Steve would hear my "Chad" voice even through his dreams—he was probably having a nightmare of him running away from a demon in his mind, and the demon was screaming in a distorted version of my alpha call.

"It looks like you are still in sigma combat mode," Stacy says, looking at me with a game face. "Well, if you want, you can continue; you have a new opponent." She pointed right at her chest as she tried to do a pec bounce, which did crazy shit with her actual tits, the tits moving and shifting across the surface of the pecs. I saw a challenge.

"Let's do it inside."

Stacy and I headed back inside my apartment.

"How about a nude mud wrestling challenge?" Stacy asked with a playful glint.

I grinned, feeling a new surge of energy. "You're on." This is something I have always wanted to do. Mud wrestling is something I'd see on television only. I at first found it to be comedic, but over time, as my testosterone skyrocketed as I aged, I started to see it as a genuinely cool kind of ritual.

We set up the pool, filling it with thick, gooey mud. It was messy and absurd, but it was exactly what I needed to show each other's strengths directly and one-to-one, in a fun, harmless way. But as the decreasingly dull activities I was taking on lately, my retard mindset was beginning to wear off and I was starting to understand the implicit true meaning behind what I was going to do with Stacy.

Stacy jumped in first, the mud squelching around her as she laughed. It served as an excellent body tan. I followed, and soon, we were both covered in mud, laughing. The tension of the past few months seemed to melt away with each playful push and pull. But this was only the starting point, and the real tension was about to be *ZOINKED!*

She challenged me with a mock-serious tone, "Think you can take me?"

I laughed. "We'll see about that!"

We wrestled in the mud, slipping and sliding as we tried to get the upper hand. It was ridiculous and exhilarating, the perfect way to release all the pent-up energy and frustration. Despite her smaller size, Stacy was surprisingly strong and agile, making the match more competitive than I had expected. Our laughter echoed through the apartment as we tumbled around in the mud. For a while, it felt like we were in our own world, free from the stress and chaos outside. But in our world, now that we felt like no one could possibly be looking and there would be no more Steves coming to strike, we did it. I eventually shifted my body enough, imagining it lurking in the shadows for a mystical cavern of life. The thing taking place from my imagined perspective is massive as fuck, but it still wasn't easy, so I could tell Stacy's body count was zero and Steve, the loser, was truly a no-life loser. But once the cave was entered, we enjoyed the moment before I passionately splurged the egg-shaped beast with my white paint gun for me to earn the cave's treasures that would be realized in nine month's time.

Eventually, we both collapsed on the edge of the pool, covered in mud and breathless from laughter. I looked over at Stacy, her face smeared with mud but still radiating that confident glow. "This was exactly what I needed," I admitted, smiling at her.

"Me too," she replied, her eyes twinkling. Feeling a newfound sense of joy and excitement after our "mud wrestling celebration," I decided it was time for my first proper outing. I invited Stacy to a trip to the zoo for our first date, and she excitedly agreed. We decided to walk there because, as it turns out, Stacy doesn't city-drive. Holy based.

Upon arrival, we noticed that the zoo, like much of the city, was plastered with the n-word pass art. We hesitated, the oppressive decorations dampening our enthusiasm. But we decided to go in anyway, hoping the animals would make this place the closest to nature we could find in the city. Let me say it now: I do not even endorse zoos in general and believe all animals should be allowed in their natural habitats. People should work towards traveling there if need be. But holy fuck, what we were about to see magnified the unfreeness characteristic of zoos by a ton.

As Stacy and I entered the zoo, we noticed people weirdly chanting the word "Nature!" repeatedly. It was unsettling and robotic. If any parents are reading this, you probably can recall watching elementary school sing songplays. The average ones sound pretty damn creepy if you ask me—monotone and resembling demonic dolls. These "nature!" repeating robots were adult children. Curious, I approached one of the chanters and asked why they were doing it.

"The animals are all staying perfectly still and passive," he explained with a serene smile. "This is nature in its purest form. It's so clean and calm, without any unpleasant bits; that is the whole definition of pure, am I right? For example, pure drinks are the drink alone while unpure drinks have other fluff and dirt in them."

His words hit me like a punch to the gut, both because his analogy was unnecessarily gross and he syllogized like a mainstream academic. I hate the sound of beverages that are designed to replicate the beauty of nature, but then some asshole doesn't have the decency to carefully drink after he eats, so bits of food are just left floating in the drink, and so that drink can't even be shared anymore. I knew this guy was brainwashed by the city's propaganda. Nature isn't supposed to be stagnant and sterile. It's dynamic, vibrant, and full of life. This perverted version of wildlife was nothing more than a façade.

As Stacy and I walked through the zoo, we saw that the animals really were overly behaved like the behavior commands of video game engines that rigidly force an animation rig of a model to repeat a line of code over and over. The lions lounged without hinting of their natural majesty outside their caves for a long time and stood on the hill way too perfectly. They were roaring, but they sounded so perfectly like the default movie intro lion sounds that it was just scripted. When I visited the lion exhibit at a zoo in Singapore, their "roars" were more like honks and grunts rather than stereotypical, but they were genuine and could be heard from inside the body.

And the chimps sat quietly, their usual playful energy replaced by a disturbing stillness. I could see some male ones were about to jerk off out of boredom and during that, I saw a mainstream scientist who was making some observations, probably syllogizing human fapping as natural. It was eerie.

We came across several textual walls displayed throughout the zoo. One sign caught my eye. It read, "These hypnotizing n-word pass posters contain visual stimuli that create the same effect as stress relief for animals as they cannot understand English, keeping them almost completely still for guests to observe 'nature' more easily."

My stomach churned with disgust as I looked at the noble animals, their eyes reflecting a deep sadness. It was as if their spirits had been broken by the city's twisted version of serenity.

Then, something caught my eye. Behind one of the walls near the lion exhibit, I noticed shadows moving. Peering closer, I saw the silhouette of a zookeeper. To my horror, I realized he was putting down a lion that refused to stay still. He first tried to get the lion to follow a piece of paper, which I assumed to be the n-word pass. Then, when the lion stopped moving its head, the man tasered the lion's buttocks. It squealed and then roared in response, scaring the zookeeper, who used a suppressed sniper to finish it off.

The city had effectively mandated the zoo to implement a pseudo-eugenics program, selecting the easier-to-pacify specimens to maximize entertainment. This grotesque form of entertainment was designed to pacify the visitors just as much as the animals. Stacy turned to me; her eyes filled with sadness. "We need to do something about this."

I looked around and scanned the security levels of the zoo. They were all made of aluminum and had fancy lights that indicated the electric wire areas. Determined to free the animals from their digital cages, Stacy and I quickly formulated a plan. The high-tech upgrades to the zoo's enclosures, which were meant to align with the n-word pass propaganda, presented a potential advantage. These upgrades meant a centralized control unit had to be somewhere, managing all the gates. The zoo had never had the gates this advanced before, and I knew that the n-word passes that pacified the citizens sped up the technological progress. But there would have to be a downfall somewhere.

"We need to find the control unit," I said. "If we can unlock the gates, we can set the animals free. And once they are out, I am sure the staff will have too much on their plates."

"Like this?" Stacy said, pointing to a large switch labeled *Master Gate Control*. We exchanged a glance, took a deep breath, and pulled the switch to "unlock.

Alarms blared throughout the zoo. Immediately, we found ourselves surrounded by security officers. They rushed toward us. Panic surged amongst even them because they knew they would probably get fired and have an even tougher time getting hired then.

But then, a chimpanzee swung down from a nearby tree. The chimp, seemingly freed from the spell of the n-word pass posters, cleverly began to joke around and laugh, confusing the guards. It reminded me of when I was little, when I tended to speak less or be mute when I was directly with my father. My father was old as shit when he had me so his hearing was also deteriorating and increasingly selective, so I was sort of raised to be used to having my voice ignored. So when I'd interact with him, I'd do just what the chimp did as it did its playful dances.

The distraction worked, and the guards, now amused, offered the chimp their soda. The chimp took a sip, then spat the soda (either because it thought it tasted horrible or it was intentionally doing a tactic) into the guards' eyes, blinding them. Without missing a beat, the chimps began to rip their faces off with terrifying efficiency.

The visitors, who were the ones feeding this zoo money while endorsing its plans, began to flee in terror as more animals reclaimed their freedom. I was hoping to see some of them get trampled on because some of them were propagandized beyond saving.

"Look at the free animals killing bugmen," Stacy said, her voice filled with awe. "This is what nature is supposed to be."

I nodded, feeling a profound sense of accomplishment.

Chapter Fourteen: Istism

Clearly, the real attributes being selected for in modernity are the exceptionally rational ones, in which they reduplicate the moral framework of modern society. However, at times, archetypical individuals who behold those traits often may at first seem highly incompatible with said framework—but the archetypes insidiously morph closer to modernism's values, and whenever there is any "gap" left, there is some kind of reform to integrate that very property. It is pretty incorrect to think that "Darwinian awards" in any upper direction are even a thing in modern society. People like to cling to the cliché that it "favors the resilient" by making homeless those who cannot hold a job (which is ironically the kind of thing leftists think, as they don't give a fuck about poor people anymore, and only those who disagree with them). But they miss that the very thing not being ruled out is the hyper-meek, calm, and reasonable careerist. There is no honor in adapting to a "technocene," a term coined to describe an environment that consists entirely of technology.[288] Think about it: what would a new Heracles have to be like in modern times to succeed?[289] Would you nipple-twisters think such an ambitious "Chad" would be a successful man in this context?

The fact of the matter is, society would attempt to rehabilitate genuine "Chads" into a corporate drone (or perhaps a soy construction worker who makes ugly modern art), and if that fails, throw him into an asylum. Maybe the most badass scenario would be him being shot down (well, only because modern technology has to dwarf the raw strength of heroes) because all of the institutions turn against him? The "standardized" choice by Heracles is he would have to hide like a pussy. In the technological system where everyone has to be reduced to become the same generic averages to ensure the system's maximum smooth functioning, isn't it the case where any abnormal feature that an individual has, even if it may be an actual enhancement of function, has to be eliminated? (Think of the semantics of "myostatin deficiency," which is informally referred to as "The Hercules Gene"). It is largely believed right now, that the abnormal is lesser than normal.[290] But I think the more big-brained meaning of viewing dysfunctions is that they can potentially be beneficial or negative.[291] Could the former mindset be a motivational precondition to transhumanism?

Modern society, though it "moves" to be more egalitarian, is pretty hostile even towards neurodivergent people, but not in the way you'd think. In the system, I have noticed a strange social happening through social spheres, where "normal people" are blindly claiming that they have "divergence x," throwing it around like there's no tomorrow and as if they even have any idea of what it actually is. While it's true that they

---

[288] A. Cera, "The Technocene or Technology as (Neo)environment," *Society for Philosophy and Technology Quarterly Electronic Journal,* 21(2017): 243–281. https://doi.org/10.5840/techne201710472

[289] F. Disciple, *Resavager Volume 1* (RESAVAGER Media, 2023), 22-23.

[290] L. Dalibert, *Posthumanism and Somatechnologies: Exploring the Intimate Relations Between Humans and Technologies* (University of Twente, 2013).

[291] C. Boorse, "Health as a Theoretical Concept," *Philosophy of Science,* 44(1977): 542-573. http://www.jstor.org/stable/186939

are normies who probably want to appear quirky, this kind of quirkiness might have some interplay to some "reduced" kind of variant of that affliction. A certain kind of divergence has several things that may be incompatible with modern society: Lots of anxiety in general, easily annoyed when disturbed from routines, difficulty expressing feelings and emotions, difficulty recognizing or understanding other's emotions, withdrawal in any stressful conversation or situation, and extreme interest in a particular field that doesn't advance normie careers. When considering certain archetypes with such a wide range of properties, the severe constraining selective mechanisms of the system would trend towards modifying the average person into the meek kinds that will robotically obey imperatives — exhibit only specific subsets of the broader spectrum (such as only desiring mechanistic routines for wagecucking, robotic morality, and perhaps heavy interest only in the kind of robotic knowledge that serves the interest of the technological system). In other words, wouldn't a "real divergence" eventually be universally simplified to something to a kind of lite edition, which you may call "spergistgist"?

Now you may be wondering why I use the word "spergistgists." This term should not provoke aggrieve since, again, I hold the view that no word inherently possesses the quality of offensiveness, and I ensure that this particular term was constructed through the application of flimsy morphological principles. I know this variant word is simplified and misses information about its syntax and some semantics, but isn't this also justified because the pseudo-archetype of normies it refers to is an inherently simplified kind?

It may be the case that most of the population in modern times is already spergistgist in one way or another. It wouldn't seem that way to the normal person, because most themselves are of a divergence from a hermeneutical person too—it has just been "normalized." Spegistgists are characterized by a hyper-fixation to objects, with an inclination to interpret existence with a rigid literalness too, perceiving only the front layer manifestations rather than discerning the essences beneath. Intriguingly, their fixation often gravitates towards mechanized constructs such as automobiles—this perhaps lies in their linear determinism, automobiles captivate due to the regimented infrastructure of the road network, mirroring the predictability with predetermined routes and regulatory signals. Within the confines of an automobile, one's corporeal autonomy is surrendered, substituting chaos with the order that the progeny finds comfort in. Their yearning is for monotonous routines, replicating daily patterns in an unvaried sequence. This mindset reflects the demands placed upon the laboring masses by modern society. It is those who subscribe to this mechanical existence who often amass wealth, thereby perpetuating their lineage and its characteristic disposition. On the other hand, wouldn't those who would be considered typical in the pre-technological age flourish in free zones, while tending to be eliminated as they would tend to crash and burn in one of the overcrowded corners?

So far, I am only discussing the very mild spergistists—so what are the implications of the late-stage modernity ones? For starters, the radical transformation would offer insights into the "hard problem" of "quirk thirst" that you see in certain spergistgists as a subset of the erratic behaviors of individuals who have some autonomy left to resist the excessive order of the system. Such actions can be perceived as inefficiencies within a system, akin to anti-resistance mechanisms within a factory, which might eventually be replaced by the integration of robotic prosthetics. The latent potential within individuals currently labeled as "low functioning" is overlooked due to its narrowly defined expression. However, in the era of prosthetics, an endpoint will be fully realized. For example, have you ever heard about Kurzweilian creepy-ass dreams about transhumanism, where the boundaries of the human form are transcended to such an extent that they transform into fully calculable predictions?

Mr. Jenkins

Realizing the potential disaster that would unfold if the freed animals fled into the city, I had to act fast. Cops would likely kill the animals once they reached downtown because they are likely the biggest pussies amongst the townsfolk now that they are the ones punishing anyone who expresses any difference among the herd. I didn't want a giant out-of-zoo Harambabe moment to happen because those guys don't even have tranquilizers.

Scanning the area, I noticed an exceptionally ginormous truck clearly meant for transporting megafauna. It was highly secured, almost like a battle tank stripped of all its combat accessories and features. The wheels were almost as tall as I am, and I could see that even then, the tires were already squished by the weight of the truck without any animal being inside. With the zookeepers and visitors too distracted by the chaos to stop me, I had a chance to get a good number of the noble animals into the truck. Even though I was sure there would have been purer and more self-respectable ways to save the animals, this looked like a holy grail to me. The only problem was that I needed to learn how to drive a transport truck, especially one designed to carry elephants.

An idea struck me. I remembered that there was a daycare center for adult people (which is located in my college). I had this idea because these people would probably want to have some fun, and this was going to be the way to make their day while following my lead. I turned to Stacy, who was still catching her breath from our escape. "Stacy, wait here. I need to get help," I said urgently. "Even though you are a 'Stacy' and I am a 'Chad' who can walk far, this is going to be a hyper-anomalous situation which wouldn't happen in a sane world in the first place, where we may need a vehicle to drive the animals away, outside of the city."

Without waiting for her response, I sprinted toward the college with immense speed, hoping to sneak in without being noticed. The risk of being recognized was high even if I wore loose clothes because of my vast jawline, but I had no choice. I then walked through the hallways until I reached room 12. *Gosh darn, room 12.* Whenever I'd pass that room, a very specific song would hit me right in the head. When I was just a pre-toddler, much of what was first shoved in front of me was dinosaur documentaries. It was so much that I thought reptiles were the dominant kinds of animals universally. Then, when I first saw and listened to the intro of the Ice Age documentaries, I was disoriented upon seeing the hairier and more socially bonded creatures and thought I was looking at autistic dinosaurs. The funny thing is it would be the other way around, and reptiles would more likely be closer to the autistic-like parts of the animal kingdom due to their lesser tendency to socialize. Still, my young and naïve ass was in the phase in my life when it was undergoing the process of being propagandized.

Luck was on my side. I found a man whom I recognized, Mr. Jenkins, who also happened to be the bus driver of the college. He was eating his lunch, cookies that were shaped like various animals. It's one of those biscuits that would make one thirsty. I approached him quickly, trying to keep my voice calm because if I were to use my default voice, it would cause his fellas to go crazy.

"Mr. Jenkins, I need your help. It's urgent," I said. "I apologize, but you are going to have to have your daily routine disrupted. I know this may sound scary as fuck, but I promise you will have fun."

He looked up, surprised and a bit annoyed. "Awe, come on, man, I need to do some sitting that I have been doing for the last six hours. Also but soon, I've got to drop off some students soon. What do you need? Please, I just want to live, man."

Thinking quickly, I remembered his soft spot for animals. And I do not mean an actual spiritual thing. It is for them what appears right in what they can touch.

"Animals need help," I said. "We freed zoo animals, and they must be transported."

His expression changed instantly. "Animals????!!! You freed? Ahh fuck, stop, don't steal my animal crackers!!!" He used a hand to cover the remainder of his cookies.

"No no no, I mean real animals, the ones that are alive at the zoo of this city. I need you to drive them from the zoo to the outskirts of the city. It won't be so bad; you drive in the city all the time!"

"But what is on the outskirts of the city? Is it safe?"

"Well, um, uh, well, the outskirts aren't as bad as you think. Also, you can just drive back as I can handle the rest of the animals' trip. They just need to be outside of downtown so that the police won't shoot them."

"Ahhhh, you just said 'uh um,' which means you are uncertain about something. Ahhhhh I hate uncertainty!"

"You'll know exactly what it will look like. Remember, the city is so fucking bad that they have already eliminated the nearby nature reserves a decent distance near the edges of the city. It may even be more certain over there than you think, if anything."

"Yay, I will sure help! I can now feel like my favorite superhero!" He began flapping his arms. "Electroman (from the movie 'Electroman') by mistake!"

We hopped into his school bus, and he very thoroughly drove us to the zoo in record time. As we arrived, we were faced with a new challenge.

Standing in front of the massive truck, surrounded by the sounds of the wild animals, Mr. Jenkins and I needed a plan to get them inside. I was so overwhelmed.

The animals were no longer hypnotized by the n-word passes completely, but they were also not accustomed to the idea of getting into a truck willingly. I am probably going to hell for mentioning this, but I wished they were just so I could round them up more quickly; but yeah, they were abused for far long enough. Some of them had severe bruising, deep cuts that were either clotted or still wet and bloody, and one even had an eye that was pure grey, having been blinded by some type of "human."

I decided to start by trying to lure them with food. I dashed to the food production facility and grabbed one of its recyclable bags. God damn, did it smell so bad in there, though. It would have smelled good to the average soyboy—by bad, I mean it gave off feelings when you spend too much having fun relaxing or partying, and you begin to sense that something is wrong. The smell was strangely sterile. I filled the recyclable bag with various kinds of raw meat, berries, leaves, fish, vegetables, cubed cheese, and grass. Exiting the facility felt like a breath of mesmerizing mist because the smell of sweaty animals was just much more preferable. Waving the bag around, I tried to attract any animals nearby. I did it as slowly and intent-looking as possible, trying to mimic the natural movement of wind and water waves. But it didn't work. I opened the bag and looked at whatever the hell the animals had been eating for the past months. The very foods were ridiculously large. But they were ugly, and you would be able to tell they served to fulfill a certain function. They were genetically modified to only nourish and smell good to the animals when they were completely hypnotized and domesticated by the n-word pass architecture. Now that the animals were partially or completely out of that mental state, the food had no effect. They behaved like I wasn't even there, still wandering and confused. I saw some animals manage to find the exit and leave, but luckily, they were the less noble ones, like the giant spiders and lizards. The larger noble ones near there were just too big to fit in the standard human-size gateways.

Frustrated but not defeated, I remembered that the zoo had replaced all the normal food with these genetically modified versions. So, there was no hope of doing the classic cheap cliché of mindlessly picking out what the animals are wired to follow. I needed another strategy. I then decided to use an inverse strategy, in that I do something opposite of positively exciting the animals. I provoked the animals by doing poses that would either make them see me as a threat or just plain annoying, daring to disrespect the strong animals. I did some little tricks I learned in the past, such as wearing a sombrero that I found on the ground, whistling in a way where it sounds like a weak-throated narcissist playing the clarinet, eating the cubed cheese, stomping around as if challenging an opponent, and mocking chimpanzee sound.

I started with the lions, chimpanzees, gorillas, and rhinos, making aggressive and annoying gestures. It caught their attention, and they began to move toward me. I said, "Wow," as I saw them intensely looking me in the eye. They galloped like small but thick mal-malloys aggressively going for a trophy. As I was looking at exotic animals charging from the perspective that includes depth perception, it was a sight to beholden. The chimpanzees especially made me feel like I was looking at a reflection as I began to feel a momentary rage, not due to anger, but for the survival of the two parties.

Just as they were about to reach my flesh, I did a very impressive backflip to dodge them, leading them straight toward the truck's entrance. One by one, the aggressive animals rushed inside the truck, driven by their instinctive reactions. I quickly looked back and saw them hilariously bang their heads on the back wall. "Ya animals got some big heads, eh?" I jokingly say to them because my hunger for challenge urged me to do a rematch against them. But they were a bit too dizzy to accept it for now.

Suddenly, I heard a humanistic "GRRRRR!" and I turned back to the front. It was Mr. Jenkins, looking like a little boy trying to imitate what the animals just did. Drats, I thought. He was probably making a freak-out response to either my strategy of doing some funny shit to get the animal's attention or he himself is a damn animal. I quickly stepped to the side and grabbed his arm before he could join a box full of angry mammals. I calmed him down by telling him it was all okay and would be over soon.

After Mr. Jenkins was back to his idle state, I looked beyond him to see what other noble beings still needed to be kept. It was the less aggressive animals that weren't as responsive. Elephants, horses, and giraffes stood around, confused and uninterested in the chaos. I tried something that I'd seen in movies. I went up to each of them and attempted to slap their asses in the same direction as the truck. But that only led to the primal aggression part without the "correct direction" component—they just ran around in circles, revealing more odd symptoms of mental abuse.

As a last resort, I noticed Mr. Jenkins munching on some animal crackers he had brought for lunch. That was also what kept him passive. I asked him what the fuck the ingredients were, and I knew that he'd know because guys like him tend to have an insane ability to memorize nutrition facts and ingredient lists. As he very precisely listed the calories, fats, sugars, the other nutrients, and then finally, the ingredients, I heard a lot of vegetable stuff. I guess there was some kind of perk to the new city mandating pseudo-vegan shit in response to the pseudo-environmentalists calling for fake nature in improper response to the unnatural architecture. I gotta use the system against the system.

I grabbed one of the crackers and waved it around, hoping it would catch the attention of the more passive animals. To my relief, it worked. The elephants, horses, and giraffes were drawn to the simple snack, willingly boarding onto the back of the truck. It was way more peaceful. No need to use my reflexes and butt strength to do a backflip or even a midair split, as the elephants were really fucking tall. They smiled at me, with their for-animal good-looking dry lips that had some dried grass all over them.

With the truck now filled with the zoo's noble creatures, Mr. Jenkins and I stood back, momentarily catching our breath. The gate of the doorway of the truck's back was essentially a couple of cage-like walls. I pushed both inward until they were sealed. Interestingly, both the animals were not chasing nor running away from one another. I guessed they were just fed. What about the herbivores? Shouldn't they be scared of the eye-at-the-front creatures? The answer would have to lay deeper—something sinister.

The truck was loaded and clearly ready to transport the animals to safety. "Mr. Jenkins, get to the driver's seat, and Stacy, sit beside him," I instructed. No other seat was available, leaving me no choice but to hang in the back of the truck with the zoo animals. Confident in my acrobatic skills and strength, I knew I could handle it. I, of course, had the choice to hang onto the sides of the truck or sit on top of it. Still, that shit was illegal in this city, and given my already bad reputation after being expelled from college and just trying to be myself at the gym, a big ass truck with a three-star police chase-worthy rating surfing it in a city where badassery is illegal would be a moving target. It would have been so easy, though, because the truck had so many hold points and even a few mini platforms that I assume were meant to be markers that this was not an average Joe vehicle.

At the back, the eyes of the carnivores seemed to glow menacingly, staring at me intensely. I couldn't tell if they wanted to eat me or were simply scared. Even the herbivores bore a similar gaze, their eyes wide with curiosity amidst the sudden darkness. As I couldn't see the details of the animals (their fur, nuances of movement, and wide-opened soy mouths), it felt like I was looking around a hyperrealistic museum that simulated the sounds of the dummy animal sculptures via artificial pre-recorded speakers.

Soon, Mr. Jenkins began moving the truck. Initially, the ride was smooth; Mr. Jenkins was highly trained and adept at controlling vehicles to avoid the kind of bumps that would make him freak out. I peeked through the little window between the driver and the box that I was in and saw he was doing the zoo path curves almost perfectly. I could imagine him working for the zoo, driving one of those really long zoo buses that have multiple segments for people who are too lazy sacks of potatoes to actually walk through the zoo.

As the truck exited the zoo through the large vehicle exit and headed into the city, the road began to get bumpy—the unfixed parts of the concrete became unavoidable. This was due to the truck's really wide width. It was also running over the grass on the sides and even the curbs sometimes. Problems started to arise. Mr. Jenkins started to freak out as the order started to dissolve; I could feel the vehicle slightly swerve back and forth, indicating he was getting imprecise with his steering. I knew this would escalate to pure chaos, so I yelled through the window, "Mr. Jenkins, feel free to use Stacy's braided hair as a fidget thing if this is too overwhelming."

Stacy turned back at me with a squint. I gave her a look that sent a message, "It's either that or we crash onto a river or city building." She angrily nodded. Mr. Jenkins then used his right hand to play with her hair without much force, except for some iterations of tug. It seemed to help a bit, and his driving got straighter.

The ride was a frantic blur of dodging and distracting. The animals' growls, roars, and screeches filled the truck, making it feel like a scene straight out of a nightmare. There were many times when the animals were collectively in a position where there was awkwardly nowhere to go on the floor, so I had to climb up the walls using the large nuts and bolts that were sticking out as ladders and then crawl like a spider while doing some hand gestures. As I lay upside down on the ceiling, the elephants were the issue, their ears surprisingly rigid and almost dragging me off. I wondered how many gym plates an elephant ear could support before being ripped off. For some reason, I always imagined actual elephant ears to have about the same level of durability as the elephant ear carnival food, which is really unhealthy. DARN YOU FOOD NAMERS!

Eventually, the truck made it out of the city, and the roads became smoother. The animals gradually calmed down, their agitated noises subsiding. Despite the smoother roads, we faced a new challenge. Mr. Jenkins, disoriented by the lack of the n-word pass architecture he had grown accustomed to and already hyper-fixated to, began driving slightly recklessly. Although, luckily, the animals remained relatively calm, my confidence wavered. They were distracted by something else.

The truck now traveled through open grassland, seemingly devoid of obstacles. The animals, having sensed the natural landscape, actively looked through the back cage doors. This was what they had longed for—a taste of freedom after spending most of their lives in man-made cages. I was happy for them, and I wanted to have some of what they were having, so I looked through the cage gaps cooperatively. They snarled at me in a good way, not minding my part of the pie. From our perspective, where the truck was previously shrinking, new forms of land emerged from the outer corners of the view. It was especially neat to see the unexpected mountain ranges. It gave me a huge boner, reminding me of when my family would take me on road trips.

Just as I was starting to think we might make it without further incident, the truck suddenly jumped violently. The sound made it seem like pieces of metal were flying across, as goes for many intense car jumps that don't actually end up breaking anything. But the impact was so intense that it forced the cage doors open. The room suddenly got much brighter, and it was almost hurting my eyes. The metal below my soles quickly conducted the new heat from the sun. The resulting opening allowed the animals to spill out one by one. As I waited by the door, I made a door-holding polite gesture, and they eagerly dashed into the open grassland, finally free.

I scrambled out of the back of the truck and rushed to the front. There, I discovered the cause of the sudden stop: Mr. Jenkins had crashed into a tree that marked the edge between forest and grassland. It appeared that he had zoned out, perhaps thinking the landscape would continue uninterrupted. I guessed this ultimately also marked the limitations of his own "autism." Heart pounding, I hurried to the driver's seat, where I saw the tragic aftermath. Mr. Jenkins hadn't survived the crash. It looked dark as well— he was doing a really infamous death pose, his arms and legs being really spread apart like he was pretending to be a starfish. I guess he was doing some "autistic" limb shaking while driving, and the sudden change in the environment really fucked him up. The steering wheel, despite being a round object, managed to STAB through his torso. To be fair, he doesn't lift and would lack the meat, and he wasn't at all fat, so it makes sense.

The sight filled me with sorrow and guilt. Even though he was kind of an idiot, I had brought him into this situation, and now he was gone. I felt tears begin to trickle down my cheek because there is a special place in my heart for these people because of these helpful situations that one would not expect. I turned to see Stacy, who was thankfully relatively unharmed. Her well-trained abs had absorbed the impact, leaving her shaken but okay. I saw a giant shard of glass stuck to her abdomen, but its tip didn't seem to reach her actual belly, which was soon to be pregnant.

"Stacy, are you all right?" I asked, my voice heavy with concern.

She nodded, then pulled the out piece of glass bravely, her eyes wide but steady. "I'm fine. What about the animals?"

I looked around and saw the animals dispersing into the grassland and forest. They were finally where they belonged, free to live their lives in their natural habitat. The sight gave me a small measure of comfort amidst the tragedy. Stacy placed a hand on my shoulder, her touch reassuring and making me feel much less bad. "Mr. Jenkins didn't die in vain. He helped us give these animals a chance."

We stood there for a moment, taking in the scene. The open landscape, the animals venturing into their new lives, and the bittersweet success of our mission (actually now that I look back to this writing, I feel bad for not specially mentioning Mr. Jenkins here, so I'll say it here: Mr. Jenkin's mission).

Chapter Fifteen: Economic Reductivism

In the modern landscape, doesn't a peculiar necessity emerge, characterized by its hostility toward the foundational elements of preceding steps towards an idealized decoction? This setting rejects existing values, following a path toward self-perpetuation by revising the narratives of its real antecedents. This phenomenon usually unfolds through the decontextualization of tangible entities, replaced by their synthetic counterparts.[292] It is not justifiable to discount these predecessors to zero merely due to perceived shortcomings when put close to newer "wordly" forms—some of the naturally "missing pieces" that denote absence inherent in the former often serve as a beautiful interpretive lens, enhancing our understanding and interaction with the world (consider the immersive uncanny sensation evoked even by an ambiguous portrayal of unsettling media).[293] Is such hostility along the lines of the subtle ways that propaganda is utilized by the technological system?

There must be some way the system promotes the idea that technology is particularly "the way" to provide solutions to social issues.[294] This is kind of how Gross Domestic Product (GDP)—yet another meaningless kind of "language" that just measures how dependent a nation is on the centralized global economy—serves the interest of the system. Not many propagandistic values right now are worse than economic reductivism. This is one of the ways the system oppresses citizens, by making THEM oppress themselves—it paints a picture that "responsibility for actions, agency, and consciousness are illusions, so, therefore, all behavior is necessarily derived by surrounding milieus such as the economy." This would create a kind of surveillance (The prison-Panopticon) where the prisoner is not actually literally being watched all the time, but it seems such to the point of self-oppression.[295] It's like the kinds of paranoid fucks who refuse to do some simple tasks outside because "tHE FeDs WiLl gEt Me" (By the way, if any feds are reading this, I am "fed" too... fed up with all the modernity in our society! I am also fed raw milk), or the pessimists who refuse to start their own spaces of fellow based friends within the evil empire that we currently live in because "I aM tOo AnXiOus." There could also be pernicious feelings of surveillance amongst even their own people.[296] This is what is meant when propaganda is not just limited to shilling—it can be indirect coercion.[297] Even though there is no law that tells people to wagecuck, what space for "responsibility for self" could they see with all this propaganda?

What's also bad: if an individual accumulates economic success under such a system, they are even more inclined to be passive; historically, people who were formerly

---

[292] H. Schübel and I. Wallimann-Helmer. *Justice and Food Security in a Changing Climate* (Wageningen Academic Publishers, 2021).

[293] A. Smuts, "'Pickman's Model': Horror and the Objective Purport of Photographs," *Revue Internationale de Philosophie*, 4(2010): 487-509. https://doi.org/10.3917/rip.254.0487

[294] M. Broussard, *Artificial Unintelligence: How Computers Misunderstand the World* (The MIT Press, 2018).

[295] J. Bentham, *The Panopticon Writings* (Verso Books, 2011).

[296] I. Manokha, "Surveillance, Panopticism, and Self-Discipline in the Digital Age," Surveillance & Society, 16(2018): 219-237. https://doi.org/10.24908/ss.v16i2.8346

[297] T. Kaczynski, *Industrial Society and its Future* (Independently published, 2018), para. 37.

rebellious would often come to the conclusion that they just needed to adapt upon becoming an integrated careerist under the economy.[298] So anyone who would have the material power to change the status quo would be much less likely to even do so anyway. Perhaps this "system's trick" is a consequence of the Marxist myths that hyperfocus on economic and material conditions as the problems rather than an interplay of intangible factors.[299] Isn't it then stupid that GDP is now widely held as the main metric for determining how "epic" the people of the nation are?

Here is a rule of thumb: modernity is good at solving problems, but only the problems that it created in the first place. Start by thinking about the various sicknesses that only arose after certain ways of seeing life. Such as the common man who now pursues trivial gratifications incessantly, while meticulously safeguarding their health. For example, the people exhibiting "idiot positions" as they sleep as mouthbreathers, as industrial agriculture's soft baby foods fuck up jaw development and end up waking up tired as fuck to wagecuck as they exhaled an excess quantity of carbon dioxide, the official holy bridge from blood cells to the tissue. Or take a look at the gross night-jump-scare bedbugs and certain diseases that came about from people living in close quarters after the agrarian revolution, which came about because of certain technological advancements.[300] More insidious—since the early 20th century, which marked the evolution of nutrition science, a lot of focus began emphasizing individual nutrients rather than whole foods, which led to a reductionist approach, viewing nutrition as a technical and individual issue,[301] sidelining social science perspectives—this would lead to the rise of "mysterious" nutritional deficiencies. GDP increases according to everything "good" about modernization, while at the same time, "soy ramifications" will not lead to a decrease in the number—this perpetuates an illusion that "we are living in the best times." Along modernity's supposed progress, are these why we see reboots of initially superfluous afflictions?

All the supposed "innovators" in modernity are just pseudo-entrepreneurs who like to pretend they impact civilization in any way (keep in mind, if mankind has existed for thousands of years, they're solving pseudo-problems that only existed for 0.001% of our time in the universe). If one looks past "modern industrialism," all the way to the agricultural revolution, it would stick out that the early agriculturalists had to attune themselves primarily to the rhythms of often just one plant and a small range of domestic animals, while the pre-agriculturalists were attuned to a wide range of birds, large animals, sea life, and wild plants.[302] So if you ever cry about "WhY ThIs AniMal CaN EaT ThIs AnD HuEmAn Can"t????? I HaVe tO WaGe CucK JuSt To BuY GroCery FooD," this is probably why. Probably the same reason you have to wagecuck just to buy the kinds of tools to do things that may seem basic for other certain creatures that are so "well off" in the wild—agriculture led man to suffer bones and teeth that indicated nutritional

---

[298] T. Kaczynski, *Technological Slavery* (Scottsdale: Fitch & Madison, 2022), 241.
[299] G. Oesterdiekhoff, "The Emergence of Modern, Industrial Society — A Comparison of the Theories of Max Weber and Douglass North," *Qeios*, 2024. https://doi.org/10.32388/3BPN8F
[300] M.N. Cohen, *Health and the Rise of Civilization* (Yale University Press, 1989).
[301] S. Stevano, "Ultra-Processed Food, Depletion, and Social Reproduction: A Conceptual Intervention," *Antipode*, 2024. https://doi.org/10.1111/anti.13046
[302] R.E. Nationalist, *The Eggs Benedict Option*, (Antelope Hill Publishing, 2022), 54.

deficiencies and stress.[303] And because crowding was necessary for the Neolithic Revolution, it led to the emergence of disease.[304] This effect compounds—along with the overcrowding, nutritional deficiencies themselves led to even more disease.[305] Maybe this is why we have many bugman nowadays screaming "wE NeEd BiG PhArMA to MaKe VaX" rather than just championing leaving modern conditions. One might be misled into thinking that a rise in GDP in relation to a rise in cancer diagnosis is a good thing because it means that we have better means of diagnosing cancer.[306] But clearly, the number of carcinogens in modernity is higher as fuck than ever. When you think of it, even if new diagnoses for cancer are found, we must look at the big picture and consider that there are countless kinds of afflictions that we have YET to even construct and be aware of. Assuming modernity still advances, "time" will "invent" more entirely different ways nature will notify you that death is inevitable (trying to solve "the problem of conflict"), and therefore, more "diagnostics" will have to be laboriously "made up"—maybe to the point of inversion. For instance, the globalized system would have to find a diagnosis for testosterone, just because it's a source of what makes dudes want to create more "competition."[307] Why would such an interference with the thirst for blind efficiency be desired by technologization?

The modern education system would be willing to teach the limitations of what GDP measures in relation to the actual global production levels, but will stop right there—could this precisely also be what benefits the system? As the education system will still imply that continuing to consoom despite this is the proper choice to make, people will just shit on the truly self-sufficient individuals and paint them as quasi-criminals and continue to wagecuck to feel like they're closing the gap of "non-measured production." Would shit like this validate the argument that those who dropped out of the system are morally superior to the average bugdrone as they don't fuel corporate distractions?

Back then, it was even considered depraved, repugnant, absurd, and unnatural to work for pay.[308] One may even argue that the more workers there are saturating the market, the less effective solutions are to problems (even modern solutions to modern problems) when one notices how much managerialism has really taken over. There exists a latent propensity for almost invisible, and I'd go as far as to say quasi-abstract "experts" to subtly condition the collective "consciousness." On an individual level, the paralyzing dogmas of institutionalized interventions communicate to the populace that they are unable to be independent. But when this paradigm is reversed, considering the vested interests and exigencies of "service systems," these declarations transform into terms that are more obvious euphemisms for: "We necessitate afflictions. We must define them for you. We must address them on our terms. We require you to derive satisfaction from our

---

[303] Ibid., 55.

[304] Ibid., 56.

[305] Ibid., 57.

[306] The Cancer Atlas, "The Economic Burden of Cancer," *The Cancer Atlas*, https://canceratlas.cancer.org/taking-action/economic-burden/

[307] A. Booth, G. Shelley, A. Mazur, G. Tharp, and R. Kittok, "Testosterone, and winning and lsing in human competition," *Horm Behav*, 23(1989): 556-71. https://doi.org/10.1016/0018-506X(89)90042-1

[308] J. Evola, *Revolt Against the Modern World* (Inner Traditions, 1995), 334.

validation."[309] How can we compare this time of "necessity of universal wagecuckism" to when modernity wasn't anywhere as prevalent?

Did you know that even if we consider a sliver of time after the Industrial Revolution, there was a period of time in the 19th century when the majority of people in America were not wagecucks? Most were self-employed or entrepreneurs! And it would sound crazier when you notice that in hunter-gatherer societies, it was the norm for producers and consumers to overlap (until the agriculture societies).[310] The system today doesn't favor such affairs though because if there are so many creative ways people are offering services, it leads to an overall deviation from the system's proposed way of reaching full efficiency—once modernity and its technological system came about, there then would have to be less entrepreneurs and more wagecucks to all perform the same kind of job. This is why, as reported, franchise-granting companies in our franchise-favoring system have to overtly do a personality test for potential franchisees that indicates whether they are "uncreative" enough to quality because one would have to be docile to function in the system.[311] There is now even a word for this coming to be, "McDonaldization," where success is so tied only to calculability and predictability.[312] It is for this reason you should never perceive money nominally, and instead investigate how it's actually earned based on how much agency one has in their work. Compare the freedom of a man making six figures per year as a corporate drone and the freedom of an independent farmer making five figures. The latter does not have to worry about losing their job for superfluous reasons! Even in the 1800s, the average American kid (they ain't even fat back then) was shown how to hunt, make fire, shoot guns, build, and make tools to build.[313] These people were truly liberated. Today, wouldn't you just be called the linguistically corrupted variant of "redneck bigot," a floppy definition that the system, of course, had to mandate to ensure its own survival rather than the preservation of individual ability?

In contemplating the nature of economic growth, it would be more accurate to consider a high GDP "bad" rather than good, as it linguistically makes the most basic things into "hoop jumps." GROSS DOMESTIC PRODUCT WOULD LITERALLY BE "GROSS" AS THE NAME SUGGESTS! To illustrate this point, consider a village where textiles were labeled as the "only product."[314] Despite this economic focus, it does not imply that the villagers solely engaged in textile production while facing deprivation or scarcity, such as starving or thirsting to death. While this perspective might seem unfamiliar to some, envisioning how our predecessors would react to the notion of "corporate retail" might reveal their disapproval. Would they metaphorically shake their heads in disbelief, as if witnessing a brain slipping from its confines like a slippery sausage from an oversized, hollow bun?

---

[309] J.L. McKnight, "Professionalized Services: Disabling Help for Communities and Citizens," Paper Presented at the First Annual Symposium on Bioethics of the Clinical Research Institute of Montreal (8th October, 1976).

[310] R.B. Lee, R.H. Daly, and R. Daly, *The Cambridge Encyclopedia of Hunters and Gatherers* (Cambridge University Press, 1999).

[311] T. Kaczynski, *Industrial Society and its Future* (Independently published, 2018), para. 65.

[312] B.S. Turner, *The British Journal of Sociology* 45(1994): 325-326. https://doi.org/10.2307/591513.

[313] B. Disciple, *Barbaric Vitalism* (RESAVAGER Media, 2023), 170.

[314] L. Smith, Why It's Bad to Have High GDP," *Luke Smith's Webpage* (21st January 2022), https://lukesmith.xyz/articles/why-its-bad-to-have-high-gdp/.

A Breath of Fresh Air

A year and a half had passed since the chaotic liberation of the zoo animals and the epic gamer death of Mr. Jenkins. Stacy and I had since dedicated ourselves to building a new life in the wilderness, where we probably had the best times in our lives so far. Away from the big cities and their influences, which we increasingly became aware of. Though we categorically heard of these, we were even more disgusted by dirty sewers, the alleyways that have dirty fingers that hold clit-force-rubbing tendrils, and the number of common colds. We found solace and meaning in the simplicity of unplugging from the open-air simulation—it felt like we were literally living in the African country "Chad" (a place where the n-word is ironically more allowed with the absence of leftists) but in the beautiful wildlife savannahs.

Life was not "too simple" per se because we find ourselves having to push ourselves on both a psychological and physical level. One of our first tasks was to establish a reliable water source. We knew water was essential for our survival, especially as people who store a ton of water in our tissues as lifters. Finding a clean, sustainable supply was our top priority. I won't lie, there were days when we really struggled, and we experienced dehydration, but it made the muscles look super ripped, but this time, no bodybuilding competition was within miles of our reach. Imagine the competition money we'd easily win and buy some fucking water.

Since the first day, I started by riding the zoo horse, now a trusted companion that somehow likes me even after I probably looked like a duck dumbass in front of it at times, especially when I was hiding like a coward at the back of the truck. We would go around the surrounding area to search for freshwater that preferably moves—when you think of "still water," you'll realize it is basically the same thing as the grossness of foreign particles in long-standing cup drinks, which I described earlier.

I looked for subtle signs like green foliage, low-lying areas, and evidence of wildlife—indicators of a nearby river or pond. I always laugh when soyboys think they can't live without tap water (which is obviously poison) and would suck the cock of the government as they also directly suck the tap water when they want a quick drink. They are the same types of idiots who would think animals are magically independent of water and that humans uniquely need water and; therefore, tap water, even when poisoned, is necessary. NO, DON'T LISTEN TO THEM. Just look for fucking animals, it's that simple.

I remember that after several days of searching since we were stranded, I finally found a continuous stream flowing gently through a shaded grove. It was a perfect spot to designate as our main water source.

Next, I needed to build a water well. Drawing on my strength and determination, I began to dig a hole deep into the ground, aiming to reach the groundwater. I remember Stacy cheering me on, telling me to pretend that it was her pussy and I had to find the clitoris; I shrugged it off, though, because I ain't some coomer who is only motivated by unnatural sex. She then told me she was just joking. Phew.

Ensuring the cleanliness of our water supply was crucial, but Stacy and I made sure to maintain a balance that didn't fall too much into big city levels. I knew the water needed to be free of deadly parasites, but it shouldn't be too pure. Essential minerals and some bacteria are important for maintaining our health and training our immune systems. If you ever see people who get big red rashes on their skin, somehow suddenly after they were born, you would have to blame their parents, plain and simple.

To perfect the amounts within the water, I used basic filtration methods. I constructed a simple filter using layers of sand, charcoal, and gravel to remove larger impurities and reduce harmful microorganisms. Another thing that really irritates me about normies is they think that stone, sand, etc., are dirty only because they exist in the outdoors. RETARDS, why are you using plastic water bottles, which literally melt below the sun's heat?

Don't forget about collecting rainwater. We set up numerous rainwater catchment systems using tarps and large leaves, funneling water into containers. This was only just a backup water source to be used as a last resort because of the idiotic pollution that ruins that damn rain and makes it so acidic. I remember my mom telling me various crazy stories about rain in Lethbridge, from the raining pre-chemical frogs to the citizen's literal rights to drink rainwater because the rain was so clean back then.

Now, bugmen may be wondering thus far: HoW DiD YoU MaKe FriEnD WiTh HorSe? The answer is a good and bad thing at the same time. "The wilderness" brought Stacy and me closer to nature, yet there was still that gross remaining factor that distanced it from our new animal companions. The zoo animals, as they were still partially domesticated due to the effects of the n-word pass architecture, formed a unique solidarity with us.

The chimpanzees and gorillas quickly became more than just some blobs of flesh that sat around with their old man boobs sticking out. They sort of became part of our extended family. Their intelligence and curiosity made them quick learners; we even taught them some basic English words. You probably guessed it—we taught them both the word "nature" and the n-word. This communication helped coordinate tasks and strengthened our bond—it provided some instruction without the totalitarian excess of rules. All I would have to say is "nature," and the chimpanzees were especially helpful in gathering smaller fruits and nuts from the forest, climbing trees with ease to reach the highest branches. If I were to say the n-word, well, it's pretty obvious what they'd do.

At first, the lions made my heartbeat fast near them. But with their innate will to hunt, they went on regular searches and often brought back buffalo meat to the campsite. This provided us with a steady supply of protein, which was essential for our diet. To be honest, I don't think I would even be around anymore if it weren't for that because, without my chiseled physique that has to be maintained via thousands of calories per day and some guarantee that I wouldn't get one back, I would have killed myself.

The rhinos were incredibly useful for their sheer strength. I always imagined them to be one of those top-heavy and slow animals because their legs look puny. Before, I thought they'd only be useful for urbanite pseudo-nature lovers who don't have the balls to go out in the wild nor walk around in savannahs but are willing to watch rhino-shitting videos for the smell. But the rhinos here would charge at trees, breaking them down and providing us with large amounts of thatch, which was invaluable for constructing makeshift shelters and maintaining our campsite. The rhinos also helped clear paths through dense underbrush, making it easier for us to navigate the forest.

The elephants were literally what some of the biggest scientists would describe mammoths to do. Their ability to farm through thinner trees provided us with pre-cut logs, which we used for building and fuel. Their trunks were also adept at pulling up roots and clearing land, making it possible to create small farming plots. They even helped us transport heavy materials that we couldn't carry on our own (not weight-wise, but awkward-to-carry stuff that isn't fit for human arm shape). The really cool bonus would be using its trunks with some tribal tattoo that represents a tape measure so that I could measure the size of my biceps, making sure it doesn't shrink too much because my rule of thumb is: I become a sissy once measuring with a large instrument becomes impossible.

The giraffes played a crucial role in Stay and I's survival by reaching the highest leaves on the trees. These leaves there were the biggest and were not only a source of spinach-like food, but also essential for constructing the water funnels. The only annoying thing about these long-necked things that look like skinny ass paraceratheriums is their tongues would drool more saliva than a kind of man that already started an agriculture lifestyle that regressed their jaw size.

Establishing a sturdy shelter was a top priority for Stacy and me as we had to see how it felt to be a streetsleeper for the first time, in a very tame way. The only reason why there has to be a name for "the homeless" in the first place is that they are living in an urban area. The numerous drug junkies and weird dudes who walk with their arms twisted to the very front of their bodies will basically be the "animalistic threats." But when people teach themselves how not to be reliant on the system and decide to sleep in the plains, they shall "magically" go from being homeless to what the common folk would call "extraordinary."

Stacy and I aimed to create a makeshift yet spacious shelter that offered protection from the elements while providing enough room to move around comfortably. I recall the moments when there would be some scary sounds, which we couldn't tell if it was manmade or the wind. Either way, we wanted our privacy to be respected, even if it would be a hope for the animals.

We scouted for a dry, flat area, ideally one between two trees with splits in their trunks. Since we valued large and personal space, we selected trees that were quite far apart, ensuring that our shelter would be roomy. Only an unnoble desk drone would be able to handle small spaces if they were to be willing to survive in the wilderness in the first place. They would long for the nostalgia of sitting inside a tight cubicle creating hideous spreadsheets or dehumanizing people into blocks of data while drinking bottled water that has a slightly sweet and unnatural taste that isn't due to an intentionally added lemon tint.

We needed a large, sturdy branch to span the distance between the trees. We searched the forest, finally finding a suitable one that was thick and robust. We inserted the two ends of the branch into the splits of each tree, forming a horizontal frame. That's right; this can be a very key foundation of a reliable and functional shelter. It isn't a universal reality that there always has to be a perfect cubic frame, which characterizes the kind of modern cookie-cutter houses that people have grown used to. This part is one thing that scares people away from exiting the system; they believe that it takes a professional architect to have a roof over their head.

With the main horizontal branch in place, we began leaning smaller branches against it, arranging them closely together to form a triangular structure. Just so it wouldn't be a flimsy piece of ass, we made sure to keep the branches slightly dug into the dirt. This setup created a slanted roof that would allow rain to run off easily, which is very important, especially if said rain is acidified. Stacy and I would occasionally joke around, teasing one another about what our faces would look like if the rain were to burn our skin. I'd be inclined to believe my sharp jaw would just look even better. Probably wouldn't even be prone to infections, as the razor-sharp ends would be sharp enough to cut in half even the smallest species of bacteria.

We laid twigs over the series of smaller branches to add a layer of insulation. Next, we used leafy branches, bushes, and leaves to create additional insulation. This not only helped retain heat but also provided more cover from the wind and rain. The thick layer of natural materials made the shelter remind us less of the weird things about keeping air conditioners near the feet. I remember doing that as I would do schoolwork back then, "rationally" thinking it felt good and should stay like that for hours. Whenever I'd momentarily move away, I felt like I had a cold fever and would immediately get too hooked onto the heater. But little did I know, my entire leg got burned, and I nearly had to see a doctor (but I ate an apple).

Thanks to the giraffes, who were capable of reaching high leaves, we gathered large leaves to use as bedding. We arranged them inside the shelter to create comfortable, natural beds. There were two beds: one that was exclusively for me and one that was just for Stacy. Growing up, the whole idea of "couples sleeping in the same bed" was a bit alien to me. The funny thing is my parents slept in the opposite sections of the childhood house—my mom slept on the top floor on the north side, while my dad slept on the south side of the basement. The deep irony is I was accustomed to room sharing. When my parents had me, it turned out there was a fraternal twin sister as well, while they built the house to only house two children's rooms (one for my older brother as well).

To keep warm during the nights and cook food, we built a fire pit near the entrance of our shelter. We dug a shallow hole and lined it with stones to contain the fire. We took flat pieces of wood and scraped them until a thin groove was formed in the center. Another branch would be used, plowing up and down, and the friction eventually built up enough heat to ignite. We surrounded the pit with larger rocks that helped radiate heat into the shelter. We also built a simple tripod from branches to hang a pot over the fire for cooking. Stacy had a blast with that, allowing her to explore recipes with some challenging restrictions and continue to do her cooking. For me, I took a ton of pleasure just listening and looking at the fire. It was so fascinating to me, the pleasant taste in my mouth that would form just from me having to hear the exploding bits of spark. I see a lot of modern men who would place televisions at where a chimney fire should be in their house (now that chimneys are kind of an obsolescence now) and put on a live footage of someone else's chimney fire just to simulate it. I know it is pathetic and a waste of power, but there is something about fire that men have a deep connection to. The modern world basically takes it away from us, makes us scared of fire, and replaces it with a synthetic replica. I'll admit, I was nearly going to stoop down to that level of pussy, marked when my mom did a little prank on me at a candle store when she "challenged" me to touch a paper orange light-up strip that looked so much like fire. Even when I was literally seeing my mom move her hand back and forth through it, I was still scared to do it. Only after I went camping for the first time with a "man-friend" (whom my mom hired to hang out with me in fifth grade because I was too cool for the herdish kids my age) did I overcome the artificial fear of fire.

To further protect our shelter from strong winds, we constructed windbreaks using thick branches and bushes. These barriers were placed strategically around the perimeter of the shelter to reduce the impact of gusts and help maintain a stable temperature inside. They also served as effective general guidance for some of the semi-domesticated animals to know exactly where to sleep when the night would fall. If it weren't for that, they'd probably knock the shelter down by accident and exhibit some behavior in which they shake and do awkward stances that a child would do when their parents leave them in a grocery store.

We built an elevated sleeping platform to keep us off the cold ground. Using sturdy branches, we created a frame and lashed smaller branches across it to form a platform. This not only provided insulation from the cold earth but also helped avoid any crawling insects or moisture. I can't emphasize enough how many times those would wake me up. The cold droplets of water especially would make me jump lying down, only using my arms to launch myself into the air. When I'd fall, the weight of myself would make my back hurt so much. If you are as big and strong as me, water leakages could be deadly during the night.

Now, the makeshift shelter was all just a thing that we utilized and nothing more, so it was naturally kind of ugly. At the time, I didn't have the resources to make a beautiful work of art using stone, so what we did with the shelter was the equivalent of a skinny kid wearing oversized clothes to hide his physique. To blend our shelter into the natural surroundings, we covered the exterior with additional leafy branches and bushes.

Even with the lions and shit, that didn't mean I decided to rely on them entirely on the food. I still had an instinctive desire to keep moving, and this meant becoming adept at foraging for food. While Stacy and I had a stable water supply and a secure shelter, a potentially perverse calling for us to settle for long, we needed a consistent source of not just nourishment but the activity of searching for things that matter.

Let me clear things up first and say it is a valid concern for people to worry about eating bugs in the future. Everyone who is at least aware that the news sometimes lies is aware that this is one of the end goals of the system. The only reason why I chose to consume them is to force myself to understand more why globalists are idiots, as I feel pints of disgust having insect legs stuck between my teeth. One of the simplest ways to gather insects was to flip logs, boards, and stones in search of edible insects. It was probably mine and everyone else's deepest disgust and fear. We all have a human disgust response toward "looking under flat surfaces to find a whole cluster of different bug species that are obviously ignoble because of their willingness to stack on top of one another." The insects we commonly found included ants, termites, beetles, and grubs. Worms were also a viable option. We avoided spiders, ticks, and flies due to their potential to carry diseases or be poisonous. Insects with hard outer shells, like beetles, needed to be cooked for a few minutes to kill any parasites before we ate them. I kept remembering images of mantises or bears having gigantic tapeworms coming out of their asses, and I told myself that to have a penis-looking thing coming out of my ass would make me have to say "no homo" to each and every wildlife organism that witnesses such.

Edible berries were another crucial food source. Blackberries and raspberries were among the most identifiable and safest to eat. We learned to avoid white berries, as they were generally toxic (And I tended to associate them with dehydration because of motherfucking ARK: Surrogate Evolved). Anyway, they were nice when we were especially thirsty and slapping a hundred berries inside the mouth solved the problem, getting our thirst bar up slowly.

Edible mushrooms were abundant, especially in dark, damp areas or on dying trees. However, identifying safe mushrooms requires caution. We only picked mushrooms we were absolutely sure about, as misidentifying them could be fatal. Since mushrooms didn't provide many calories, they were a last resort. The effort of finding them often outweighed the caloric benefit they provided. I remember getting frustrated after not finding one, and the last bit of sunken cost conditioning that the system insinuated in me led me to eat a red and white mushroom and ended up causing my vision to become all rainbow and distorted while I was constantly defecating.

Using simple tools like spears and nets crafted from branches and vines, we took advantage of the stream nearby to catch fish. Fish were an excellent source of protein and relatively easy to cook over our campfire. It made our breaths stink, but we easily mitigated that by making sure we ate solid enough other foods, which acted as natural toothbrushes and flosses. We didn't waste a damn second waiting idly in a primitive w*shroom and heavens forbid, do the "wash your hands without soap 'b*throom challenge.'"

During certain seasons, we collected bird eggs from nests. We were careful to take only a few eggs from each nest to ensure the bird population remained sustainable. Eggs were a versatile food source, rich in nutrients, especially when eaten raw. I didn't have much of an issue doing this. When I was three years old, I was always fascinated by shiny, colorful objects that had peculiar shapes, so one day, I was on the porch and found a nest that a bird had built on the stairway. Three blue eggs looked like how sterile Easter graphics would depict chocolate eggs. I unhesitantly held one and split it into two pieces. I understand why my mom would remind me of that every year, but I was about to be a natural raw egg enthusiast!

Chapter Sixteen: Time and Death

In modernity, a dysphoric concept dictates our perception of temporality, leading us to adopt a linear conception of time. Historically, time was not actually perceived as a mere sequence of quantifiable intervals, as we now perceive it in terms of lame boring fiscal years. Instead, time was regarded as a qualitative continuum, where each period possessed intrinsic significance. The modern view fragments time into inconsequential events, effectively nullifying the past—this ignores the antecedent conditions that have shaped the present and precluded the possibility of transcending the current state of affairs. Wouldn't this reject both the Platonic realm of eternal forms and the Nietzschean idea of the path to a higher man?

"Amogus" this discourse would come the idea of "temporal rupture," a schism in the temporal continuum within urban landscapes, disrupting the collective perception of time. Urbanization blurs the boundaries of place and time, leading to this rupture. Ideological factions have engaged with this concept, challenging the theory of duration, which posits that time's essence resides in a continuum of transformative moments.[315] Modernity's tendency is to anchor individuals in the "immediate," thereby diminishing their appreciation for historical continuity and its foundational role in shaping the present. The replacement of good antiquity with dull modern constructs obscures historical legacies. Would this render even the most "high self-esteem" historians unable to decipher their significance?

Transitioning to the realm of aesthetics, do we encounter a process that strives away from the idea of "process"? Clearly, we no longer prioritize the experiential and introspective dimensions of creation—the artist's engagement with the world contrasts with object art, which is concerned with the aesthetic attributes of artifacts.[316] Throughout time, there has been a historical emphasis on object arts, which has led to the neglect of process arts, which has left several key questions unanswered, such as the role of the artist and the attribution of aesthetic qualities.[317] The unique value of process artworks lies in their ability to inspire aesthetic activities that are dependent on their design.[318] Furthermore, process art uniquely inspires aesthetic engagement, contingent upon its design, emphasizing the artist's agency in shaping their interaction with the work. This active participation highly contrasts with the passive appreciation of object art, where the observer merely contemplates external aesthetic qualities.[319] The so-called progress today marks a hermeneutical demise as art appreciation shifts from questioning beauty to pondering its mere depictions on meaningless alternative platforms (like screens)—historically, process art dominated until modernity enabled the preservation of art in textual forms and then made it overly standardized. How many people nowadays actively want to see a live performance, when we juxtapose it with other points in history?

---

[315] K. Wang, "Time rupture in urban heritage: based on the case of shanghai," Geojournal, 88(2023): 1865-1977. https://doi.org/10.1007/s10708-022-10732-2

[316] C.T. Nguyen, "The arts of action," *Philosophers' Imprint*, 20(2020): 1-27.

[317] Ibid.

[318] Ibid.

[319] Ibid.

There should instead be an exploration of temporality and aesthetics, which reexamines the notion of an individual turning themselves into "a work of art" without being domesticated by a dread of dying someday and longing for infinite self-preservation. It is said that in the modern world, overcoming time is no longer spiritual, but only an illusion via speed, immediacy, and simultaneity.[320] This is massively scaled in the technological system, where those who don't have the balls to explore beyond quantitative time are at the top. On the other hand, societies embracing qualitative temporality inherently cultivate virtuous leadership. The leaders stand above the temporal fray, inviting the world to them, sustained by the timelessness of their epic coolness legacies. In these societies, would leaders be revered not out of fear but through a sense of deep-water motivation?

In modernity, time is perceived as consecutive, irreversible, homogeneous, quantitative, and there is a "before and after."[321] However, in the Evolian view, time was qualitative, not as a series but rather a rhythm, broken into cycles and periods where each moment had its own meaning and value in relation to others, as well as lively individuality and functionality.[322] Yet, it is crucial to recognize that while traditions can offer a "Lindy effect," vigilance is necessary to prevent their overemphasis. If traditions are adhered to merely due to their designation as such, they risk dissolving into "teleological regression." In such cases, the oppressive elements of modernity may insidiously infiltrate, eroding the foundation they are meant to uphold. Or we see some traditionalist LARPers who want to view time as a kind of cyclical phenomenon where the past and present are one of the same things. Doesn't this just discourage people from being exceptional too? "Surfing" the times may end up getting people to become bound by time all over again, not taking action against the system. I don't know, although I like the idea of qualitative time, it just rubs me the wrong way to commit to the idea that "real events or people may have repeated or dramatized a myth."[323] This might just be what reduces myth to mere language. Would you rather be your own warrior or be a backyardiganian roleplayer?

With time being so cucked, has modernity diverted the essence of "being alive" to something that has to be merely formless, and therefore killing the warrior spirit? This shift makes it increasingly difficult for ordinary individuals to accept death, heightening anxiety and fostering a pathological clinging to life—risk and potential suffering are crucial to the warrior's path. However, the modern world only presents suffering in the form of unbadass illnesses such as drugs and psychological illnesses. These artificially induced afflictions just stifle progress and regress mankind across generations—the kind of suffering that is "senselessness."[324] In contrast, the physical challenges of the pre-modern world imbue life with meaning, offering individuals the chance to transcend and become stepping blocks to a greater existence. Through the will to overcome adversity, one might even prefer death to a life of mere idleness and IRL hunger bar management—like the strong having a sensitivity for making life "safe" while the weak having a

---

[320] J. Evola, *Revolt Against the Modern World* (Inner Traditions, 1995), 325.

[321] Ibid., 143.

[322] Ibid., 144.

[323] Ibid., 148.

[324] F. Nietzsche, *On the Genealogy of Morals* (Penguin Classics, 2013), 144.

sensitivity for making life more profound.[325] Time appears to accelerate with age as one experiences monotonous repetition, signifying that choosing idleness is essentially spiritual disappearance—are the truly great only under a dichotomy of being either free or nonexistent?

One could regard the Ancient Roman Republic, not the Empire, as the zenith of vitality. Though modern institutions suggest that the Roman Empire was the pinnacle of human achievement that America should model after, in reality, what started before then was the Roman Republic, which always strove toward fighting the bigger enemies and actually lost most of their battles, but nonetheless exercised a powerful will imposed on their enemies.[326] Symmetrically, contrary to the technological system's artificial tendency to pretend to care about "animal welfare, we would be "helping" wild animals by not intervening so that they can enjoy their share of kinful life (we can notice a contradiction in the bugthought of leftists who would say "that's nature" at a lion eating a zebra but would scream "tHaTs NoT FaiR" when seeing a society conquer a society they self-project to, even though the latter has been proven to have done the same to others). Real "wildlife welfare" would be eliminating the technological system, which would mean abandoning the artificial national parks and zoos that are only needed because of the system's destructiveness in the first place. Additionally, this helps them self-master themselves as kin, not just for predators that win prey trophies, but for the satisfaction of making an escape (at the same time, exercising "man as beast of prey"[327] is also still possible). Only an intervention would cause their suffering—the suffering of weakness?

A possible objection to this is that ethical concepts like "good and bad" apply to wild nature just as they do to civilized contexts, which would suggest a need for interventions, including genetic engineering, to alter predator behaviors and creating wildlife parks.[328] Or that death harms animals by depriving them of potential future positive experiences, thereby contributing to overall disvalue in nature, which would critique theories that value ecosystems or biocenoses over individual sentient beings, arguing that such views conflict with the moral consideration of individual suffering, and that they are less credible when considering the significant aggregated disvalue experienced by countless sentient beings.[329] I would say that these prevailing stances often overlook important aspects regarding the whole phenomenon of death. Firstly, death essentially allows an ascendant process to continue (not in the literal sense of how time should work, but making higher the limiting factors that allow the discrete points of time to continue standing out), which fosters the proliferation of higher lifeforce later (Likewise, life doesn't just exist in a natural space, but because of it[330]). Additionally, we can observe, with the right trail of thought, that the utopia of universal "all death is a no-no" is impossible in the long term—such idiocy is dubious even if we pretend it's logistically possible. Even the dreamy notion of solving death by engineering mankind to morph into a theoretical "super-life" similar

---

[325] F. Nietzsche, *The Gay Science* (Vintage Books, 1974), 98.
[326] F. Disciple, Resavager Volume 1 (RESAVAGER Media, 2023), 109.
[327] O. Spengler, *Man and Technics* (Alfred A. Knopf, Inc., 1932), 19.
[328] O.M. Moen, "The ethics of wild animal suffering," *Etikk I Praksis - Nordic Journal of Applied Ethics*, 10(2016): 91-104. https://doi.org/10.5324/eip.v10i1.1972
[329] O. Horta, "The Problem of Evil in Nature: Evolutionary Bases of the Prevalence of Disvalue," *Relations Beyond Anthropocentrism*, 3(2015):17-32. http://dx.doi.org/10.7358/rela-2015-001-hort
[330] J. Dewey, *Art as Experience* (Perigee, 2005).

to the tardigrade—capable of enduring a so-called "perfectly peaceful" vacuum-like existence within a controlled space—strikes me as a default route towards further mediocrity, as "supermanish" as it sounds. This would be analogous to a colossal captivation because it would be a relaxation area that renders beings as literally having to be passive entities devoid of the impetus to engage in conflict or conquest and other adversities. Such an existence, an absence of external resistances (not even air resistance), would inevitably regress life to its most base form (like not having lifted weights for too long), akin to a giant Petri dish of the same simplistic blobs—would consciousness itself become THE weight that a being's leg has to drag?

In a void of pure blackness, there would be no point in perceptual faculties and, therefore, consciousness, and they would seem to "get in the way like an uncarefully moving elbow that accidentally knocks someone else's drink off a desk" and becomes a misstep. The emergence of consciousness in life may be a gamble, with many perishing in the struggle against more primitive entities, as consciousness does not confer immediate self-preservation advantages. The technological system, even though it comprises concrete objects, is just a motion towards a functioning void, a captive space metaphorically extinguishing the spirit of the captive life—wouldn't it nullify its essence and so kill it in advance long even before its physical elimination comes to fruition?

To cultivate a warrior mindset in practical terms, may you consider viewing recorded history as a narrative punctuated only by conflict? It is often said that periods when civilization is insulated from external challenges are the "empty archives" of history. When individuals perceive their material needs as fulfilled or soon to be, they lack the motivation to transcend their comfort zones and address intangible deficiencies. In such times, the truly heroic—those who are constants throughout history—remain hidden from view. It is said that this was the time when there was the necessity for civilizations to rise to the occasion.[331] And in the world of tradition, there was a concept of heroic death, where a warrior's willingness to sacrifice his life in battle is perceived as a pathway to immortality.[332] A way of viewing "modernity" is that it is actually a misnomer—only a return to a form of ancient totalitarianism, but reskinned.[333] Or heaven's forbid, the modern condition is actually just the default kind of life, like how there was no need for technology (individual machine devices) to subject us to a restrictive society.[334] Those who are into the idea of "if it happened for most of history, it should be how things ought to be" should listen—you really aren't living if you are not considered a part of the historical timeline. That should be a great objection against the obsession with mere life if there is one. We should have an aversion to the notion of mere self-preservation, the view that sees plain life itself as THE burdenous challenge. The modern individual only has a propensity for a constant urgency that leads to nothing. In contrast, the free man, unencumbered by such pressures, could enjoy a more thoughtful pace, thereby cultivating an appreciation for leisure. Wasn't "leisure" in its purer form not mere idleness but rather an "interval" devoted to self-cultivation beyond the mere instinct of survival?

[331] J. Evola, *Metaphysics of War* (Arktos Media, 2011), 52.
[332] Ibid., 86.
[333] B.A. Pervert, *Bronze Age Mindset* (Independently Published, 2018), 62.
[334] Ibid., 83.

New Generation

Even though the mainstream media always likes to pretend that life in cities is what makes people sociable, living in the wilderness has brought Stacy and me closer than ever. However, one of the most significant events in our journey was the birth of our child. It crept up on us, and I don't mean that the nine months went by fast. We were just so concentrated on the many ways we were allowed to live. In city life, there are very few ways to do this, so as one spends all their time actionless trying to determine who they really are and then chooses one of the few paths that involve sitting all day in an office, what else would they have to think about? Nothing except waiting for the inevitable moment their boss tells them they must work even after having the child and suggesting they allow their child to enroll in the public daycare, to be both motherless and fatherless.

Stacy and I faced an "obstacle." The mysterious thing called giving birth... without a *hospital... DUN DUN DUN!* But we were determined to overcome them together. What the hell do the majority of birth-giving-helper-workers at the hospital even do anyway? I heard most of them are just fresh college graduates who are just looking to see some pussy without having the life experience of seeing the realities of what an actual birth looks like—all the blood and feces that people don't talk about.

As Stacy's pregnancy progressed, the challenges became more apparent. I had to hunt and gather more intensely as her hunger skyrocketed. Her puking at various times motivated me to eat bugs because the latter is relatively less gross. Sometimes, she would have the same mood as an oversized gorilla with fiery eyes, raging as it navigates through the trees of burden.

When she began to feel the immense pain that came with the later stages, I did everything I could to support and reassure her. "Remember, Stacy," I said gently, holding her hand as she grimaced through another contraction. "Visualize the timeline as if it is a collection of independent segments, separated under categorically different conditions, not just quantitative. Focus on the different events, not just the length of the pain. Each moment in our lives brings us closer to the moment that will trump all others, whether good or bad—the birth of our child. When you look back, the pain, though prolonged for weeks, will appear to be a single increment."

She nodded, tears in her eyes. "It feels like I'm going to die," she whispered, her voice filled with fear and exhaustion. She sounded like a hyena who speaks too loud relative to its own relaxed default vocals, and I tried not to laugh as it reminded me of when my mom sounded like a funny robot when she cheered at my older brother's soccer game, but I remained sincere.

I squeezed her hand, looking into her eyes with all the love and strength I could muster. I dead-ass teared up as well, which is saying something because since I never teared up in movies before, as a soyboy who used to watch movies, I thought I was immune to my emotions. "You're going to survive this," I said. "And even if, by some impossible chance, you don't, remember that every event in your life has led to this moment. Whether you know about those events or not, are you paving the way for the next generation? You would be like a human bridge to something higher. Think of yourself as immortalized as the future generations will carry your essence."

My words seemed to give her strength. She nodded, taking deep breaths as she prepared for another wave of pain. As she did her battle screams, I could feel an intense heat that radiated not into the air but into my internals, us feeling the connection. Holy shit, this was a pretty unique feeling and you would have to stop being a coomer to know what I am talking about.

Hours felt like days as Stacy labored, her strength and resolve inspiring me to stay by her side, unwavering. I was truly seeing how men and women both have their own struggles, with barely any overlap. But I kept reminding her of our shared values, emphasizing the significance of each moment. I had my eyes closed as well and would hover my head near her pregnant belly. Her abs remained defined, and I noticed she resembled one of those big open-class male bodybuilders with a massive bubble gut due to all the insulin, growth hormone, and sheer food they consume. Whew, that looked overwhelmingly powerful.

Finally, after what seemed like an eternity, the moment arrived. I remember when Stacy called me to the shelter, where I was hanging out with the chimpanzee and the gorilla. I told the two apes, "Oh shit George probably coming soon," and rushed inside. I saw Stacy lying in her bed as usual, but doing the birth-giving pose that we all know about. She looked like herself when attempting a new personal record in her leg press, but the screaming was even louder. I bent over in between her legs and looked into the baby launcher as I yelled out, "PUSH PUSH PUSH PUSH!"

With one final, powerful push, I saw a batch of head hair that added to the already hairy pussy (we didn't know how to make a shaver in the wilderness yet), and then there was a dramatic *POP*. Our baby entered the world, crying loudly, announcing their presence. His announcement was tremendous, though. The crying sounded like a weak grown man who just lost a video game match, but I don't mean this in a bad way because the baby literally sounded like a man now, indicating he, fortunately, inherited Stacy and I's "Chad"-like genes, or Stacy was so well fed without all the soy foods. In addition, we saw how shredded he already looked, and it was no wonder Stacy felt so much pain. He looked like one of those professional arm wrestlers, and I knew he'd grow in golden proportions with time. That all added to the single event we had been waiting for so long, and it was clear that both our legacies would be carried over.

Tears of joy and relief streamed as we looked at our child. The culmination of our love, resilience, generations of smart nice booba/chest breeding, and determination was now in our arms. The pain and fear melted away, replaced by an overwhelming sense of accomplishment and gratitude. Stacy, exhausted but radiant, held our baby close. "We did it," she whispered, her voice filled with awe.

"We did," I echoed, my heart swelling with pride and love. "Welcome to the world, albino gorilla." I referred to him as such because he looked like it. But that was a mistake.

I heard a roar coming from outside. It was followed by a series of galloping, the sound of hands and soles heading closer. Bits of leaves from the shelter's roof were falling, and I was first struck with a sense of worry when the swigs supporting it moved horizontally and creases formed on the dirt. As a giant hand punched through the makeshift door, I prepared for impact. It was thick and rubbery from a big fella. The rest of the body then squeezed into the doorframe without a care of what it was made out of, breaking the edges and not minding the splinters it caused. I met eyes with a gorilla, who gleamed at me suspiciously. He then looked at the baby that was in Stacy's hand. He inhaled and hit his chest with his fists in a series, bits of voice exhaling incrementally in sync with the beats. This scared the baby, but he wasn't backing down; he went from crying to sitting up intently, heading towards the gorilla. He beat his chest back. The gorilla appeared concerned. *What?*

"You two, chill!" I spoke. But the baby took it as something else and rolled off of Stacy's arms. He crawled on the dirt, getting his hands dirty, and then came face to face with the gorilla. Immediately, I tackled the latter. The big furry monster wrapped his arms around me, and it felt much like how I would be when I was relaxed on a bed in a self-cradle position. Although not that high, I managed to take the gorilla into the air, and we crashed through the leaf walls. Outside, we were separated by the ground's force, and we thudded from each other like an explosion did. The gorilla was quicker than me to stand back up. I did it after I shook my head to regain focus. The gorilla, now facing me at nose distance, me being in front of the now severely damaged hut, did a final roar. I did my best to still remain gazing into its eyes, ignoring its mossy breath. After, the gorilla walked away as if nothing had happened. I then peeked into the hole I made (not going to give the gorilla credit because all my force induced it to fly over in the first place) to see my baby son clapping. Stacy was amazed at the fight and our son's reaction to it. Most babies would have just made a squinty, scared soy face. Ours proved his emotional rigor.

The birth of our child had become even more of a transformative moment, and this cool bit served as a ceremonial sacrament for Stacy and me. I paid my respect to the gorilla for putting up a good fight, handing him a leaf as a snack that he already would have been able to gather in the first place, at *ALL* times, if it weren't for the psychological conditioning of the zoo. But I could see the gorilla improving in his sense of freedom.

Stacy and I decided to name our baby "Suko," a name that resonated with the mental and physical strength and resilience we hoped to instill in our child. As we settled into our new roles as parents, I became deeply committed to raising Suko with the values and skills necessary to thrive in a cruel but large world that offers all kinds of uncountable paths. Not necessarily in the wilderness but generally in a world of uncertainty and wonder. Teaching him how to be with it.

One of my first actions was introducing Suko to the river where we collected our water. As I held him in my arms, I could hear the crashing of mini waves against the rocky shores. I started attempting to line up my sight with Suko's and mentally minimizing the scope of my body to gauge what this body of clear white would look like to him. Somewhat overwhelming. Inspired by the myth of Achilles' heel, I wanted to ensure that Suko would be comfortable and unafraid of water. After all, who the fuck would want to fear what takes up over 70% of their planet's surface? And as I mentioned before, water makes up a similar ratio in one's body mass. Imagine being scared of your own body.

I dipped Suko's tiny body into the cool, dynamic stream with great care. His body went limp momentarily, like he went into pause mode, but then resumed moving his arms along the fluid. To my relief, there was no panic. Having been submerged in liquid for the past nine months in Stacy's womb, he seemed at ease in the water. I could tell he was intelligently comparing this "new liquid" viscousness with what he was used to. I repeated the process in increments, allowing Suko to regain his breath between dips. He raised his head above the water while performing calm breaths, rather than most people's response to inhaling and exhaling as if a shark were beneath the surface. As I continued, I couldn't help but recall my childhood and the slight bitterness I felt toward my mother (I love her. I mention this window of resentment to represent a mistake that is very common among parents in the modern world). She never taught me how to swim, leaving me with a lingering fear of water. My dumbass couldn't even bath alone until an embarrassingly old age. And the bathwater never went any deeper than the height of my feet.

Suko aside, as time passed, I noticed a significant change in the behavior of the animals we had once considered companions. The longer they spent in the wild, the less domesticated they became. It felt like I was looking at something as gradual as blood-stained tissue going from red to dried brown. I didn't notice the behaviors change from one day to the next, but when I would check in the resource outputs to see them decreasing, it prompted me to check on them more closely.

The rhinos, our reliable source of thatch, started conserving their energy for more practical purposes. Instead, they did it more for procreation purposes, the males fighting each other to determine who has the right to mate. It reminded me of my encounter with Steve, as one of the rhinos was a runt and only lived because his buddies allowed so. Previously helpful in gathering wood, the elephants began to travel in their herds, paying less attention to us. They copied my journeys to the river, drinking out of it using their trunks, washing away the tape measure marks I painted on them. The giraffes migrated deeper into the forest, reveling in the paradise of abundant trees. I was mainly glad because that meant no snottier drool dropping on the shelter's roof and leaking into the interior. The lions, their primal instincts rekindled, began to exhibit aggressive behavior towards the herbivores, driven by a fierce hunger. Although many claim that lions don't go for humans because they aren't worth the calories, the lions would occasionally salivate at me, admiring my muscle gains for the wrong reasons. Interestingly, the horses remained at the same level of domestication, still willing to give us rides and stay close to our camp. All they needed in return was foot cleaning and some other general grooming. The gorillas and chimpanzees, while becoming freer, continued to express friendship and loyalty towards Stacy, Suko, and me. They moved around more, swinging from tree to tree after regaining more arm strength, which was in contrast to the zoo's evil decision not to include playground stuff in their exhibit sites.

One night, a breaking point was reached. Stacy, Suko, and I were sleeping peacefully in our shelter when sudden chaos erupted outside, jolting us awake. It was like waking up to an alarm clock, but it was not annoying. I opened my eyes, thrilled at the sounds of elephants whining, rhinos loudly doing their bull-like hums, and lions doing their main roars. "It's about time." I said to myself.

Suko started crying, and I quickly calmed him. "It's all going to be all right. Father's here." (The modern world really linguistically ruined the word "daddy" in favor of a world stripped of family bonds, so I refuse to use it).

We hurried outside to see what was happening. What we saw was nothing short of an open circus. The lions were chasing down packs of elephants, giraffes, and rhinos. It wasn't what you would expect because they ran more circularly. The scene was brutal, though. The lions, driven by their primal hunger, took down the giraffes quickly. Those defenseless spiritual daddy-long necks couldn't stand a chance, getting their tongues ripped off and the rest of their throats coming out of their mouths inside-out.

The elephants and rhinos, however, put up a fierce fight, using their size and strength to defend themselves. The elephants reliably broke the bones of one of them, injuring him to the point of immobility. Rhino charges tended to require a lot of skill, as concentrating in one direction would lead a rhino to commit to that way, while the lions had more flexible direction-changing. As the packs grew more cohesive due to the increasing threat, they managed to gnaw at the grey-armored skins. The battle was not clean, and many animals lay injured or dead on the ground.

I looked up into the forest trees and saw the chimpanzees and gorillas hiding among the branches, their eyes wide with fear. Nearby, I spotted our loyal horse smartly hiding behind the shelter, away from the fray. Holding Suko close, I whispered reassurances to him. "This is just how nature works," I said softly, trying to mask my nervousness. "Nature only cares about who wins. Think of it like a final 'game of tag' session for the prey, coming out with a bang."

A few hours after the remaining corpses of the animals left room temperature, Stacy, Suko, and I remained awake, our minds racing with the events that had unfolded. We didn't speak to one another verbally. It was all just amateurish sign and face language. But our shocked and exaggerated expressions made it easy to tell what meant what. However, we were also incoherently thinking, so communication was easy.

Just when we thought things had calmed down, a distant noise broke the silence— the unmistakable sound of a helicopter. It was like "patrol patrol patrol," substituting what I would expect a helicopter blade-in-wind sound to be. It quickly increased in volume, perhaps decreasing the horizontal distance between it and us. I had to find out.

"Stay inside," I instructed Stacy and Suko, my voice filled with urgency. "I'll check it out." I stepped out of the shelter, my heart pounding as the helicopter approached. I was shocked that it was heading to land next to our camp. I felt the thrust of the blades spinning, causing the grass and my hair to swerve. My hair was grown by now, and I never cared to cut it, so it was blown right before my eyes. I used my hands to remove the excess fluff from my field of view. Then I saw…

Two individuals in armed clothing exited the aircraft, their authoritative demeanor unmistakable. I recognized them immediately—they were city bureaucrats. I was able to tell because of their robotic movements and inhuman gazes. They wore belts holding all sorts of gadgets that I didn't recognize.

The bureaucrats started by telling me they were visibly alarmed by the sounds of wild animals. Now, seeing our primitive survival base, they were even more concerned.

One of them stepped forward, his voice cold and commanding. "We are rapidly expanding the city's size and require all non-official buildings in rural areas to be exterminated. After all, the government has purchased this land already."

Puzzled and frustrated, I asked, "Why is our encampment such an issue already? It took a long drive to get here from the city."

The bureaucrat pointed to the horizon down south. For the first time, I noticed a series of peculiarly white rectangles—city buildings encroaching on the natural landscape. The realization hit me hard. Stacy and I have been doing well and thriving in the wilderness for years. This whole time, we hadn't accounted for the fact that the city would, of course, decide to accelerate its growth via its easy-to-manufacture n-word pass structures, and now, it threatened our home.

"You have a choice," the bureaucrat continued. "Either you, that ridiculously ripped woman, and you guys' baby return to the city as a normal family and allow this encampment to be destroyed, or you go to prison."

Dissatisfied with both options, I replied that I didn't care and was unrelated to their inquiry, "You don't deserve to be in positions of power. If the city were well governed, it would have been cool enough for us cool people to become citizens of it naturally. Accelerating the quantitative scope is not going to make it any better. You guys coming here and yapping for us to be welfare receivers over there is like a failed entrepreneur who has to discount his trashy chocolate bars that can't sell."

Offended, the bureaucrats pointed tranquilizers at me. Tension filled the air. I started sweating because who knows what they would do to my body as I fell asleep. *Kill? Thugshake twerking? Rape?*

Just then, a miracle happened. Suko walked out of the shelter remarkably early in his development, startling the bureaucrats. "How is that baby even walking?!" one said.

I smiled, happy with how Stacy and I parented Suko so far, but I was worried that the bureaucrats would have to have empathy so shitty to be willing to kill a baby.

But as they remained distracted, the gorillas and chimpanzees dropped to the ground from the trees, speaking the basic English words I had taught them. Confusion spread among the bureaucrats as they pointed their tranquilizers at Suko and each animal, unsure of what to do. Seizing the moment, I tackled both of them, taking a tranquilizer rifle from one of their hands, and then shot both of them. Within seconds, they made orgasmic faces and then fell unconscious.

After a pause, I uttered a concern. "We can't stay. Surviving in the natural world is great, but we must face the enemy—the city itself. I need to stop them once and for all."

Stacy's eyes filled with worry, but she nodded, understanding the gravity of the situation. "Take care of Suko," I told her, my voice firm. "That's your mission. There's no guarantee I'll make it back due to the city's violent law enforcement."

Mounting the horse, I turned to face the direction of the city.

Chapter Seventeen: Non-Player Characters

Paradoxically, isn't the act of labeling random individuals in public as "NPCs" (Non-Player Characters) profoundly revealing and unsettling? While this term is rooted in the language of video games and modern cultural phenomena, it transcends the fakeness of the modern era. Consider, for instance, a primordial area where life is within the bounds of the unicellular stage; governed by a simplistic idiocracy of matter. These entities were essentially indistinguishable from one another, akin to a singular pseudo-organism. Yet, this archetype has persisted throughout history. Another notable manifestation can be found in the medieval witch hunters, who embodied the archetype of the social justice warriors—don't today's NPCs operate with an eerie resemblance to those ancient uniform lifeforms?

While seemingly kind due to their passivity and aversion to conflict, the NPC's true menace lies in their method of "replication." Despite their disinterest in meaningful growth, they propagate by mindlessly echoing programmed directives, disseminating these notions with surprising "smoothiness." May the ideas that spread effortlessly, therefore, often be the most illogical? This process is less about defending against coherent ideas (even if they may be clearly bad) and more about responding reflexively to specific symbolic patterns, akin to a subject in a quasi-translation blind room thought experiment. Experiencing one of these responses would signal to the NPC that such information is a "prerequisite" of "unthinkable"—almost demonic. Among political ideologies, would the technological system's leftism actually be particularly antagonistic toward diversity? This may be mirrored by the reality that many political or technological entities thrive under the euphemism of formal algorithmic fairness, claiming "fairness" without any kind of impact.[335] Yet, this kind of theoretical society that those parties preach about, in which every individual is precisely identical, might just be a metaphysical impossibility. Reflect upon the fact that within any social group, actual differences inevitably necessitate some form of hierarchy—wouldn't a Paretoistic effect unavoidably manifest?

This does not imply the existence of a universal criterion that objectively determines superiority, but the system's commitment to solidarity with marginalized groups is merely a euphemistic façade, concealing its intent to erode cultural barriers globally. This process aims to transform as many individuals as possible into complacent, mechanistic participants, which is an acceleration toward a communistic matrix. This is why many today and, in the past, would refer to "stakeholder capitalism" as communistic or socialistic,[336] as they have a tendency towards introducing socialist political systems. And as such, why should the notion of capitalism in its pure sense be blamed for the mechanistic NPC phenomenon? Isn't it strange that even though woke marketing is proven to cause negative reception, companies still go out of their way to do it at the

---

[335] B. Green, "The false promise of risk assessments: epistemic reform and the limits of fairness," *Proceedings of the ACM Conference on Fairness, Accountability, and Transparency (FAT*)*, 2020. https://doi.org/10.1145/3351095.3372869
[336] R.E. Nationalist, *The Eggs Benedict Option*, (Antelope Hill Publishing, 2022), 19.

expense of profit, even insincerely? Likewise, there is so much cliché about artificial intelligence hype driving early adoption and market expansion, often at the expense of marginalized communities.[337] I think this distracts us from important "before and afters." Market expansion, under modern technology, eventually to the scale of a "universal" is what may push a machine learning model to be inclusive of marginalized communities— but it just would not seem like it at the start. Marginalized people tend to be outnumbered initially, so speaking of chances, a non-marginalized person will much more likely get their hands on something first when it is released to the market. But once the market expands so broad that the "data" of marginalized people begins to reflect how much they are now integrated into the technological society, that would be when the pressure to "push for accountability" for more inclusivity begins. In what way is this a function of the system? Under the technological society, where living conditions are so dehumanizing, characteristics of self-augmentation and monism come into play—unnatural living conditions created by certain technological advancements generate new needs and demands, leading to the development of additional machines to fulfill these requirements.[338] Those technologies would effectively be the linguistic technologies of "inventing" fake persona archetypes such as corporate brands and pronouns (which semantically sound significant, but aren't culturally significant enough to interfere with the system's efficiency) as techniques that only exist in the realm of language. What else would it do to sedate a crass resistance to the massification of society?

Ultimately, what transpires within the minds of those we term "NPCs"? Consider how increased social crowding leads individuals to perceive their surroundings through more concrete, low-level construals. This crowding infringes upon personal space, triggering a defensive mechanism that elicits tense arousal and avoidance motivations. As crowding intensifies, individuals experience heightened arousal, prompting avoidance behaviors and the adoption of concrete mental frameworks.[339] This phenomenon exemplifies how overcrowding and a lack of personal space compel individuals to become indistinguishable from one another, driven by strong prevention goals. The aesthetic deficiencies of modern suburbia exacerbate this trend, making self-improvement unlikely. In this context, individuals increasingly turn to consumption as a form of escapism, denying the whole point of life even as their thoughts become more concretely focused. Moreover, many individuals exhibit learned helplessness—a state where, when faced with persistent stimuli and no apparent means of escape, the human mind surrenders. This condition further entrenches their passive existence, reinforcing their detachment from genuine experience and deepening their conformity, something that the ruling class uses against the populace so that there wouldn't be resistance against them.[340] Sounds familiar?

To illustrate, it has been discovered that it was unnecessary to force-feed geese to achieve the desired liver yield. By removing their cages, it's seen that once the geese

[337] D. McAra-Hunter, "How AI hype impacts the LGBTQ + community," *AI Ethics*, 2024. https://doi.org/10.1007/s43681-024-00423-8
[338] J. Ellul, *The Technological Society* (New York: Vintage Books, 1964), 111.
[339] A. Maeng and R.J Tanner, "Construing in a crowd: The effects of social crowding on mental construal," *Journal of Experimental Social Psychology*, 49(2013): 1084-1088. https://doi.org/10.1016/j.jesp.2013.07.010
[340] V. McLeod, *Clown World Chronicles* (VJM Publishing, 2020), 71.

perceived freedom, the presence of physical barriers became irrelevant, as they still acted as if they were still there.[341] This reflects the intricate dynamics of control, in which the NPC, their spiritual goose heads stuck below dirt ground in the seemingly autonomous flow of everyday choices, assumes that all choices that are already mere illusions within their reach are the only paths out there. Much like domesticated animals that are technically free to act otherwise but rarely deviate, NPCs may have the illusion of choice while remaining within the bounds of an environment. Could you go as far as to say that even those who appear so ambitious to do well in modernity are those who have the most kind of apathy resulting from learned helplessness?

It is foolish even to think that the elites themselves are free, as their choices are often dictated by "the inside"—achieving actual glory in such a world necessitates mastering from "the outside." It can even be argued that rather than the wagecuck, the technophiles are actually the biggest NPCs[342] (Even today, the "orator"[343] maintains relevance whether conscious or not, capable of bamboozling those who are more technically apt than they are). They may be deprived of the cognitive faculties required for the aspiration for higher values, diminishing even their nature on a fundamental level, thus transforming the entire collective into a docile and unthinking herd. Would all entities eventually "evolve" into hyperbolic expressions of their lower nature over time?

Municipal Apocalypse

Arriving at the city, I was immediately struck by how drastically it had changed. While I had expected to see the n-word pass architecture, the reality was far more disturbing. The cityscape was filled with painful, brightly lit structures that seemed to pierce the sky like razor-sharp blades. The clouds were no longer visible, and even the sun was beginning to suffer the same fate as the stars suffered when regular streetlights had already obscured them. These structures didn't touch the ground; they floated slightly above it, creating an eerie, unnatural effect.

As I moved further into the city, I noticed that some of these structures were flickering, alternating between white and black in a disorienting strobe effect. It was enough to make me feel like I might have a seizure.

The buildings reached thousands of feet into the air, dwarfing any "worldwide wonders" towers I had seen in the past. It was as if these monolithic forms had appeared overnight, completely transforming the skyline. The crazy thing is you'd think they would be in some world record book or article. Though I hadn't used the internet in years leading up to then, how would I know?

The realization hit me suddenly: these were not solid structures—I could see them "glitch out" and reveal some of the real physical objects behind them. Instead of concrete and steel, the architecture was composed entirely of artificial holograms. I assumed that some distant projector was out of sight, casting these holographic images across the city.

---

[341] D. Barber, "The farmer who makes 'ethical' foie gras," *The Guardian*, (18 January 2015) https://www.theguardian.com/world/2015/jan/18/the-farmer-who-makes-ethical-foie-gras.

[342] C.A Haag, *The Hermeneutics of Ecological Limitation: Ecophilosophy Beyond Environmentalism* (Independently Published, 2019), 87.

[343] Plato, *Gorgias* (Hackett Publishing Company, 1987).

The more I looked at them, the more nauseous I felt, but it was an indulgent kind of nausea reminiscent of getting drunk. I have never been drunk before, but it was pretty close to a combination of how people describe the "feeling cool" high from drinking and the shitty hangover the morning after. I quickly understood that I was succumbing to the n-word pass architecture hypnosis.

Desperate to regain my composure, I began blinking rapidly and focused on the ground, breaking the spell the holograms were trying to cast. I knew I probably looked like I was doing a virgin walk as I did this, but the deeper irony is I would become virgin-like if I were to succumb to the holograms. I attempted to do some funny things with the rest of my body, trying to do "Chad"-like movements. With my senses somewhat restored, I continued moving deeper into the city.

As I walked, I encountered the citizens. The streets were overcrowded, teeming with people packed within half a meter of each other. It was clear that there had been a massive population explosion. The city was expanding rapidly, but somehow, it was much more mechanistically advantageous for this population-space ratio mismatch.

But what struck me most was the people's behavior. Everyone was glued to their phone screens, engaging in the same mindless activities. Yes, this is striking. They were either spamming "n-word" or the now fake word "nature" on the dean's forums, watching unoriginal remakes of classic shows laced with characters saying "n-word," or using the word "nature" in the shows that are supposedly "dystopian" but are projected by the mainstream to make it look like the state would be willing to fix ecological problems. Or following the latest boring gaming streamer who raged using the same vulgar language, and saying he misses nature when he gets kicked into the respawn screen, preventing him from seeing the fake pieces of grass and trees that are just meshes in a game engine.

Curious about what was keeping them so close together, I reached out and touched one of the holographic structures. My hand passed right through it. There wasn't even any "fancy" light reaction to my skin's contact. It looked as expected if you cast a hand shadow on a flashlight's beam area.

As there wasn't even a "scary" look that came with going through the holograms, there was not at the slightest a physical barrier forcing the citizens into such close quarters; it was purely psychological. The holograms, combined with the hypnotic architecture and their mind-numbing phone activities, kept them packed like sardines and seemingly okay with everything. They were breathing into each other's faces (granted, they all seemed to have unnaturally white teeth, probably because of a widespread new corporate dental product). This revelation was both horrifying and enlightening (no pun intended). The city had managed to enslave its population without even having to remain a traditional physical police force, relying instead on manipulation that pushed the right buttons.

I stood amidst the crowded streets, the oppressive weight of the city's control bearing down on me.

With the horrifying realization of the city's transformation weighing heavily on my mind, the first people I thought of were my parents. They were both intelligent businesspeople even though businesspeople in this age are usually also easy to manipulate using propaganda mainly because they have a sense that they have so much to lose in the system.

My first stop was my mother's dental clinic. It would be quite a distance to there, as it was near the city's center and I was still near the edge. Mounting my horse, I rode through the altered cityscape, my heart heavy with anxiety. On the way, I was traversing much faster than I thought. Even though a ton of concrete buildings got in the way, and it was still technically taking me longer than it should have, being able to ride the horse through the holographic architecture made me feel like I was in ghost god mode in a video game. I, of course, made sure no security guard or the like watched me do so.

When I arrived at the dental clinic, I was devastated by what I saw. I remembered its previous branding—a memorable logo of an oyster with a white pearl inside, symbolizing pearly white teeth. The oyster looked more robotic, with the jaws of the clam being prosthetic.

The once-proud digital billboard used for marketing had been replaced with a holographic n-word pass. It made me feel sad. Thinking back, the dank memes my mother would add to the slideshows to be trendy toward the Zoomers were cute.

I entered the clinic, my worry intensifying. If you have ever gone to the dentist before, you'll know about the particular smells. Sometimes, you get a hint of blood. Sometimes, you get a hint of filling. Sometimes, if you are the optimistic kind of sniffer, you even get a whiff of the candy. I actually picked out none—there was no smell at all.

Inside, I found my mother working on a patient's root canal. Her movements were disturbingly uniform and robotic, as if she had been reduced to a machine but could be replaced by a machine at any moment.

I waited until she finished with the patient, watching her with concern and disbelief. I resumed sitting in the waiting area, bored as hell because the dental office had to remove all the cool decorations. I looked to the counter to see it was just the clerk who patients walk up to sign up or confirm their bookings. Usually, the accountant would sit beside the clerk. But that, I didn't see. Curiously, I went to the side of the counter (the clerk didn't question me because she recognized me as her boss's son). I was shocked that all the accounting work was being automated, and the clerk was checking to see if the bot program wasn't glitching. I should have received a 100% in my introduce-yourself-to-class assignment in COMM.

I met her in her office once my mother was done with the patient. Her teeth were unnaturally white, almost glowing. They looked so fake, contrasting the vibrant, natural smile I remembered.

My mother started barraging me about my imperfect teeth, criticizing them for being slightly less than pure white.

"Wait, what does that have to do with anything? Mom, I'm fine," I insisted. "I've survived in the woods for years without dental issues. The pre-agriculture food I ate acted as natural toothbrushes. Humans only needed to start flossing and brushing manually after we began relying on agricultural food."

She looked at me with a mixture of pity and frustration. "The hygiene standards in city life have become much higher, and you can't scrape by without perfectly sterile artificialities. Here, let me clean your teeth with this new instant bleach-like chemical. It's revolutionary, though it hasn't had much testing yet."

I recoiled at the offer. "No thank you."

"You are all grown up now. You'll have to have good hygiene in the world in front of you. Brush, floss properly, and brush the tongue. If a person has bad breath, that is the only thing that sticks in their mind, and they will always remember that's the guy with bad breath and unclean teeth. It can be a cruel world out there."

"The world in city life is cruel?" I questioned her. "What does the word 'cruel' mean to you? 'Cruel' isn't saying 'hello' to the bugmen you see every day, who don't care about you anyway. Cruelty isn't saying, 'Hi Bob, nice clothes you got today,' but having to hold back your real beliefs only because that would lead you to lose your job. Vital cruelty in its purest form is facing a cruel world with immense struggle, experiencing a bronze-age-like world as a barbarian, your life being at stake because of some jacked animal who may come to fight you, not being at the stake of getting kicked into the streets only because your boss doesn't think you're using the latest corporate mouthwash product, both literally and figuratively. I have amazing breath right now, the natural human pheromones."

I began to wonder if my mom herself was losing actual dental knowledge, even though she was considered one of the most excellent teeth persons in the city. You'd think that she'd know that people naturally lose their natural sexual-partner-attracting odors once they start using an external agent to replace them.

"Well then, FUCKING FUCK!" I said firmly, storming out of her office before she could argue further.

As I exited the clinic, I noticed the little basket where free lollipops were usually kept. Each lollipop now had a cockroach inside. It was like the one thing I wouldn't want to touch. Dead rats and insects with beady black eyes—you wouldn't ever want to see them submerged even in mediums you know you wouldn't consume because they don't deserve to touch anything. I couldn't help but laugh bitterly, realizing that this grotesque addition would artificially boost demand for dental cleanings. The combination of candy and insect legs that would get stuck in people's teeth would ensure more frequent visits, playing perfectly into the city's desire for more tax money.

Determined to see if my father had fared any better, I mounted my horse and sped to his restaurant, conveniently near the dental clinic. I felt sick to my stomach for a moment, contrasting the new clinic's ways of operation and the idea of food. Fake teeth coming in contact with something you are going to swallow are just a smaller-scale version of consuming bits of whatever the hell the material of the teeth is. Plus, you'd be smelling the metallic sensations while swallowing.

Shaking my head, I entered the restaurant.

Inside, no customers were eating. The once-bustin' place now stood empty, contrasting its former glory.

My father sat at one of the tables, engrossed in a live hockey game. He immediately noticed me and invited me to sit beside him. "Come, join me," he said, smiling. I should have been more careful when referring to his expression as "smiling" though. If you ever see the uncanny "long eyes" you should imagine how freaky the long mouth looked like. I almost thought my dad had become one of those creepy pot-bellied, long, scraggly hair, short torso, long legs, and nose apple witches that are always used as cheap jump scares in horror media.

I sat down, taking a deep breath. "Dad, you need to stop watching the hockey game. All the advertisements in the arena are just those bland default letters that would make you want to see ads from your competitors that list their food praises from celebrities and magazines."

He frowned, clearly annoyed. "What? It's so exciting to see who is going to score next!"

I sighed, trying to make him understand. "It's not even about sports now. The cardboard posters slid onto the white shiny walls that prevent the puck from hitting the expressionless eyes of the audience is what's keeping people away from your restaurant. It's everywhere, and it's affecting everything."

But he ignored my point, selectively hearing only what he wanted. "You need to meet more people and learn from them. You have to identify with our team! We are them! Go buy a jersey with the name of your favorite player!"

I couldn't help but visualize antennas emerging from the sides of my father's head. "It's all just the conventional way people practice to feel like superheroes. Imagine seeing one of the anonymous helmet-wearing mouthguard chipmunks who just so happened to wack the stick at an angle, which just so happened to be where a black rubber disk, and the angle just so happened to be towards a plastic frame covered by a web of fabric, and the glove-wearing fat man just so happens to fail to use his pity ability to be where the disc is flying. Then, the rules happens to increase a number in the corresponding time. Then you be like 'Oh mY GoD I JuSt AchIevEd SuCh CoOl ThiNG,' even though you as a television viewer are miles away from it and the pixels on the screen are delayed by a millisecond due to stream lag."

But despite my intellectually deep lecture, he rambled on, blaming everything on the economy, which had become the mainstream scapegoat for any business trouble. "The economy is bad. That's why there are no customers. The economy gonna be bad!"

"You got jokes, sir; the economy in our area, at least, is actually at its peak," I argued. "The city's so-called anti-stress protocols are just euphemisms for viewing people as mere utility. Everyone is staying home because the moment they are not as willing to hang themselves on a noose, they are more able to continue doing nerdy birdy trash. After that, it's immediately their bedtime."

He waved off my concerns, sticking to his old habits of selective hearing. "You should wrangle up with more regular people. You'll understand then. Don't be shy, you will be similar to the smart people if you are around them."

Frustration mounted as I tried to reason with him. "Words thrown around over frivolous things will be at risk of manipulation. I have nothing to say to the robots that roam the streets. Even the word 'shy' itself is already undergoing severe butchering. The issue is the system's tendency to reward those who can parrot the usual 'Good, how are you?' and 'Good weather we are having' or, better yet, the latest punchline in the trending sitcom shows because those are the easiest sentences to find a response in a 'response' toolbox. If I mix myself with the caste of the robots, they will talk over me because they can't handle anything more complex than what somebody decided to write on a script. If I become the sum of the people who are here, I would be as lame as going to the local fried chicken restaurant and buying the meal that comes with a card."

But my father, old and hard of hearing, misheard every word I said. Realizing that I wasn't getting through to him, I finally gave up. I stood up and left the restaurant, feeling a deep sense of despair.

As I walked away, I couldn't help but feel the weight of the city's control bearing down on my family. Both my parents were trapped in the system, unable to see the truth.

Riding out of the city, I felt a growing sense of despair. My parents, once people who at certain times were pillars of wisdom that actually kept me alive in a giant industrial cooker at the start, had been reduced to mere shadows of themselves, images of their actual forms being trapped in bulbous lights held by a monstrous beast with goat-like horns.

I rode my horse to the nearest mass of robotized citizens I could find, feeling a desperate urge to yell out, to shake them from their stupor. It was the only way I could feel like I could impact things at the time. Sure, I had things in the tips of my fingers out of the city, but it just seems cucked to plug out of the system without attempting to seek ways to destroy it.

Out of sheer frustration, I decided to go all in. "All of you need a spiritual awakening!" I shouted at the herd. I was surprisingly quiet in my eyes. I was so mad, feeling like I was talking through a telephone with hopelessly bad reception because all of them were broken. Yes, they deserve to be dehumanized to such depersonification.

Unsurprisingly, the response was immediate and aggressive. "Did that guy riding on the horse just say 'spiritual'?" one person in the crowd exclaimed. "Holy crap, he just said the word 'spiritual,' and therefore, he must be a witch who can summon evil demons and ghosts! Let's get him!"

My heart sank as I realized my mistake. Spirituality had become such an alien concept to these people that the word had lost its true meaning. They now associated it with "spirits" in the most literal sense, viewing it as something sinister and dangerous.

The crowd ran toward me in unison, a uniform mass of rage-fueled bodies. I spurred my horse into a gallop, rocking back and forth. Even as we gained distance, I noticed the crowd's relentless stamina. Horses are fast indeed, and that's why we domesticated them. However, human endurance is formidable, so we managed to reach the top of the food chain. I needed to find high ground to escape them.

After what felt like an eternity of riding, I saw a gigantic power dam looming ahead. Glancing back, I saw the herd not far behind. But I calculated that they would reach a danger zone if I stopped the horse for ten seconds. For any bugman who knows how to drive, shit like that is why the two-second rule is a thing. A plan formed in my mind: I would lead them to the dam's edge and let their momentum carry them over.

As we approached the pit, I prompted my horse to reevaluate. It turned on a dime and "errrched," forming massive dust clouds. I coughed as I unexpectedly inhaled some of it. But luckily, it was loud. The old lady cough produced some soundwaves that made it appear that we were right on the edge, and the zombified crowd continued running straight, unable to stop, and one by one, they plummeted off the edge into the water below. Their cries echoed in the air as I breathed a sigh of relief, safe for the moment. I looked down into the abyss to find out they all either drowned to death or got their frontal bodies scraped by a thicker water laser stream of death.

Calming down from the close call, I turned my attention to the peculiarities of the power dam. It was much larger than most built ones, both in terms of height and width. The herd that just fell probably even died because the impact on the water molecules was just so high of a force. I studied the mother of it all. There was a gigantic metal structure extending to the clouds. It resembled one of those magical pyramids with a beam of light shining from the top, except hundreds of beams emitting horizontally and descending downward gradually. I soon discovered that this was from a place of evil—I traced the beams of light and saw they all each led to a building in the urban area. So this projector produced all the city's holograms, powered by the dam itself.

Chapter Eighteen: Body

How the hell has modern man and the pseudo-culture that he didn't even mindfully craft, plummet to a status beneath even that of what some people laugh at for "being animals"? Observe, if you decide to at last admit to being a panty wearer, the force of the kind of life that at first looks like old men with overgrown hair. Look past, and you will reveal a hint of superior physique that would make most wear a soyboy face. Most modern men, within their frailty, would melt even with the aid of sharp dildos against the might of this. This difference shows that an authentic culture presents upon a kind of life a great power, even in the realm of the physical. Unlike humans, who have to now kiss ass to the pernicious seduction of skipping forces that signal needs for the next iteration and endlessly technologizing their tools based on mere energy and availability, even animals retain a purity of function. In a blind pursuit, mankind has just forged a chasm between individual capacity and technological output, a gap ever widening. This is typical of societies devoid of culture, ensnared by a lack of interest in first going through the synthesizing of hard knocks, crafting intermediaries that fail to bridge the gaping asshole between subjective input, the movements of their unique branches, and the teleological aspirations of their creations. Now, seriously, compare the pseudo-culture of the declining West to chimps as they are right now. There are, in fact, differences amongst chimps in which the influence of cultural transmission exists. It was revealed that Kasekela chimpanzees used a greater variety of raw materials and produced longer and wider tools compared to Mitumba chimpanzees, with significant differences in tool length and width indicating cultural influences.[344] Kasekela tools were made from various plant species, while Mitumba tools were predominantly made from twigs, reflecting cultural preferences rather than availability.[345] How is there so much normie-ification of human cultures in relation to other life?

There is significance to the Foucauldian notion of conditioning the individual into a docile body, which is favorable by governance,[346] and the fact that there is increasingly a prevailing phenomenon where there is a singular role only partially focusing on the cognitive parts of a person's form.[347] Aren't these both yet massive negations of the self? Transitioning to the realm of innovation, this degradation of "progress" lies in the dissociation of purpose from action, reducing higher forms of consciousness to automatisms. True innovations of the past were those that accounted for increasing human potential rather than stifling it. In the good times, individuals compensated for deficiencies in tools with strength and dexterity, preserving the potential for generational growth. Considering the idea of a "cyborg" where the boundary between life and technology is increasingly ambiguous,[348] we could see that cyborgism is already happening implicitly

---

[344] A. Pascual-Garrido, "Cultural variation between neighbouring communities of chimpanzees at Gombe, Tanzania," *Sci Rep*, 9(2019). https://doi.org/10.1038/s41598-019-44703-4
[345] Ibid.
[346] G. Burchell, C. Gordon, and P. Miller (eds), *The Foucault Effect* (University of Chicago Press, 1991).
[347] Y. Moulier-Boutang, *Cognitive Capitalism* (Polity, 2011).
[348] D. Haraway, *The Haraway Reader* (Routledge, 2004), 7-45.

without the cliché of us having to overtly replace our literal morphological features, though it has to do so slowly. And it IS BAD ALREADY. Further exploring this notion, viruses symbolize a regression from complex life forms into entities dependent on external agents for existence. Relating to this, humanity risks a similar fate within a milieu devoid of authentic space, where individuals sacrifice private spheres and familial bonds in favor of mechanical existence and the dissemination of degenerative ideologies. Isn't the reliance on external technological agents symbolic of a euphemistic transformation into viral bodies (Ironically, in our modern age, nonconformists are often viewed as the parasitic entities)?

Furthermore, a far cry from this viral form, the BAPist view of higher life isn't just limited to animate/idleness, but also differentiation and structure in that higher life has different parts with different functions (like organs and systems, differences in sexes).[349] In fact, preservation of this differentiation would sacrifice an ability to aimlessly replicate homogenously; or, in more Nietzschean terms, a reduction in mere number can be a symptom of growing strength and perfection.[350] For instance, it's seen that for man, his inborn character and biology are in contrast to the more uniform character of life, especially yeast.[351] Given this, what could then be said about the system's negation of individual and social differentiation?

For instance, amongst the more uniform life, perhaps from the lens of a technologized system, asexual reproduction embodies several "efficiencies," such as the expeditious augmentation of the populace under auspicious conditions, the solitary sufficiency of a singular progenitor, and the superior economy of time and energy devoid of the necessity to stop being a no-life virgin. Yet, this mode of reproduction is not without its vices; it engenders a death of differentiation within the collective, thereby confining the kind of life to a singular role and rendering the entirety of the collective vulnerable.[352] Thus, it may be stupid to conclude that we would hypothetically attain greater potency and efficacy by regressing to asexual reproduction—these contributors would perhaps tend to lead each individual attuned to a limited range of natural contexts. There is an observation in which Darwinists would be perplexed by traits like the peacock's tail because they seemed maladaptive in terms of natural selection.[353] Distinguishing between sexes (as significant biological categories) and reproductive dimorphism (species having two distinct types that mate with each other), one might argue that reproductive dimorphism better fits explanations of sexual selection, as strikingly, many traits associated with sex are not consistently correlated across taxa.[354] But this would seemingly imply to some that the concept of "sex" as a strictly biological and fundamental category is probably a social construct, which is yet another idea that some leftists would use to try to convince us that they can invent 68 genders out of thin air. Besides the fact that a peacock tail is only seemingly obsolete because it may be some technical error in a

---

[349] B.A. Pervert, *Bronze Age Mindset* (Independently Published, 2018), 29.

[350] F. Nietzsche, *On the Genealogy of Morals* (Penguin Classics, 2013), 63-64.

[351] B.A. Pervert, *Bronze Age Mindset* (Independently Published, 2018), 41.

[352] BBC, "Inheritance - OCR Gateway: Evaluating sexual and asexual reproduction," *BBC*. https://www.bbc.co.uk/bitesize/guides/zqv6gdm/revision/5

[353] A. Evron, "What Do Sexes Have to Do with (Models of) Sexual Selection?" *Philosophy of Science*, 91(2024): 310-328. https://doi.org/10.1017/psa.2023.86

[354] Ibid.

technological society, studied by a Darwinist who only theorizes under faulty assumptions, it is perhaps a kind of an example of "the naturalistic fallacy for leftists." For example, morphologically speaking, in some forms of life, males are larger than females (like many mammals), while in others, there is no systematic size difference between the sexes. Furthermore, among mammals, parental care is typically female-only, but in some other forms of life, care is biparental or entirely absent after egg-laying. All in all, using fundamentally different lifeforms as points to prove that sex should be merely a social construct is really just an insult to mankind. Do we really want to stoop to the level of the kinds of creatures that, again, contradict the assumption that parental care and meaningful social relations are universal traits associated with one sex? No! And modern society heading to this state is a sign of us going down the path of regression as familial structures are deteriorating (increasingly, we see women having thicker thighs than even dudes who train quads while bulking). Food for thought, there are many cases of automaton life that can change sexes in a whim—though this may sound like some fun cartoon character shit that sounds unmundane, I'd argue that this could illustrate how the dissolution of sex roles is so perversely favored by the technological system. Mankind under the "tyranny" of "sex-individualism language" may seemingly sound quirky at first, but in actuality, this is to result in the increase of the net number of potential uniformly efficient wagecucks of the technological system—in the end, wouldn't it slowly average out to one single synthetic wagecucking pseudo-sex?

Plus, how unbadass would such a uniformity sound to you? The direction towards this is perhaps how there is a decline in war when it comes to the individual warrior—the concept of war becomes more collective and internationalized, moving away from the individual heroism of the warrior to a more impersonal and mechanized form of conflict. There is a phase that marks the decline of war, known as the bourgeois phase, where the warrior archetype is transformed into that of the soldier, and the motivations for war become more aligned with economic interests rather than heroic ideals.[355] Following that would be the communist phase and technological age in which war has been reduced to combat between machines.[356] And so far, it really does seem to be the case that it isn't actually the soldier who is actually fighting (and may even be regressed to the form of the kind of "primitive" who exist today who disappear definitively rather than "evolve"[357]). How would even mere life itself prevail under this?

Could mitigating the lack of embodiment that characterizes the modern world potentially be initiated by understanding embodiment as a form of enactment? Exiting this virtualness may be facilitated by physical actions that mimic actions that are portrayed in the output.[358] So, perhaps a solution to the unbadass technological hellhole would be focusing on developing indemocratized/uncommunistic technology that is much less alienated from the body, akin to the bow and arrow. It is held that unlike much of modern technology, archery involves both technical efficiency and aesthetic experience.

---

[355] J. Evola, *Metaphysics of War* (Arktos Media, 2011), 90.

[356] Ibid., 19.

[357] Ibid., 67.

[358] L. Hjorth and E. Milne (eds), "IE '07: Proceedings of the 4th Australasian conference on Interactive entertainment" *IE07: Australian Conference on Interactive Entertainment Melbourne Australia* (3-5th December 2007) Melbourne Australia.

Instinctive archery, for instance, is described as flexible and versatile, fostering a deeper connection with the environment and one's body.[359] The aesthetic experience in it is compared to the Aristotelian notion of virtue acquired through habituation—it allows for more improvisation and creativity compared to non-instinctive methods—archers can adapt to various conditions and switch between different types of bows, emphasizing spontaneity and versatility.[360] For traditional archers, the aesthetic experience does not detract from technical efficiency; rather, it complements it. For example, observing the arrow's flight allows the archer to gain quick feedback on the shot's quality and make necessary adjustments.[361] There is much importance in developing a habitus—a stable disposition involving the integration of numerous skills and movements into a unified, fluid, and smooth bodily expression, which requires repeated practice and a deep familiarity with the process, enhancing the archer's overall skill and physical coordination. It appears that "devices" like this are the good "bodily extensions" that have no inherent mechanism to degrade their users. Instinctive archery, in particular, fosters versatility and spontaneity, allowing the archer to adapt and improvise, thereby sharpening their intuitive and creative skills. The notion of trying to "become the arrow" would emphasize the engagement required in archery. This transformation underscores the unity of mind and body, enhancing the archer's self-awareness and control. Archery demands the continuous development and refinement of skills, fostering a deep mastery that involves both body and mind. Modern technologies like fully automatic guns, while requiring some level of skill, do not necessitate the same depth of physical musculature and mental training, potentially leading to a less comprehensive development of abilities. This depth is less prevalent in activities that rely on simple, mechanical actions like pulling a trigger. Assuming other factors are equal, who would be more likely to have 22-inch biceps; a man who works his ass off with a bow, a button-pusher, or your mom?

Let me make things clear: I don't mean to necessarily sneer against the concept of firearms, as, in general, they were invented before the Industrial Revolution, the 14th century.[362] I mostly sneer against the ones that require a clunky organization and an alienated long supply chain just to get into the hands of the user. Firearms were at least feasible to make if one could find the right scrap materials and other shit and build by an individual (hammers having the same degree of man-directed motion as archery) which also could be handmade. An individual within a vast, orderly organization (which itself may compromise substantial investment in self-defense to invest more in efficiency) would likely only contribute to about 5% of the weapon's production, which is nowhere near enough to not be alienated when he would theoretically start operating it. Essentially, the closer a technology's function is to the motion of one's conscious body, the less likely it is to require a strict organization to produce because the man's body would ALREADY be a crucial component of the tool's mechanism. One could notice a newer permutation

---

[359] E. Bianchi, "Towards an Aesthetics of Archery," *The British Journal of Aesthetics*, 64(2024): 33-48. https://doi.org/10.1093/aesthj/ayad007

[360] Ibid.

[361] Ibid.

[362] D.A. Tegegn, "The role of science and technology in reconstructing human social history: effect of technology change on society," *Cogent Social Sciences*, 10(2024). https://doi.org/10.1080/23311886.2024.2356916

in the technological society in a cyclical fashion where "democratizing technologies" elevate businesses, but only until "corporatization."[363] This may highlight the importance of the Haagian term "ergonomic," in which one has to understand the full process of the work of an object to understand the object.[364] Honestly, things wouldn't be so bad if people were either significantly involved in the creation of "bodily extensions" if they make such; or if they aren't the manufacturer, the technology's input-output function is significantly tied to the body's movement. The biggest problem is that everyone in the technologized society has neither of those qualities—could this also lead to a feedback loop? It has been speculated that people's revulsion for life ascension is partly because modern man no longer has to even do farming work himself, which alienates him from the heredity decisions that would have to be made to net the most productive plants.[365] So, is the nature of wagecuck consumerism, paired with the prevalence of the Haagian counter-sense object, favorable in modernity because it would more likely lead to this decline of the body and, therefore, more technological state control?

Under modernity, at the very best if we get lucky, the individual who'd "stand out" would be "democratized" superheroes—superheroes who don't have powers but instead are "superconsumers" who buy their way into their power.[366] But little would they know, the "powers" are "stealable" abilities—for example, one can theoretically take a B*tmobile and run over B*tman (from the movie "B*tman"; Woke B*tman be like: "I'm B*t-them" lol). I am not implying that we should even worship the fictitious superheroes as well—even the ones many times stronger than the normal man. Some would even say all these fictitious superheroes are a psyop, being fabricated by the system because that would discourage man from becoming a hero without a super serum.[367] Rather, "primordial heroism" should be the proper heroism—one who though has strength that isn't attainable naturally by most, is meant to inspire men and to teach us about nature.[368] What would be a real-life example of a virtuous "superhero" that isn't so catered to the soyboys, and what could have led to their downfall? More curious, what could lead to their uprise?

It is believed back then: the Spartan Hoplite understood that skill and martial excellence made up around 80% of his chances of survival and glory, and the rest was luck. However, obviously for the modern man, this ratio is inverse with the advancements of technology.[369] This may continue to worsen, until a certain tipping point—a logical step of the technological system is said to be a scenario where human soldiers and cops in the future will likely be replaced by robots who will shoot down protestors without

---

[363] F. Phillips, "Interconnections: A Systems History of Science, Technology, Leisure, and Fear," *Journal of Open Innovation: Technology, Market, and Complexity,* 7(2021). https://doi.org/10.3390/joitmc7010014.
[364] C.A Haag, *The Hermeneutics of Ecological Limitation: Ecophilosophy Beyond Environmentalism* (Independently Published, 2019), 146.
[365] E. Dutton, *Breeding the Human Herd* (Imperium Press, 2023), 295.
[366] C.A. Haag, *Hermeneutical Death: The Technological Destruction of Subjectivity* (Independently Published, 2020), 19.
[367] F. Disciple, *Resavager Volume 1* (RESAVAGER Media, 2023), 90.
[368] Ibid., 91.
[369] B. Disciple, *Barbaric Vitalism* (RESAVAGER Media, 2023), 131.

hesitation in the future.[370] But given that killing has less of a hesitation factor when it can be done from far physical distances,[371] made possible by technological apparatus, would this make a system superior to a group with personal subjective agency, militaristically?

Now consider that machines depend much on predictableness, which can lead to aimless firing.[372] That may create room for ever more predictable blind spots. For this reason, the Hoplites did ritualistic dances back then, which, from a superficial view, doesn't seem militaristically efficient but creates confusion in enemies (which may especially be the case for the "literal thinkers"[373]). You shall also acknowledge the idea that loss in morphological diversity increases the likelihood of universal disappearance[374] (Ye boys, meaningful divowsity cool/epic). If a technological system needs its members to all be somatically identical, why would their blindspots not subject them to unadaptability at an existential level in the event of a sudden change?

When you think of it, the globalized technological system is basically a giant uniform mass—in a sense, that make them much more militarily weak. It's pretty obvious that a legion of brotherhoods has a better chance of fighting against an extraterrestrial invasion than if an entire globalized civilization were to chuck its entire army of anonymous husks—whose only factors of differentiation are linguistic pronouns—into a combat mosh pit. Think of the fighting as if you're using an area-of-effect weapon in a video game that can slay multiple small enemies at once—when one is fighting a decentralized legion of brotherhoods, they are less predictable, and a single tactic wouldn't be sufficient to wipe them. There is significance to the idea that even though some athletes employ "suboptimal" means of winning, such as playing beautifully, their actions are still considered rational, and the aesthetics are considered a win in and of itself.[375] Overall, would you say such a non-technical society could be superior even on a technical level?

The War

Determined to confront the heart of the vehicle of the tyrant and the tyrant itself, I entered the legislative building's entrance. The tiles underfoot were filthy, with pieces of debris stuck in the grout lines. If anything, this was what my "teeth person mother" should have been complaining about regarding "plaque." The smell was overwhelmingly foul—a combination of swimming pool chlorine and the stench of urine and feces that the chlorine was supposed to mask.

Since I had spent so much in the wilderness, developing natural pheromones and a branched tubule connection to both the earth's ground and the sky, I needed to maintain it—the artificial, pungent smell of this place was an assault on my senses. If any coomer

---

[370] T. Kaczynski, *Anti-Tech Revolution: Why and How* (Scottsdale: Fitch & Madison, 2020), 189.

[371] R. Sparrow, "Predators or plowshares? Arms control of robotic weapons," *Technology and Society Magazine*, 28(2009): 25–29.

[372] B.R. Duffy, "Fundamental Issues in Social Robotics," *The International Review of Information Ethics*, 6(2006): 31-36. https://doi.org/10.29173/irie137.

[373] N. Wiener, (1961). *Cybernetics: Or Control and Communication in The Animal and Machine* (2nd ed.) (MIT Press, 1961).

[374] R. Frankham, "Genetics and extinction," *Biological Conservation*, 126(2005): 131–140. https://doi.org/10.1016/j.biocon.2005.05.002.

[375] Y. Eylon, "The Contest Paradox," *Sport, Ethics and Philosophy*, 2024: 1-16. https://doi.org/10.1080/17511321.2024.2331679

has ever decided to start a cum jar for some reason and eventually they accumulate enough that they wouldn't dare pour it down a sink despite *not* actively taking any initiative to do so, I *oppositely* felt similar, except I did take the initiative to endure nature's forces. I ran to the end of the hallway, my footsteps echoing off the grimy tiles.

As I burst through the door at the end of the hall, I found myself in a markedly different room. This space was more formal and decorated, befitting a legislative building. The walls were lined with dark wood paneling, and ornate chandeliers hung from the ceiling, casting a warm, golden light. Plush carpets muffled my footsteps, and the air was filled with the faint scent of polished wood and leather. As I took in the surroundings, I met eyes with one of the guards stationed by the door. To my surprise, he smiled at me, a gesture so out of place that it caught me off guard. Confused but determined, I moved on, the contrast between the squalid hallway and this refined space highlighting the duality of the city's decay. My resolve hardened with each step. I felt like I was in the bedroom of a man-child who refused to get his life straight together. The smell of saliva from blankets is ever-increasing, with sweat that only accumulates because of one area of an epidermis that touches another for too long rather than movement. Even though there was a momentary freshness, I could feel the air growing thick again. The visage, initially a cold color with a hint of teal, also grew in warmth.

As I moved into the next room, I found myself in a reception area dominated by a large desk. Behind the desk sat a clerk who looked profoundly sickly and weak. His skin was unnaturally smooth, yet his features showed signs of aging—his hairline was receding, his eyelids drooped with heavy folds, and his face and limbs had lost their natural bone mass. It was as if he embodied the worst of both worlds: the appearance of an immature child combined with the frailty of an old man. The overall effect was unsettling, making it impossible to take him seriously because anyone would assume him to be unqualified to do even the most mediocre jobs. Simultaneously, they'd think he has Alzheimer's, but then one would wonder: how are so many people with Alzheimer's getting themselves into presidential positions?

I approached the desk, trying to mask my revulsion and concern. "Hello," I said, forcing a friendly tone, about to spit out some funny jargon that would excite a robotized person no matter how many questions there would be to ask. "I am an associate of Boobcorp Industries, and I'm here to see the mayor. I have some new, innovative ideas to help the city flourish and expand. CuTtInG EdGe."

The clerk looked up at me with tired eyes, expressing mild confusion. "You can just email the mayor," he replied in a monotone voice.

I pretended to be taken aback. "Email? But I have a piece of new technology to demonstrate. It's something that needs to be experienced in person. It involves touch and feel. Besides, with the powerful algorithms in the city, anyone can create deepfake video footage of technology that doesn't exist."

The clerk stared at me, processing my words slowly. After a long pause, he finally spoke. "Touching and feeling don't matter these days. That component of the five senses has been a useless feature of humans all along; there must have been some anomalous mistake in the past that made us adopt them. Ultimately, prosthetics programmed to invoke any stimulus we want in our brains will be available for everyone."

Thinking quickly, I leaned in slightly, maintaining eye contact. "I really need a way to get the technology into their hands. I assure you, it will introduce a new sense that will simulate the greatest p0rnography in new ways that we previously couldn't imagine. Can you tell me where I might do that?"

The clerk sighed, then relented. "Well, me and our people would love that! Alright. You can make a proposal to our technical experts. They are in room 314. You can take the elevator at the end of this hall. But remember, this is highly irregular."

"Thank you," I said, pretending to give him a reassuring smile before heading toward the elevator. The hallway leading to the elevator was dimly lit, with flickering fluorescent lights casting eerie shadows on the walls. The air smelled of stale disinfectant, a sharp change from the sickly-sweet chlorine and urine scent of the previous hallway—I still had that setting in my head even after I left it since the clerk looked like he would smell like it. I stepped into the elevator, the metal doors creaking as they closed behind me.

Inside the elevator, the walls were lined with scratched and dented stainless steel. The buttons for the floors were worn from years of use, but interestingly, the "fingerprints" that I saw on them didn't at all have patterns, just straight-up circular stains of solid mist. The ride felt like an eternity, the only sound being the creaking of the cables and the faint hum of the motor. As I neared my destination, my mind raced with the possibilities of what was going to be behind the door.

But that door 314 turned out to be not really a door. Think of yourself as a dog running around the house, and you can only access the parts of the home that your owner permits. These are usually already-open doors or one of those smaller paddle doors at the bottom of person-sized doors. This one right here was a combination of those. As I pushed, it rotated on its axis really easily. It was only a psychological barrier that would have prevented me from entering.

Entering room 314, I was taken aback by what lay before me. The room resembled a museum-like storage facility, showcasing the top tech companies' contributions to the city's government. Ironically, these very companies were funded by the government in the first place, very carefully cherrypicked. The space was filled with sleek displays and glass cases, each housing advanced technological artifacts that looked both futuristic and outlandish. The first thing I noticed was the militaristic theme of the exhibits. However, something seemed contradictory. The so-called weapons appeared to be made of plastic, yet they were described as incredibly durable. Intrigued, I approached a series of plastic boxes enclosing the technology.

The first box was labeled "Dorabae Basic Gun 3000." It was described as an automatic ranged firearm, but remarkably lightweight. It was designed to be so light that even small "organisms" could easily carry it. It featured an "aim assist" function, where an articulated barrel would "intelligently" aim at anything that moved and looked distinctly different from what was pre-programmed when the gun was being engineered.

Next to it, I found another striking piece of military tech: the "Dorabae Basic Helmet 3000." This helmet had giant goggles attached, offering the wearer a rose-tinted view of everything, even during wars. If you see anyone die, it will make it look like they are disappearing as if "GaMerS DoN'T DiE, ThEY ReSpawN" in a way that's perverse because the visual falsely implies their crude intellect would carry over, and if the algorithm fails to do that if the in actual life death animation is too irregular, their blood is converted to a green color instead of red similar to how China censors violent gore media right now. The helmet had a tinfoil texture, supposedly to make the wearer feel "rebellious," when really, they are just servants to a dysfunctional, pathologically altruistic government, fighting for an entirely different country.

Then, there was the "Dorabae Basic Armor 3000," a bodysuit that looked like spandex but was described as being both very light and indestructible. It claimed to prevent any pain completely and was flexible enough to fit any body size.

The more I inspected these technologies, the more suspicious I became. They all seemed powerful and efficient, yet the descriptions were filled with words that felt like oxymorons—phrases that sounded like something a toddler would greedily put on a Christmas wish list. Despite their seemingly fantastical nature, they were right in front of my eyes. The room's walls were lined with more bizarre displays than the last. A holographic roadmap outlined the future upgrades for these technologies. It indicated that these were just the beginning. The problem was that these technologies were hardwired to upgrade themselves, destroying their predecessors before any "consumer" could learn how to make their own, even with complete information.

As I stood there, absorbing the implications of this technology, I realized how insidious it all was. A man should ideally experience the pains of war to understand its true cost. A man should personally strike an enemy to recognize who the enemy is. A man should see some of his allies get struck to internalize the realities of war and psychologically reinforce himself. This artificial, sanitized version of warfare removed all the human elements that made war something to be dreaded and avoided. It turned the conflict into a sterile, emotionless process, stripping away the very experiences that could lead to a deeper understanding and, potentially, real peace.

I nearly jumped when I heard a group of people enter the room. Turning to the back doorway, I saw more than ten individuals arriving, all equipped with the combat technologies I had just been examining. But their helmets were off, allowing me to see their faces clearly.

What I noticed about their facial features collectively was unsettling. Individually, they might have passed as "normal humans" of our times, perhaps the type of manlets to take off their fedora hats for a moment to insincerely greet someone else and feel like they are in an old classical movie of "during-industrial factory" workers. But as a group, their similarities were striking. Each face seemed like it could morph into the same face as all the others, which is the very same face they had all along. One can take a face generated by one of those "this person doesn't exist" websites and paste it onto the head of one of those soldiers, and they'd give off a "prettiest ugly person in the world" look. They all resembled the old clerk I had seen earlier, who was young yet simultaneously old-looking, a disturbing blend of agelessness, except their blend of identity ambiguity was sex-related. They moved the same, neither doing a hip sway nor a perfectly straight leg-o-man walk.

But it wasn't just their androgynous features that were disconcerting. These soldiers bore an uncanny resemblance to the stereotypical grey aliens, with their necks barely able to support their heads (only possible with the armor they were wearing), who would mindlessly say "shore" quietly to every command given by even a subordinate. I was tempted to say, "Hey, you guys weren't bald before," but I had to keep my mouth shut because they looked like they had the kind of aggravation propensity that one of those classmates in elementary school physical education class who have lightning bolt patterns as their buzzed haircuts and take the sports too seriously.

The strange-looking soldiers approached me, their faces lighting up with excitement. "Oh boy, oh boy, what new technology do you have that we may use?" one of them asked eagerly. They started to do an ass shake, imagining themselves operating whatever the fuck they were expecting, my "fake, made-up invention" they had in their fake imagination. Knowing I had lied to get this far, I tried to think quickly. "Hold your horses. Sorry to break it for you all, but this technology doesn't fit you guys. It's just too big and heavy. Maybe someday you guys may grow into it."

Drats, I spoke too honestly, but I just didn't feel like lying at the time. Suddenly, the atmosphere in the room shifted. "HOW DARE YOU MAKE IT UNACCESSIBLE!" one of them shouted.

In the midst of the escalating tension, one of the soldiers latched onto my phrase. "You want us to hold horses? I'll do it," he said and then abruptly left the room.

As the tension mounted, another soldier took out a tablet and turned it on, then turned it around to face the screen to me. They showed me live security camera footage. To my horror, I saw the soldier who had left the room strangling my horse that I left outside before entering the legislative building.

"MEHEHEH!" my horse managed to cry out amidst the asphyxiation. Fuck, now I regretted not riding it in because the doors and halls would have been more than big enough to fit it—they designed the structures to be accommodating to increasingly obese people. Rage boiled within me. "Enough!" I yelled, my voice echoing through the room. "You want a challenge? Fine, let's fight."

The androgynous soldiers' ambiguous faces twisted with anger, making them look like insecure low testosterone baby-faced young adults who intentionally scrunch up their faces to look like "tough older men" as their way to "looksmax," but only to end up looking like they were born with progeria. The room, with its sleek displays and gleaming gadgets, seemed to close in around us, turning into a battleground.

Suddenly, there was a knocking on the door through which I had first entered the room. The sound grabbed my attention, as did that of the androgynous soldiers. The knocking grew slightly harder as the soldiers quickly put on their helmets and aimed their guns at the door. I glanced at the gap between the door and the floor and noticed strange-looking feet—too narrow and unlike any shoes I'd seen before.

The knocks seemed more forceful as if the being behind the door was trying to break in, albeit weakly, rather than politely indicating their presence. That was when I began to feel slightly relieved because there was no way this wasn't an outsider to the government. Finally, the door flew open, and I was shocked by what I saw. It was my three pet cats that lived in my parent's house: Boe, along with Mochi the Calico Cat, and Yuki the White Cat. Behind them were the chimpanzees (one holding the bloody corpses of guards) and gorillas from my time in the wildlife. Ryan, out of all people, was also there and looking freakier than ever without his eyes. And then I saw Stacy, holding Suko in her arms.

"Stacy, what are you doing here? You were supposed to stay outside the city and focus on taking care of Suko," I said, my voice filled with concern and surprise.

Stacy met my eyes with determination. "I had so much hope that you would successfully revolt against the n-word pass city that I decided to bring Suko along to witness such a historical event. He needs to learn how to be a warrior. So, I brought the animals to help sniff out your natural pheromones and find you. Ryan also offered to help, as he diligently trained his smelling abilities to compensate for his lack of eyesight."

As we spoke, I noticed through my peripheral vision that Ryan, the cats, and the apes were quietly beginning to equip some of the spare militaristic equipment in a poorly organized storage box at the center of the room. The designs, with slightly hypnotic patterns resembling the n-word passes more subtly than the regular propaganda architecture, were apparently meant to attract any creature to use them. Ryan just had an attraction toward firearms, period. Once the androgynous soldiers noticed the outsiders touching what was supposedly their own shit, they opened fire.

The animals, using the democratized equipment, fired back. The equipment was designed without trigger guards and had multiple triggers around them to accommodate various body types. The guns could even be voice-activated by saying the "n-word" word. The androgynous soldiers shouted the word, activating their guns and filling the room with the deafening noise of gunfire.

The animals were initially startled and instinctively pressed one of the many buttons on each of their firearms. The chimps and gorillas, quick learners, began repeating the "n-word" words and firing back. The auto-fire feature of the guns led to chaotic crossfire, but the soldiers' armor protected them from their own shots. The chimpanzees and cats ran around sporadically, making it difficult for the soldiers to aim accurately. Mochi, who usually does this when in a heightened mood, twitched her back in excitement and made her calico pattern look trippy, causing bullets to miss her. Yuki darted about quickly while Boe, the door opener, left the room. The bar of domesticated animals was crazy low.

In the midst of the chaos, one of the soldiers accidentally shot a technological grenade. It exploded, creating a massive hole in one of the walls. I guess the building was designed to have a much lower air pressure to accommodate the structural order of some of the unstable technologies for storage because there was a massive force that emerged— the difference in air pressure between the inside of the building and the outside caused a powerful gust of wind to pull everything outward. The cats used their sharp claws to cling to the rubber mat that spanned across the floor, and the apes clung to furniture with strength. Stacy and I held on tightly, but Suko and the androgynous soldiers were being dragged toward the hole. My heart pounded in horror as I realized the broken wall faced the power dam, meaning a fall would lead to the water far below.

In a split second, one of the soldiers, wearing a rose-tinted helmet, aimed his gun at Suko, ready to shoot even though he was just a baby. In a desperate move, Suko jumped off, falling toward the water. I rushed to the edge of the broken wall, watching in horror as the androgynous soldiers drowned. But to my amazement, Suko flourished in the water, swimming proficiently thanks to all the times I had dipped him in the river earlier.

Realizing that we needed to face the main enemy once and for all, I knew navigating the legislative building—a sprawling maze—would take too long. I had to act quickly. I spotted a collection of technological explosives in various bins, each sizzling with a blue light. The urgency weighed heavily on my chest as much as when I accidentally dropped a barbell on myself during a bench press session; everyone else was barely hanging on.

Grabbing a gun, I aimed and fired at each of the bins. The shots rang out, one after another, prompting a series of explosions that set off a chain reaction. The room shook violently as the explosives detonated in quick succession. The air pressure, formerly threatening to pull us all into the dam, stabilized as the explosions created new openings in the building. As the dust and debris settled, the once impenetrable maze of the legislative building lay exposed. Walls were blown apart, and hallways were laid bare.

Amidst the destruction, a starkly contrasting village-like set of structures came into view, nestled at the far end of what seemed like a backyard of the parliament building. I thought it was bizarre that I hadn't noticed this before entering. Without wasting any time, I dove into the water to rescue Suko. His little arms flailed, but his automatic swimming instincts still kept him afloat. I scooped him up and swam back to the edge, then climbed back up with him securely on my back. At the top, Stacy, Ryan, the cats, and the apes were waiting, feeling thankful they no longer had to fear for their lives.

Together, we made our way to the village-like setup. The structures looked primitive—made of mud and straw—but something felt off. As we approached, I first noticed a gigantic hot tub filled with people. The vast majority of them looked identical to the androgynous soldiers, except they were all naked, seemingly secure about their horribly weak physiques because every one of them was weak. Their presence was unnerving, but the sight at the pool's far end truly caught my attention.

It was Mr. Lester and the mayor, lounging together and drinking beer.

I told my allies to stay back and approached the mayor and dean. They seemed lost in their own worlds, unaware that half of the legislative building, right in their lines of sight, had been blown up.

My focus was on the mayor. "You," I yelled, pointing at the gluttonous one with glasses. "I know exactly what you're doing."

The mayor looked at me with a mix of confusion and disdain. "And who might you be?" he asked lazily, sipping his beer.

My anger boiled over, mostly because anyone should recognize me by my massive, shredded physique by now, but I focused on the point. "This entire setup is a sham. This pseudo-village is just a facade for the leftist's moral superiority. You sit here, in your wasteful hot tub, next to a power dam that's increasingly draining the city's resources as you are pulling more and more citizens to overcrowd this area."

The dean scoffed. "You have no idea what you're talking about. This village is a symbol of living in the simple times."

I pointed to the buildings. "These buildings are made of mud and straw, yet they're filled with thousands of electrical wires, which can be seen between the straws. This dam is just a front. I know you are just trying to make this city resemble the communal longhouses that housed pure idlers who propagate their own kind, just on a larger scale. That was never 'wholesome.' Now, you're going to pay."

Without hesitation, I ran to the edge of the power dam, one explosive still in hand. The dean and mayor shouted behind me, but I didn't stop. I reached the edge, took aim, and threw the explosive across to one of the dam's walls. It struck with a thunderous impact, and the wall began to crumble. Water gushed out in a torrent, and immediately, the apparatus powering the city's n-word pass holograms began to shut down.

In a matter of moments, from a distance, the city lost the majority of its so-called buildings as the holograms flickered and disappeared. The skyline, once dominated by towering illusions, now lay bare and exposed. The hot tub, too, lost power, and the water quickly cooled. The people inside, including the dean and mayor, began to panic. Their bodies, accustomed to the hot water to such a degree of life and death because they were literally idle in there for months, went into shock as the temperature dropped rapidly. One by one, they passed out, and many were even dead, indicated by the shit that was coloring the pool brown, as it is impossible for a dead body to hold in shit.

I guess I cut out the entire city's power supply because I could even hear collective screams from all the way, the downtown robots finally knowing how it feels to live without electricity.

"The city has fallen, millions must die because they can't use power," Ryan said, coning his ears with his hand. "Many are going to commit suicide, starve to death, cannibalize each other." He wasn't joking. Even I could hear all those future actions in their calls.

But the power cut didn't matter because there was going to be another force on our side. We stood at the edge of the power dam, watching the water rush out and the city's facade crumble. But I knew this was just the beginning. This was only one city where we had revolted against modernity. This may formerly be the city with the most technologically fast corporations, but it is just a matter of time until a corporation in any other place in the globe does a similar state-company collaboration and starts another dystopian cancerous growth that will spread to other cities, countries, and continents.

The Aftermath

Here, I intend to engage with these inquiries: What if I told you the real "word" that the soysystem took away from us is the word "nature," and succeeding this is the elimination of other "-word passes" and "epic gamer terms"? What's the "nature" of the perpetrators of this denatured system? And what moral dilemmas does it present?

Regarding a conscious entity's relation to nature, the word "nature" was originally actually in opposition to "convention" (nomos) when it first emerged.[376] The philosophy revolving around "nature" would be considered dangerous to orderly convention because it was associated with lawlessness,[377] a far cry from civilizing—a form of de-civilizing and re-barbarization, a return to the wild in order to escape from "nomos."[378] Nomos functions as homogenization, tribal survival, and the continuation of mere existence via a regime of commands, speech, and teachings that obscures nature."[379] Similar to the tight restrictive technological system? Years of conditioning under modernity have led us to associate the exercise of individual will outside the bounds of the technological order, even when it involves acts of excellence, with so-called "evil beings," setting them in opposition to the concept of good. Consider why America is populated by individuals who appear so lethargic that they might collapse at the slightest provocation. Contrary to popular belief, the phenomenon of modernity's mercantile elites isn't exclusive to "all-embracing individual interests" as much as many think. Other more hidden factors are so compelling that they give rise to a curious phenomenon of "void-interests" or even "reverse-interests" (Think of a pirate LARPer trying to use a cranky wooden ship for the first time in his first-time adventure. He brought some friends and acquaintances along the way, after telling them they'd find some hot booty (literal and figurative form) in some remote tribe island. The problem is that the pirate LARPer's arms are too skinny and weak to properly steer the wheel of the ship. Every time he attempts to, he takes too long for the damn thing to rotate to a sufficient degree of movement change, there are literal tactical time lags. Eventually, they do end up near one of the tribal islands that this pirate LARPer promised so wholeheartedly. But because he can't steer properly, he prematurely crashes the ship into the shore, beaching the ship itself, and the tribal women of the island tribe quickly begin doing the Amazonian position on the pirate LARPer along with the other ship passengers (death by snu snu)). Does a significant dilemma of our era also lie in the lack of virility among those who helm the neoliberal order, other than their "malevolence"?

These figures evoke a sense of uncanniness akin to encountering a living zombie. Such individuals, found beyond the symbolic leaders such as presidents we recognize, represent a pernicious network. These hierarchies maintain control by diminishing the vigor of the whole order, all the while further eroding their internal fortitude. In this manner, they embody a parasitic disease-like class, nearly ineffectual when removed from

---

[376] C. Alamariu, *Selective Breeding and the Birth of Philosophy* (Independently Published, 2023), 29.
[377] Ibid., 165.
[378] Ibid., 221.
[379] Ibid., 140.

their entrenched systems of influence, reliant on external mechanisms to uphold a pseudo-supremacy. It must be questioned, however: Does the metaphor of necessarily labeling "proliferating desires" as something akin to a "zombie virus" fall short of adequately capturing the nature of "desire," as it reduces desire to a universal negativity?

Whatever the case, it is widely understood that desires possess a potent capacity to diffuse through individuals, in ways that can be both good and destructive. This interplay of desires would create a complexity of motivation and multifaceted ways in which aspirations can influence "society time" structures. The phenomenon of mimetic desire, in particular, can spiral into destabilization—yet also a certain kind of uniform force?

Normies usually covet objects only because they observe others do, especially ones that are easy to conceive independent of real creativity. Furthermore, as they increasingly mimic each other's desires, obstacles increase—wouldn't attention seemingly shift to what opposes "desire"? Such "destabilization" tends to be "mitigated" in which the masses, whether or not deliberately, select a scapegoat to be sacrificed if they find that the obstacles get too big.[380] This kind of thing is evident in myths where a guilty victim restores or establishes order, symbolizing the resolution of crises through sacrificial violence,[381] and beyond a certain threshold of belief, the effect of the scapegoat is to reverse the relationships between persecutors and their victims.[382] A clear example today could be how entrepreneurs often transition from being widely loved to actualizing a kind of derangement affliction, as more people attempt to achieve this archetype and end up in a state of resentment. Modern society is afflicted by two predominant "desires": attempts of differentiation via the pursuit of consumer goods once exclusive to the bourgeoisie, and the quest for absolute equality. These two "feel good" yet contradictory infections result in irrationality, exacerbating the issue. This perpetuates a future with diminished freedom, as there is a noticeable tendency for normies to begin targeting small entrepreneurs (today's folks who at least have more agency than wagecuckery but not so high up as to have to shift back to chronic oversocialization) rather than the big corporations. Aren't the very same leftists who accuse "the other" of "making up scapegoats" literally just this as seen when they do their riots?

Could we then draw a parallel between anti-introspective propagandistic messaging and the absence of the "will to unique desire" among the mercantile elites and the so-called peasant rabble? Now suppose that negations—language that isn't open-ended and requires little thinking to obey—in messaging, which indicate what is not to be done or what is not true (like "Don't miss this opportunity"), have been shown to offer a stylistic alternative to affirmative statements.[383] While they are often associated with negativity, negations in branding were shown to project a sense of power,[384] suggesting that marketing messaging should incorporate negations to project strength and engage

---

[380] R. Girand, *The Scapegoat* (Johns Hopkins University Press, 1989), 130.

[381] Ibid., 42.

[382] Ibid., 44.

[383] T. Pezzuti, J.M. Leonhardt, "What's not to like? Negations in brand messages increase consumer engagement," *J. of the Acad. Mark. Sci*, 51(2023): 675-694. https://doi.org/10.1007/s11747-022-00894-3

[384] Ibid.

consumers, particularly those seeking higher status.[385] But then, is not status merely a motivator for enhancing one's social position and garnering respect and admiration from others? It would make sense for it to drive individuals toward benefits such as financial rewards, bland social recognition, and mere preservation—are these incentives not precisely what today's elites desire, structurally identical to those of the rabble consumer?

You can also consider the striking impact that media portrayals of company CEOs (chief executive officers, but they start to become cucked executive officers in our current context) have on consumer perceptions—and, therefore, their own behavior.[386] For instance, the political ideologies of CEOs shape consumer evaluations over time,[387] then consumer reactions to the related news strongly correlate with stock returns, confirming the link between consumer evaluations and investor behavior.[388] The implications for management would suggest "Given the observed negative financial implications of CEOs prone to misbehavior, it is crucial for boards to rigorously assess the character and past behavior of CEO candidates."[389] Other than the technological system's linguistic favor of having the higher pressure for companies to deceive their messages to the media, consumers would be happier to consume whatever the company is producing if there are good public relations. This stuff should already be intuitively clear, but what would happen if a company were to indulge in corporate irresponsibility? Sure, they wouldn't spend as much money on stuff, but there is a more subtle way that it would go in favor of the technological system. It goes along the lines of controlled behavior, which the CEOs already have to conform to because of their already rigid need to be under high scrutiny if they so desire the mere preservation of a firm's existence. Is it then significant that firms would face the risk of elimination as new technologies are implemented,[390] rather than the cliché that they have "special" desires beyond necessity?

To take things further, these pseudo-entrepreneurs themselves are depraved under our technological society—a communistic system. Ironically, even the idiotic idiology we know as Marxism has some terms that could explain the loss of agency of these normie entrepreneurs. With "reification," social relations and human actions are perceived as inherent attributes of things (commodities)—as these become fetishized, the human labor and social processes behind them are obscured. This could be translated to "entreification," the process by which individuals and their actions are objectified and commodified within the entrepreneurial discourse.[391] At the initial stage, entreification enables entrepreneurship by creating a socially reified entrepreneurial position, allowing individuals to act within a structured role that society recognizes and supports. But at a later stage, as entrepreneurs become more integrated into the market, they start to lose their sense of personal agency. Their actions and decisions become increasingly abstract

---

[385] Ibid.

[386] S. Stäbler and P. Gala, "Breaking the news: how does CEO media coverage influence consumer and investor evaluations?" *Mark Lett*, 2024. https://doi.org/10.1007/s11002-024-09720-y

[387] Ibid.

[388] Ibid.

[389] Ibid.

[390] A. McAfee and E. Brynjolfsson, *Machine, Platform, Crowd: Harnessing Our Digital Future* (WW Norton, 2017).

[391] A. Örtenblad (Eds), *Against Entrepreneurship: A Critical Examination* (Palgrave Macmillan Cham, 2020), 53.

and detached from the concrete social relations they initially navigated.[392] This would be "entrepomorphization," where there is the endowing of entrepreneurial "things" (brands) with life and human-like qualities. Entrepreneurs start to worship these entities, seeing them as larger-than-life figures that act independently of human control. This fetishistic relationship further strips entrepreneurs of their agency, as they become mere facilitators of the entities' perceived will. Wouldn't this make a "pseudo-reproduction" of entrepreneurship, ensuring that "entrepreneurship itself" only continues to be driven by abstract market forces rather than individual agency and creativity?

We see a paralleled real-life example where some "online store" employed subcontractors to develop its technological platform, but without accurate coordination (The founders were unable to steer the development process effectively, resulting in fragmented and inefficient work), and they ended up with a bunch of technical flaws in their system with the delays and order processing, damaging their reputation.[393] They faced pressure to promise "revolutionary" features such as a virtual assistant while the technology was not mature enough at the time. The ongoing technical problems contributed to its high burn rate, as funds were continuously diverted to try and fix issues rather than being invested in growth and customer acquisition.[394] Effectively, entrepreneurs in this scenario are caught in a deterministic cycle where their actions are dictated by the very forces they sought to harness, leaving them as mere drones of an out-of-control process, because they themselves envisioned and then tried to rush to the very same pre-determined cliche of what technology would end up like, which aren't actually innovations but reduplications of what is insincerely extrapolated. If an entrepreneur is reluctant to embrace substantial risk, they can mitigate uncertainty by aligning their creations more closely with pre-existing conventional paradigms. This involves crafting content that resonates with familiar themes or employing repetitive, easily memorable elements. Such strategies constitute the essence of what would be propaganda, and nothing more. The system does not inherently generate value. Instead, the audience is cultivated for the type of content being produced—it is more straightforward to cater to an established market than to engender a new one; why would that mean the market itself confers value?

In the end, the present "innovations" in the technological system are merely vehicles for the preservation of the system's convention, whether personal or societal. For instance, we may posit that we rigidly constrain ourselves to the established taxonomies of technology in these four types: incremental, adaptive, radical, and frontier. Incremental innovations involve minor adjustments to existing technologies to satisfy existing societal preferences, like smartphone upgrades.[395] Adaptive innovations modify existing technologies to create new societal preferences, such as hybrid cars generating demand for more environmentally friendly vehicles.[396] Radical innovations develop nascent technologies under conditions of extreme uncertainty to meet clear societal needs, like the

---

[392] Ibid., 54.

[393] Ibid., 51.

[394] Ibid., 52.

[395] D. Chiffi, S. Moroni, and L. Zanetti, "Types of Technological Innovation in the Face of Uncertainty," *Philos. Technol*, 35(2022): 94. https://doi.org/10.1007/s13347-022-00587-3

[396] Ibid.

creation of the first smartphones or the development of renewable energy technologies.[397] Frontier technologies represent cutting-edge advancements that emerge in highly uncertain contexts, creating previously unrecognized societal preferences, such as quantum computing and machine learning, which open new opportunities in healthcare, finance, and space tourism.[398] This proposed taxonomy accommodates some uncertainties in technological innovation, offering a more holistic perspective than traditional economic-based approaches. However, the taxonomy under our current paradigm underscores that post-industrial technologies are often mere iterations of the same concepts. Phone upgrades are euphemisms for infrastructure that invades psychological space, necessitating global connectivity through tedious virtual meetings that make wagecucking so much worse. Eco-friendly cars and solar panels facilitate increased traffic efficiency but constrain individual mobility freedom. Frontier innovations, like quantum computing and machine learning, are marketed by elites as means to extend life spans or transcend human limitations, representing the overt elimination of humanity while appealing to the primitive drive for mere existence. Space tourism panders to the desire for space, yet it would actually merely be for "pre-owned space." It, especially when accounting for societal needs, inevitably makes technology more indispensable as it integrates into the system. Where would the free independent actor be?

There is a normie inclination to equate capitalism with any problem that aligns with the technological system's relentless pursuit of maximizing efficiency for its own sake at the expense of genuine innovation. But in reality, this drive transcends any single economic model, often finding even greater extents in other systems. For instance, within a communist construct, the development of space exploration technology might be directed exclusively toward enabling transport within pre-established, institutionalized boundaries of space to serve idleness. In this sense, the drive for blind efficiency reflects the impoverished technological paradigm itself, rather than the inherent characteristics of any particular economic system. Capitalism, as it currently functions in the system, becomes a stepping stone toward an anti-innovative communistic system. Certainty, then, is always present when raw desires are apparent. These desires are reduplicated to replace real desires, creating simulations that perpetuate our servitude to the system. A truly innovative path might be to transcend even these four taxonomies, seeking a "sixth sense" equivalent of desires and needs. After all, the autonomous pursuit of excellence is often constrained by the need for market approval when one chooses to lead a market rather than follow it. What about the numerous cases where business leaders create products that the market was initially averse to[399] (although, again, normie-ized since the system institutionalized them into hedonistic homogenization)?

For a supposed "master" to refuse to ascend a taxonomy would be a sign of insufficient courage or strength—always relying on pre-existing models is ignoble. One could view the striped individuality due to fetishized objects as a form of self-domestication—their failure to transcend conventional collective norms, taking on the

---

[397] Ibid.

[398] Ibid.

[399] N. Bhuyan and A. Chakraborty, "The Problem of Autonomy: An Alternative Notion of Excellence in Business Ethics," J Bus Ethics, 191(2024): 253-267. https://doi.org/10.1007/s10551-023-05454-5.

same "job" as other entrepreneurs. They are literally on the same level of nobility and strength as the weak leftists. Although this doesn't absolve the mercantile elites of their doings—they still should be spotlighted because of their pseudo-accelerationist actions. Now, if the weak leftists are in much higher masses than the masters, why are they stuck in their state of actionless resentment rather than taking on their perceived elites head-on—if that would theoretically be possible in a non-mindfucked scenario?

Modern leftists lack the capacity for intellectual thought and impactful conflict all while civility paradoxically plays a minimal role in their "rebellious" mechanisms—clearly, this is their ulterior submission to the technological system's need for an excess of orderly passivity. Their methods of "going against the establishment" are largely because incivility (like causing inconvenience) often draws more raw attention (their chief motives) without much thought.[400] Another one would be "triggering reason-giving," political disobedience that manipulates the environment to trigger a conditional reason for the audience to act against a law or policy, creating a circumstance where it makes it rational for the audience to act differently—like the system's pseudo-environmentalists blowing up pipelines to make certain environmental policies economically unsustainable.[401] These are in contrast to more conventional things like testimony,[402] which just plain doesn't do shit. Doesn't it kind of seem like there isn't any possible way to change the system, in which both language and traditional ways of gaining power are doomed? The explanation may lie in the observation where we see all the violent leftist rioters everywhere who are seemingly so "versus the elite," while they don't at all get punished by law enforcement. What gives?

The system already has an arbitrary "list" of what kinds of "violence" to mandate. Leftists will commit violence but only in ways that are so weak as to grow the system even more, being an outlet that prevents them from violently attacking the real source. It is especially shown when they directly attack the stores at the end of the supply chain just to steal the consumerist goods, which they will become even more used to being dependent on (products of the technological system), yet they say "bLaMe cApItLism." One might go as far as to say that it is the ultimate purified example of conforming to capitalism.[403] The system is "a single, centralized worldwide organism in which every part is dependant on the functioning of the whole."[404] So, the only things mandated to be attacked are the nodes of the system that don't function as its vital organs. Small mom-and-pop stores and brick-and-mortar stores, in general, for example, are just the "average biomass." Attacking those is literally just the equivalent of one of your small micro arteries being cut—it won't be an interference to the system at all. Instead, it would make things worse, conditioning people to accept the system's advancement even more—the pure rational step forward, which is shifting the control of goods to the ownership of the state, or control by the technological system. The system's more vital parts, such as power

---

[400] S. Coyne, "The Role of Civility in Political Disobedience," *Philos Public Aff*, 52(2024): 221-250. https://doi.org/10.1111/papa.12258

[401] Ibid.

[402] Ibid.

[403] C.A. Haag, *Hermeneutical Death: The Technological Destruction of Subjectivity* (Independently Published, 2020), 169.

[404] T. Kaczynski, *Technological Slavery* (Scottsdale: Fitch & Madison, 2022), 212.

plants, are not interfered with often because leftists know deep down that they can't live in nature. By the way, this major kind of interference has happened before (one incident preventing the movement of millions of computers and putting one of the largest cities to a halt).[405] So why would it be an unrealistic method of rebellion?

Generally, when a party does a grand "rise up," they free themselves from Nietzschean "ressentiment." However, if they instead rationalize their own powerlessness into a perceived virtue of rebellion and instead pretend, they remain in a state of passivity, permitting their indignation to grow and subtly corrode their spirit.[406] Leftists are just this; to rationalize their weakness, they only imaginatively demonize their perceived oppressor, but they end up denying reality, creating an illusion of strength amidst their weakness and spiritual idleness. What the modern leftist action will turn our society into will perhaps be similar to what happened as a result of the Russian revolution... except something more technologized of course. In the Russian Revolution, the people who were massacred were not only the aristocracy but also independent entrepreneurs... it witnessed the elimination of anyone with the capacity for freedom. Russia became a communistic universally slave state, something reflectively economically favored in the paradigm of modernity, as exceptional individuals would be too absent to overlap their will into the system. While "revenge" is natural, this is bullshit. Leftists feign their nonexistence out of weakness despite burning down all the mom-and-pop stores. But because they and the elites are of this passivity, they are effectively one and of the same thing (while both are enframed as powerful by propagandistic caricature). What else explains well that we are "ruled" by a giant mass that longs for self-preservation for its own sake?

A grand but scary irony is that even though the current paradigm overvalues the commitment to self-preservation at all costs, this is actually the opposite of what we need to do for mankind's survival in the long run. There will come a time when we have to move beyond one planet to avoid putting all eggs into one basket. It is said that "blood" is most important—although the soil was crucial for providing us a foundation for launching ourselves away, it is inevitable that we have to move into the greater unknown.[407] Elaborating on the challenges arising from space travel, what kinds of horrible space travel implications will the modernity paradigm have created for us, even though modernity is widely believed to be what would lead us to space travel? There has been mention of spaceplanes allowing for efficient travel to space,[408] and discussion about space elevators, providing cheaper and more continuous access to space.[409] Considerations also include engineering mankind to better withstand space conditions.[410] Astronauts on long-duration missions, like a trip to Mars, would also face severe psychological stress from isolation and confinement, emphasizing the importance of mental health support and crew compatibility,[411] favoring astronauts who can work well

---

[405] T. Morris-Suzuki, "Centralisation and Decentralisation in Japan's 'Information Society'," *Media Information Australia*, 44(1987): 48-54. https://doi.org/10.1177/1329878X8704400112

[406] F. Nietzsche, *On the Genealogy of Morals* (Penguin Classics, 2013), 25.

[407] B. Disciple, *Barbaric Vitalism* (RESAVAGER Media, 2023), 111.

[408] S. Webb, *All the Wonder that Would Be: Exploring Past Notions of the Future* (Springer Cham, 2017), 78.

[409] Ibid., 85-87.

[410] Ibid., 89.

[411] Ibid., 82.

as a team. Although these space colonization solutions sound hecking epic, what philosophical problems would arise regarding meaningful exploration in its pure essence, beyond the semantics? Start by considering the proven reality that individuals despise prolonged confinement in enclosed spaces; subjecting them to conditions akin to an airplane or space elevator would drive them to extreme distress—if the irritation of hearing real literal crybabies on a flight or the displeasure of seeing the ugly-ass reflection of your ugly-ass face in an elevator shiny wall for ages resonates with you, the point is clear—it could easily slip into equating to relinquishing human autonomy and the capacity for hermeneutic appreciation of cosmic beauty at an increasingly substantial level. The advocacy for engineering to enhance human resilience to space's harsh conditions appears promising. However, this approach trends towards maladaptive modifications within the collectivized artificial rationality of modernity. Similar to what was mentioned earlier, this combination would transform human morphology to resemble efficient but idle lifeforms, replacing original human attributes with hackable electrical appliances—these appliances lack the intrinsic ability to consider reproducing after a spontaneous expression of self-mastery, rendering them incapable of having descendants of the ascending type. The notion of selecting astronauts with robust mental resilience and teamwork skills will likely be a euphemism for choosing individuals who lack genuine enthusiasm for the true mastery of space. Instead, they pursue space exploration only at a standardized careeristic level in modernity (as they are told they should value by propaganda), devoid of authentic exploratory spirit. Their ability to function well in a team, despite the natural tendency to feel claustrophobic over extended periods, typifies a Kaczynskian oversocialized individual incapable of innovative thinking and thus unable to hermeneutically engage in a comprehensive spatial conquest. Maybe a good "test" to determine whether we'd be fit for space conquest can be done if we stop rushing towards mere collectivized space travel for the sake of itself—there may at some point come a great "philosopher Chad" type who'd know how to address such challenge and with corresponding big gonad-like inborn feelings, exercise imposition accordingly. It is possible that our current space wouldn't technically have the resources to enable space travel but think about it; either we regress ourselves into hermeneutical idiots who will cannibalize ourselves before traveling meaningfully enough, we do attempt the noble way of real travel, or we simply don't exist at all. Though "natural selection" would favor systems that hog efficiency over the ones that go for human values,[412] wouldn't it be those same systems that are entirely ignoble enough to desire mere existence over expansive existence?

At this point, it appears highly unlikely that a significant shift will soon occur, as there comes a paradox in modern society: the lower social classes, often having comparatively little to risk or lose, encounter fewer constraints on their freedom, while those in higher social strata find themselves increasingly bound by tangles of obligations. A distinct force subtly imposes new demands, ensuring that the upper classes remain bound to specific roles and functions. In the modern world, where the definition of "freedom" has become inverted, the elite liberate themselves from the immediate necessity of wagecucking; yet this liberation fails to translate into the pursuit of deeper existential purposes. Rather than evolving into individuals who channel freedom into

---

[412] T. Kaczynski, *Technological Slavery* (Scottsdale: Fitch & Madison, 2022), 188.

creative interests, what comes is a fake ruling class that is only there because of what a paretoistic principle would determine—a "pseudo-aristocracy" that lacks true nobility?

We might argue that, in a technological society, those occupying universally subordinate positions (lacking true creative power) are inherently dependent on those who hold dominant positions. They now rely on the "algorithmic"[413] structures that govern and generate the machines—frameworks they then invert. It is now those unequipped to create and hold power, only with the capacity to negate. Though it is often a cliché that the suffering of society results from an elite overly absorbed in "leisure," this misses the point that the modern understanding of "leisure" has become impoverished, implying mere idleness or unproductive time. Originally, however, leisure signified time freed from the demands of wagecuckism—an interval intended for pursuits of higher value, such as artistic creation. In its true form, leisure allowed individuals to transcend mediocrity, providing the space to engage with philosophy. Not even the wealthiest elites today spend time on this because they have already been so cognitively stunted and can only think in terms of dollar figures, without any life-world context. It is the case that it's the technological system's subconscious doing of this definition, mangling to shame every single conscious agent, no matter what place in the social order, from getting to begin to dabble into the kind of philosophy to question the innateness of the technological society—worse still, necessarily being at severe mercy of impersonal forces?

Returning to the idea that modern man is universally degenerating into a viral mode of existence, though real viruses might not be technically alive, they seemingly align with the definition of life, characterized by growth, reproduction, functional activity, and continuous change preceding death. A virus is a borderline case in defining life—it cannot propagate without hijacking other living organisms as resources. Unlike a single cell that can replicate independently, a virus requires a host cell for replication. But one might argue that humans, too, cannot reproduce in isolation because, after all, they may have to feed on the resources provided by the ecological whole. Therefore, the point still stands that the degeneration of modern man can be compared to an empty memory drive as a form of "malware." This malware can alter the computer and be duplicated by it. It can remain dormant for years yet function perfectly when reinserted into a computer. However, it cannot replicate or innovate independently. It requires the computer's mechanisms to operate, and the empty drive remains passive, incapable of self-replication or independent action. Likewise, human parasitism's drivers would only fit the modern man, reproductive drives (when prioritized before self-mastery), and exponential growth, manipulating and exploiting their environment similarly to other parasitic species.[414] Both biological and computer viruses satisfy this criterion, don't they?

Amidst the "disease state of man," the notion of disease as a social problem has never been more accurate. After all, diseases in general are undesirable conditions that induce suffering or constrain capabilities and are addressed by societies through the development of institutions and practices—they must encompass "social dimensions,"[415] and are said

[413] C. Steiner, *Automate This: How Algorithms Came to Rule Our World* (Portfolio, 2012).
[414] S.J Bartlett, "The Ecological Pathology of Man," *Mentalities/Mentalités: An Interdisciplinary Journal*, 20(2006): 1-18.
[415] C. Saborido and J. Zamora-Bonilla, "Diseases as social problems," *Synthese*, 203(2024). https://doi.org/10.1007/s11229-023-04468-w

to possess three critical characteristics: they affect large numbers of people, they impact individuals in a uniform manner, and they necessitate collective solutions.[416] They also affect more than one individual in a similar way, enabling "categorization and classification," and so the resolution of these issues is effectively achieved through measures applied to the problem as a whole, thus requiring organized action.[417] Paralleling this to the kinds of externalities of modern man, our existence is fundamentally grounded in the concept of disease, confronting us with trivial and vexing social issues rather than grand challenges worthy of heroic feats. It cannot be repeated enough that propaganda has become the dominant affliction because of this. A challenge then lies in the fact that one cannot simply target and eliminate an individual, nor can the technological apparatus simply be reduced to nothing—the insidious nature of modern propaganda, facilitated by its horizontal spread among the masses, demands a hyper-collective solution that addresses everyone to be effective. The institutions are thus designed to address this perceived nonconformity. This is the virophage phenomenon we are witnessing, where natural herd members occupy positions of power while those who resist herdish thinking are marginalized, resulting in a conflict of "disease versus disease." LAME! WHERE IS ALL THE EPIC GAMING PEEVEEPEE?!

However, I must be careful to remind you that the "herdish archetype," such as the "empty drive state," isn't necessarily a bad thing in all contexts—there are automatistic actions that mankind exhibits that are actually of benefit, despite the limited appreciation of the roles and significance of virality.[418] Understanding broader ecological and social contexts, philosophers and anthropologists argue for viewing them as dynamic processes rather than static entities,[419] in which via "intra-action," humans and viruses emerge from their interactions rather than pre-existing as separate entities.[420] Perhaps, this can be likened to how general propaganda may be judged as neutral.[421] Obviously, mere language will inevitably have a deviation from the truth. Historically, sophists weren't necessarily the opposite of philosophers.[422] But one must still remember that modern conditions will inevitably eventually turn good propagation into bad because when people eventually atrophy due to the impediment of creation in a restrictive space, they will then spread that descending weakness, and we go back to bad square one. The noble types shouldn't wrangle with herdishness for too long, is all. The whole notion of "floppy disc" should not necessarily be outright diminished; the existence of herdish types is almost inevitable due to its laxness and relativity—they may even bear following out of necessity with no other alternatives.[423] It just shouldn't be the predominant governing body. This is our current liberal democratic society, or for us, the global technological system; it is plagued

---

[416] Ibid.

[417] Ibid.

[418] S. de Chadarevian and R. Roberta Raffaetà, "COVID-19: Rethinking the nature of viruses, *History and Philosophy of the Life Sciences,* 43(2021):1-5. https://doi.org/10.1007/s40656-020-00361-8

[419] Ibid.

[420] Ibid.

[421] I. Ramos, "Propaganda Does Not Have to be Good or Evil," *Disputatio: Philosophical Research Bulletin,* 8(2019).

[422] C. Alamariu, *Selective Breeding and the Birth of Philosophy* (Independently Published, 2023), 208.

[423] F. Nietzsche, *The Gay Science* (Vintage Books, 1974), 176.

by herd morality, masking itself as master morality. Instead, the noble life versus the other should be a constant battle, and they must hold their "respective distance." So, when there is a "rise up" attempt, it encourages the masters to practice competence to stay upright in their position. The problem with the conditioning in the technological system is there is no actual revolt happening because the masters are so decrepit and weak, so they use petty tactics to pacify the masses while simultaneously stooping down to the herd—what life force do they have to self-improve?

The Nietzschean discourse on "the herd" may even transcend what the system embodies, where regarding the "bad," there can be a rightful appreciation of all that is "outrageous." For instance, a formidable villain whose defeat brings glory to a Übermensch figure.[424] The hero's identity is intertwined with the presence of an adversary—the desire for power signifies a desire for growth, but this necessitates overcoming obstacles—the mightier the adversary, the greater the growth upon their defeat. An adversary is not necessarily "evil," as elucidated: for some, an enemy was often a "good" man.[425] But what kind of adversary would be the right type? And to what extent would the technological system "despise" this type, and instead replace it with artificial ones?

Simply put, one should examine whether imposing a risk of harm can itself constitute harm (an aversion of risk being one of the most prevalent desire infections amongst the herd) by differentiating between subjective risk and objective risk. Subjective risk is based on an individual's belief about the likelihood of an event, and objective risk is based on actual probabilities independent of beliefs.[426] The former, which depends on the risk imposer's belief, theoretically cannot harm the victim as these risks exist only in the mind of the imposer (Like a person aiming a gun at someone without him knowing—the risk exists only in the gun holder's mind, not affecting the prospective victim's welfare).[427] Objective risks can also be argued not to theoretically harm because they do not interfere with a victim's interests (For example, a lottery machine with a low probability of deciding on an action of shooting someone. The risk does not set back the potential victim's interests, as the objective probability does not inherently harm him).[428] Interestingly, subjective risks in some cases may appear to contradict "autonomy" and "preference" accounts—there can be a separation between "wrongful acts" and the risks themselves, in which even though wrongful acts may potentially harm dignity, the risks themselves do not constitute harm.[429] Furthermore, doesn't the technological system often impose restrictions on the citizens to avoid potential risks, "believing" they are preventing harm, ultimately to achieve its need for full efficiency? The system, a vast collective of technical factors that form a giant propaganda mass, may base its regulations on pseudo-subjective risks, replacing individuals' capacity to be subjective, where the perceived dangers exist primarily implicitly, abstractly initially in the fully rational "other world."

---

[424] F. Nietzsche, *Human All-Too-Human: A Book For Free Spirits* (George Allen And Unwin Ltd., London, 1910), 358.
[425] F. Nietzsche, *On the Genealogy of Morals* (Penguin Classics, 2013), 27.
[426] T. Rowe, "Can a risk of harm itself be a harm?" *Analysis*, 81(2021): 694–701. https://doi.org/10.1093/analys/anab033
[427] Ibid.
[428] Ibid.
[429] Ibid.

This is while the world outside the soystem might actually pose objective risks much lower/different than what the system tells the citizens to perceive. Initially, it may seem that the system's mandated risks cannot directly interfere with our legitimate interests, as these risks are not actual harms. However, the regulations that must control those risks would harm them by restricting people's autonomy and opportunities for development, which are legitimate interests. In the case of an autonomy account, the system makes many options unavailable to us and, ironically, has a sufficient range of safe options to choose from. Regarding "dignity," overprotective behavior might send the message that one is incapable of handling risks, affecting their self-esteem and dignity (hence the feelings of inferiority felt by the leftists). This perception coerces actions more than actual, objective risks. At the very least, a better framework for technology would be along the lines of "preparedness" ones (does not rely on past events but instead focuses on readiness for a range of possible future events) rather than risk ones (deals with possible uncertainty by converting future uncertainties into calculable risks. Examples include insurance and statistical methods that manage these risks based on past data).[430] Isn't the system's seemingly peaceful development a petty kind of violence that is so bad it deserves to be retaliated against?

The gradual "technological peaceful development" works like the boiling frog metaphor, where if a frog is placed in a pot of boiling water, it will hop straight out, but if it is placed in lukewarm water and it is slowly heated enough so the increase isn't noticed, by the time it realizes it is boiled, it is too late.[431] Is it ironic, though, that in our pseudo-accelerationist world, it still works a lot like the philosophy behind why accelerationism might be beloved by some in a time when there's so much insidious badness?

Arguably, while risky things like war itself are terrible, the prevalence of universal peace is worse, as men would lose meaning.[432] In modern society, it is funny how it seems like there are more wars going on than previously. But those are only the dehumanizing meaningless wars—soldiers are only sent to fight to serve for foreign land, to rid the country of the fighters who would otherwise use their virility to revolt against the idle class of elites (Principally, those fighting in war should be driven by their own kin rather than sheer politics[433]). Moreover, a society anchored in hedonistic values will eventually make apparent its inherent fragility when it encounters a true adversary. While it might succeed in sustaining internal equilibrium and efficiency, it lacks the resilience required for genuine conflict and the needed pressing demands of innovative problem-solving. Would the governing structure of such a fruitful society be intimately shaped by modes of IRL combat gaming?

An example of a better state would be Spartan culture ("Spartan" here is not to be literally confused with the "Call of Halo" game where you "shoot" the bad guys and "own" the noobs). In a strikingly paradoxical justification, the Spartan ethos rationalized their "relationship" with the Helots as a means to secure time to enjoy some IRL gaming. Now take the time to compare the modern bugman with the life of the Helots that the

---

[430] L. Samimian-Darash, "Governing Future Potential Biothreats," *Current Anthropology*, 54(2013): 1-22. https://doi.org/10.1086/669114

[431] V. Mcleod, *Clown World Chronicles* (VJM Publishing, 2020), 38.

[432] F. Disciple, *Resavager Volume 1* (RESAVAGER Media, 2023), 99.

[433] D. Reiter and A.C. Stam, *Democracies at War* (Princeton University Press, 2002).

Spartans conquered… and you tell me, what you would rather be? At one point when the Helots grew enough in numbers, Spartans would be sent to attack them in fear of an uprising—as the Helots defended themselves, this would favor strength, cunning, and intelligence. Assuming you are too big of a pussy to be a Spartan, be honest; would you prefer to be a Helot than a modern wagecuck, if that means your people would at least be fighting and therefore STRONKER, comparing that to the forever descending virility of modern man? How cool would it be to live those epic gamer gladiator combat films IN REAL LIFE? How can we enable epic IRL gaming Chads into power?

Food for thought, would "tyranization" in a specific sense of the term be better than the tyrannical technocracy we have now? One may argue that "true" tyranny is the only way to overthrow the current bashful tyranny.[434] Now, it is obviously important to distinguish the contexts of tyrannies, to avoid confusion with undesirable modern totalitarian rule. To simply differentiate the styles of this type of rule, the Platonic political cycle begins with a higher form of governance to a degraded form—it starts with an aristocracy of philosopher-kings, then a timocracy, an oligarchy, democracy, and lastly "tyranny"[435]; it then "cycles" back (the descension typically caused by successors giving less of a shit). Following this cycle, the 21st century so far interestingly seems to hover between the democracy and tyranny phases; in this paradigm, the dominant masters are incapable of passing ramifications through any philosophical meddling, and thus, tyranny under technological determinism is taking place. Although, the Platonic envision of favorable governance can be interpreted as a form of tyranny—tyranny under the rule of educated philosopher-kings is considered good as it is tailored to personal agency, unlike the modern narrow totalitarian caricatural definition of tyranny. Regarding tyrants in the ascending state: the "guardians" live dynamic lives, continuously adventuring—favored for their intellect, athleticism, and strong will. With their massive ambitions, they undertake an initial sacrifice by enduring hardship or risk of death, in opposition to mere life. In return, they are granted power. But because their strong wills would translate into individual interests that are so alienated from the herdish masses (unlike submitting to lame desires like pure numbers and raw pleasure), their rule would start to be "foreign," upholding the "respective distance" as they adventure out in the outskirts to earn rightful power as warriors upon return (just like epic action gaming IRL). Could this arrangement actually allow other citizens to pursue their relative desires and interests freely, depending on their capacity for agency (whether or not their capacity for freedom holds following a conventional system; or assuming a perverse technological system doesn't ravage the natural resources to facilitate a "necessity" for modern consumerism)? Does that sound sexy and good enough for you "nature"-loving leftists?

Heck, it is said that two alternative ways to preserve the idea of "nature" (in its purer sense of the term, in opposition to a strict imperative convention) are both philosophy and tyranny,[436] the latter being an active form of philosophical rule. This is unlike early kingship, where the king wasn't powerful, and they were, under the convention,

---

[434] Doonvorvannon, *Barking at the Herd* (Independently Published, 2018), 10.

[435] Plato, *The Republic* (Penguin Classics, 2007).

[436] C. Alamariu, *Selective Breeding and the Birth of Philosophy* (Independently Published, 2023), 161.

diminished into some sacrificial figure for the preservation of the order.[437] Just like the cucked executive officers as the mercantile elite?

The envisioned unconventional philosophical rule is very different from theoretical elucidations of supposed "philosopher-kings" attempting to steer a society with a fixed system of values (which would inevitably lead to failure for various reasons[438]). In the advent of significant societal transformations that would be regularly facilitated by dynamic "nature-based rule," the disruption of the entrenched order would be inevitable, guiding us toward an uncertain trajectory. We might even consider the role of innovating itself, where ideas of sufficient significance (especially beyond what current conventional language can encapsulate) destabilize and desuffocate the existing suffocating order. This suggests that the rise of tyrannizing in the form of active philosophy can emerge independently, fueled by the catalytic influence of genuine innovation. The point is to save us from an age in which as machine culture develops, the role of both individual leaders and inventors diminishes.[439] So, the innovation would have to be new either in a way where it isn't cumulatively bound to an existing step of the system or it isn't appropriated by the state in a pacified way compared to how the individual innovator originally intended it to be (remember, one of the deepest ironies of the technological society is that it is actually hostile towards any genuinely new out-of-convention invention because that would cause interference with its necessity for excessive order to maintain an equilibrium of full efficiency, and therefore its progression to its ugly logical conclusion—of course, again, if you don't allow its orderly appropriation). You wouldn't even need the help of modernism or "the technological society" for these innovations to come to be, you just need to actively use mind and body to bridge the gap. It is argued that even the hardest technical solutions are "right in front of your face" (For example, while the Incan Empire had toys with wheels, no one thought to use the wheel to make an actual cart[440]) and many of the innovations in our paradigm are actually ineffective— aren't those just effective to serve modernity's teleological endpoint (for an unconscious collective at best), rather than personal needs?

So guys, if we want to return the possibility of lively free Chads to exist and therefore substantiate "meanings," we must remember the following: if the technological system were eliminated now, much could be saved because the longer it runs, the worse the outcome for the biosphere and the human race, and the greater the risk that the earth will be a dead planet.[441] When a technological system gets close enough to its teleological endpoint, to what extent would the "bar to disrupt its order" be so lowered?

Good Rex

Okay, so basically, I farded and shidded out a pencil sketch of a dark skin man with my bare-ass hands (look at me guys I am such an inclusive artist) and then showed it to the

[437] Ibid., 80.
[438] T. Kaczynski, *Anti-Tech Revolution: Why and How* (Scottsdale: Fitch & Madison, 2020), 190.
[439] O. Spengler, *Man and Technics* (Alfred A. Knopf, Inc., 1932), 92.
[440] L. Smith, "The hardest technical solutions are right in front of your face.," *Luke Smith's Webpage* (12th July 2022), https://lukesmith.xyz/articles/obvious-technical-solutions/
[441] T. Kaczynski, *Anti-Tech Revolution: Why and How* (Scottsdale: Fitch & Madison, 2020), 76.

remaining members of the pseudo-aristocracy, right in front of one of the barely-surviving city architecture—it was beyond their comprehension, so they short-circuited and then fucking died. Stacy and I then soon had ad*lt time together. Okay, the story cl*max (censored, because it is the same word as a graphic word that refers to orgasm) is now over, and I don't really give a damn about the story resolution, so I'll end the book here. Don't forget to like, share, and comment.

About the Author

I am not quite as "cool and based" as I make myself out to be in this book, but I still live a relatively awesome life in beautiful nature, and I am not a terminally online soyboy unlike most people nowadays.

Anyway, here is my email for practical purposes: mackentoshder@gmail.com.